BIG SNOWY MTS.

LITTLE BELT MTS.

JUDITH GAP

HARLOWTON

TWO DOT

MUSSELSHELL RIVER

CRAZY MOUNTAINS

COFFIN BUTTE

BIG ELK CREEK

AMERICAN FORK

FISH CREEK

PORCUPINE BUTTE

CAYUSE HILLS

BIG COULEE

BUTTE RANCH

DRY CREEK

SWEET GRASS CREEK

OTTER CREEK

MELVILLE

"NO BUSH"

BLACK BUTTE

HOME RANCH

VAN CLEVE'S
DUDE RANCH

WHEELER CREEK

SOUTH FORK

10 MILE CREEK

BIG TIMBER CREEK

SOUR DOUGH

RASPBERRY BUTTE

MOUNTAINS

YELLOWSTONE RIVER

BIG TIMBER

"THE MELVILLE COUNTRY"

# 40 YEARS'
## GATHERIN'S

BARBIE VAN CLEVE

Spike Van Cleve

# 40 YEARS' GATHERIN'S

Introduction by
DEAN KRAKEL

THE LOWELL PRESS / Kansas City

*A Persimmon Hill book*
*published in cooperation with*
*the National Cowboy Hall of Fame*
*and Western Heritage Center,*
*Oklahoma City, Oklahoma*
*by The Lowell Press,*
*Kansas City, Missouri*

**Library of Congress Cataloging in Publication Data**
Van Cleve, Spike, 1912-1982
Forty Years' Gatherin's.

1. Van Cleve, Spike 1912-1982
2. Ranchers–Montana–Sweet Grass Co.–Biography.
3. Cowboys–Montana–Sweet Grass Co.–Biography.
4. Sweet Grass Co., Mont.–Biography.
5. Ranch life–Montana–Sweet Grass Co.
I. Title.
F737.S9V36        978.6'64'0922
[B]      77-71679
ISBN 0-913504-39-4

FIRST EDITION
Eighth Printing, 1995

Copyright © 1977 by Spike Van Cleve

The Natural Cougar Opaque paper on which
this book is printed meets the guidelines for permanence
and durability of the Committee on Production Guidelines
for Book Longevity of the Council on Library Resources.

Printed in the United States of America by
Constable-Hodgins Printing Company, Inc.
Kansas City, Kansas

*For Barbara*

*Also by Spike Van Cleve:*

# A DAY LATE AND A DOLLAR SHORT

# Contents

# Introduction

SPIKE WILL FOOL YOU, sure enough. The first time I met this pigeon-toed, bow-legged, sunburned son-of-a-gun with a pointed chin wearing a grin as wide as the Powder River, I asked myself just what kind of a bird is he? "A pure quill Montanyan," he calls himself. A native son, third generation under the Crazies (Crazy Mountains) north of Melville in Big Timber Country. "Gramp's cousin was killed by Indians in the Custer fight," he says casually. "I go back a long way. More'n a hundred years. My roots are here on our ranch . . . I love it, heaven can't be any better than this."

Spike carries the presence of the West better than anyone I have ever met. He's real; he's a rare combination of man. To see him on his range in the saddle chasing fillies in a hell-bent style is poetry, it's the style of the West personified. He has rhythm to say the least. My God, how that man can ride.

Stand off to the side in his barn some evening when he's feeding his mares and listen to the tender conversation: mares chomping and grinding oats, chins rubbin' feed boxes, blowing, Spike talking soft and gentle. "Ol' girl, how you feelin'?" Or, "You sure did work well today. Almost left ol' Spike sitting on air near Otter Creek when you made that sudden turn . . . 'Course that's what I get for daydreaming, dammit. Git over there old girl now. Easy there. S . . . tick, s . . . tick . . . what's matter girl, hoofs need trimmin'? Spike will see that the job gets done right away."

To see this man, wearing a tuxedo at the podium before a microphone in front of a large banquet crowd with his attractive wife Barbara in a formal gown beside him, is to know he's something extraordinary. They are a handsome couple. Spike is not fully at ease, but he's confident. He's sure of what he's going to say and how he'll say it. He's a natural showman, and whatever he says will be worth remembering. Somehow you know he had his tussle with higher education. He won't tell you much about his years at Harvard, for at heart he's a modest man. But you know he was there and won. He left the eggheads or the academics, whichever you choose to call them, with more to think about than he probably got in return. But he had to go to Harvard because he loves reading. He loves English literature. He wanted to hear of philosophy as it should be taught . . . the world's great religions deeply expounded— and politics and history. Spike had to find out. He wanted not a degree but a yardstick for the mind to carry with him the rest of his life. Of course he grins and laughs and says the best damn thing about going to Cambridge was coming home . . . each spring. "God, how homesick I got. I missed everything—'specially the smell and feel of the soft breezes that blow down from the Crazies and the sound and rush of snow water cascading over rocks. And ma' horses. Oh God, don'tcha know I missed 'em. When I came back I vowed to never leave again and I didn't."

Spike and Charlie Russell have a lot in common, aside from their Montana kinship. More than anyone realizes, unless you stop and think about it. What a pair they would have made on a ride at a roundup, around a campfire, or anywhere in fact. They are both original word painters. The finest critique I have heard of a Russell bronze was done by Spike: *"Spirit of Winter,"* he said, "Lordy, what a piece of sculpture! The *Spirit of Winter* personified by the hooded skeleton, wearing a robe, with savage dogs at the figure's side. My God, man, that's art I understand—it's our country. Hunger, fear of freezing to death, winter—it's all there. Charlie Russell knew the spirit of winter because he had been on the edge of it . . . Russell not only spoke the language of the West, but he felt it in his art."

Spike not only speaks and feels Montana to the marrow of his bones but he can write about it. The first story of his I read I stumbled onto by chance in the lobby of the Northern Hotel in Billings, Montana. The magazine was published by the Dude Ranchers Association. "Cody and Terry" was the title of Spike's story. In it he builds up the reader to the qualities of the matched team of work horses and then, before you know it, he's forced to do a terrible thing. To destroy Terry. But not before he feeds him oats and pets and consoles him for a spell. By this time my eyes were filled with tears as I waited and waited for the fatal crack of Spike's rifle. His writing is often poetic and has beautiful timing. "Cody and Terry" was one of the most sensitive pieces I ever read. Returning to the Cowboy Hall of Fame, I telephoned and asked permission of the Dude Ranchers Association to reprint it in *Persimmon Hill,* Cowboy Hall of Fame's quarterly. They agreed. To illustrate the story we chose New Mexico artist Robert Lougheed. It was no surprise to me months later when Spike's piece won our Western Heritage Award for magazine contribution in 1973. The story is currently under consideration by a major firm in Hollywood to be made into a motion picture.

*40 Years' Gatherin's* is a classic manuscript and will stand alone. It's all West to the core. It need not be compared with any other, because like Spike, it's individual. At the Cowboy Hall of Fame, we are proud to put our brand on it as a remarkable book, a *Persimmon Hill* book.

DEAN KRAKEL, Managing Director
National Cowboy Hall of Fame
Oklahoma City, Oklahoma

# Preface

I AM A LUCKY MAN. I was born, grew up, and have lived all my life in what I figure is the prettiest country God ever made—under the Crazy Mountains at the western edge of the high plains of south central Montana.

It's a good country. Where a man can sit his saddle and see, southwest to south across the Yellowstone valley, the dark flanks and white peaks of the Absarokas. To the southeast rises the Beartooth range, and beyond their eastern end, two hundred miles away in Wyoming, the Big Horns lift in the clear air. Eastward stretches rolling rangeland broken by creeks and tumbled hills, the grey rims of the Big Coulee barely visible on the horizon; and to the northeast the Bull Mountains break the skyline. To the west of them, beyond and along the far side of the Musselshell, stretch the Little and Big Snowies. At their western end the Judith Gap lies as a gentle swale between them and the sprawling bulk of the Little Belts; the gate to northern Montana and the upper Missouri. All across to the west stretch the Crazies, and, swinging in the stirrups, a man has to throw back his head to follow their abrupt shoulders up to the white crests of the peaks. A pretty, clean country where a man can see a long way—and have something to see.

Even the names sing. Creeks like Otter, Whitetail, Big Elk, Big Timber, Little Timber, Horse, Cayuse, and especially, Sweet Grass. The buttes: Porcupine, lifting above

xiii

the foothills, in shape a lot like its namesake; Black, with its covering of heavy timber; Raspberry, stretching its length along South Fork; Coffin; Wolf; Battleship; and the Cayuse Hills. The first settlers must have been discerning men, and I'm grateful to them for their choice of names.

The area carries the name, "the Melville Country." It has been called a backwater as far as progress is concerned. The horse age lingers, and the ranchers still hold with the idea that a man works for what he gets, helps his neighbors and takes care of his own, and that a handshake and a man's word are as good as his bond. Maybe even better.

The town of Melville sits on a bench above the Sweet Grass, and when I first saw it, about 1916, it had a post office, two stores, two saloons, a church, a blacksmith shop, a hotel and perhaps a half dozen homes. There was a livery barn, a stage barn and a dance hall, too. Not much of a city physically, but not only those who lived there, but all of us in the Melville Country were, and are, fiercely partisan; we might fight among ourselves, but we brooked no outside interference. To such an extent that if the sheriff of Sweet Grass County, with his office in Big Timber, was not from the Melville Country himself, he usually had a deputy who was, to tend to that part of his bailiwick.

Before the Milwaukee and Great Northern Railroads built through Montana in the early part of this century, most of the produce of central northern Montana funneled through the Judith Gap on its way to the Northern Pacific on the Yellowstone. A lot of it came through the Melville Country and Melville itself. Beef cattle, sheep, jerkline freight outfits, bull teams hauling wool, and each with its attendant uncurried retinue. It was no wonder that for some fifty years Melville was known as "the toughest little burg in the state," a title it relished!

Over and above that was a civic pride which was shared for miles around—we had the slickest horse thieves and nerviest rustlers, fastest running horses and rankest broncs, best riders and hard case fighting men in Montana. Truth, and my heritage, compels me to say that, by God, it was absolutely so!

Today the Melville Country is essentially the same as when I was growing up fifty-odd years ago, though there have been a few changes. There is a paved road through the heart of the area; most of the ranches have power, either REA or Montana Power; and for every five people who lived here fifty years ago there are about one-and-a-half, or less, now. The homesteaders came, starved out—though it took some of them about thirty years to do it—and once again we are a stock country. Grass is our crop, and we convert it to beef or mutton, just as for thousands of years it was converted into wild meat for the Indians.

The region was never easy on people, or horses, and it was tough to get by, but it marked its own with a wry humor, deep toughness of character, individuality, a streak of nonconformity and an innate decency. Today, the people, their lives and the way they thought would be more or less unique. They were good people, and I grew up with, fought with, played with and worked with them all my life.

The old-time ranch hand wasn't exactly top heavy with worldly goods. His horse gear, a bedroll, and a warbag—as a rule a seamless sack holding a few clothes—was about all, and in total it was always spoken of as, "my forty years' gatherin's."

These are mine.

SPIKE VAN CLEVE
Big Timber, Montana

# The Melville Country

FUNNY THING, but say "Big Timber" to people from around the state and you are liable to draw a blank look. I've found, though, not only in Montana, but in a good deal of Wyoming and Alberta as well, if I say, "I'm from Melville" or "I'm from the Melville Country," I get a way different reaction. Invariably the response will be, "Sure enough!" or "The hell you are!" and whoever I'm talking to will grin, always.

Naturally I savvy that, for I was raised in the Melville Country, have ranched there all my life and figure on dying there. Just like my Dad did. Melville has a reputation that is a lot bigger than the town ever was, and it's well-deserved! It gave its name to quite a scope of country east of the Crazy Mountains, too; from Porcupine Butte on the divide between the Sweet Grass and the American Fork of the Musselshell—which is the same as saying the divide between the Yellowstone and the Missouri—south to Big Timber Creek, and from the heads of the creeks between the two east to the Big Coulee—an area roughly 1200 square miles.

When I first remember the town, the peak of its population explosion had passed. The homesteaders were beginning to starve out, so I imagine it had around twenty-five residents, give or take a few, and not counting grub line riders, drunks blowing their summer wages nor ranch hands wintering there.

"Hub" Hickox founded the town along about '79 or '80, supposedly with two pack horse loads of stock in trade—mostly cartridges and whiskey I imagine, in light of later events. I have no idea why he picked the bench east of the Sweet Grass, pretty though it is. Probably a horse went lame, or something. Puts me in mind of the man with the wagon load of whiskey back in the early days who broke an axle crossing a creek. He unhooked, unloaded, set a sideboard across two barrels and waited.

Directly a rider came by, bought a drink or two and, in the course of the ensuing conversation, remarked that it was a funny place to be in business.

"Hell," said the proprietor, "any place in Montana's a good place for a saloon. I ain't been in business but since I broke down, an' you're here, ain't you?"

Anyhow, Melville's still in the same place and still alive. But the old joie de vivre is about gone since the last saloon closed down.

In the strict sense of the term I don't believe it could be called a ghost town, but for a lot of us it sure has a lot of ghosts; a lot of memories of happenings and people. Especially people, for—from those I have known over the past sixty-odd years, and from what I've heard tell of those before my time—Melville, the town *and* country, has had the damndest collection of characters you could imagine. They are not plumb extinct either, nor were they considered as characters—just par for the course. I have a deep affection for them all, too, because, hell, get the right sort of wet year and there's lots of loco on the rocky ridges in the Melville Country. Even now!

Seems like the earliest settlers sort of set the pattern. The Cook brothers came down from the Alder Gulch country and located on the Sweet Grass in '79. John was long gone before I arrived on the scene, but old George Washington Cook lived to well over a hundred, and I remember him well.

A hard old man, nice, and set in his ways. He never owned a shod horse and claimed that, "If God'd 'a wanted iron on horses they'd 'a been foaled that way." But I noticed he never went barefoot himself.

There was the time, too, when he and a neighboring rancher were working stock one bitter November day. The old fellow had on a hat, no gloves and a sorry henskin jacket, while the neighbor was wearing, and appreciating, a scotch cap, heavy gloves and a mackinaw. When they got the stock shaped up and were about to start them for the winter range, the man suggested that George put something warmer on before they left, for they had a good four or five miles to push the cattle.

The old man's answer was, "Nope. I've put in better'n sixty years in Montana, an' it's jest too early in th' season for a man to humor hisself," and he opened the gate and fell in behind the stock.

Cole Puett settled on the Sweet Grass early, about a mile below where the town later grew up. Mrs. Puett was a fine horsewoman, and they brought a really good stud with them. Because of Indians the stud lived in the house with the family—in a stall at the far end of the kitchen. Just imagine the howl that would go up from health authorities nowadays, but the Puetts lived to a ripe old age, and as far as I know the stud did, too.

The Puett's niece, Mrs. Hersh Franklin, lived in the same house when I was a youngster. A little woman who was built of spring steel and rawhide, she scorned anything modern—except for her "Yankee" woodbox and her "running water." The former a woodbox that filled from outside and tipped into the kitchen, and the latter a ditch under a trapdoor in the floor. The water, I suppose, was a holdover from the Indian days, and handy for the stud, too. I was very much in awe of Mrs. Franklin because she always called my Dad, "Sonny," and I figured she surely must be at least as old as God.

Another typical early Melvilleite was Sam Garvin, wagon boss for the Floweree & Lowry outfit that headquartered some six miles further down the Sweet Grass. This was one of the big, early day outfits in the state, and their "22" brand was well known east of the mountains. Seems that one time the cook wanted to quit, but he was such a good one that Sam wouldn't let him go. But, when the foreman was gone one day, the cook packed his warbag, saddled a pony and quit the country.

When Sam came back and discovered the state of affairs, he caught up a fresh horse, tracked the errant, roped him out of the saddle and led him back to the ranch. At first the cook set back pretty badly, but by the time they got home he was keeping the rope pretty slack and Sam told him, "I got you halterbroke to where you lead good. Now, by God, maybe you'll stand hitched." I guess the man did, for he was still on the job when Garvin quit later on.

Sam was a shade salty! He had a roundup crew camped on Sourdough, and one evening they all decided to make a trip down to the stage station "hog ranch" at the mouth of Dead Man's Canyon. This had a pretty rollicky reputation, and a number of cowboys that had visited it had turned up missing, hence the name, and the crew decided to clean it out. Nobody ever said much about what happened that night, but by daylight the boys were back in camp and the station had damn sure been cleaned out. The name of the canyon had added meaning, too.

Sam finally quit the Melville Country, by popular request I imagine, and "went to Wyoming." I strongly suspect that the Garvin Basin down there between the Pryors and the Bighorns got its name from Sam, for its reputation and his sure matched. Maybe not, but they were rough, both of them.

Sim Roberts was the foreman for the "22s" after Sam left, but Sim had a propensity for shooting people and soon left to take up a homestead just above Melville. Where targets were handier, maybe, or because the general atmosphere suited his talents better. He didn't stay there long, though I never learned why, and moved down on the Yellowstone near Reed Point.

His popularity never seemed to be overwhelming, however—I have the definite impression he always took the long end of the stick in his gun fights—and he finally left that country, too. During his stay there he had a falling out with Nate Young and killed him on the street in Big Timber in '99. A rather dim view of the fairness of the deal was taken by Nate's brother, Bill Young—or as he was commonly known, "Pistol Bill" Johnson. It was the accepted fashion to swap names back in those days, particularly if a man had held up a stagecoach and served time for it, as Bill had done down in Idaho. In any event, "Pistol Bill" laid for Sim and caught him on a bobsled with a load of hay one winter's afternoon. In this case he used a rifle, and Sim only escaped by dropping down on the eveners back of the team and whipping over and under. Even so he was nicked a time or two, but not badly enough to keep him from deciding he would enjoy a change of scene, and he pulled out of the Reed Point country that night.

A man can still stir up an argument about him among the few remaining old-timers anywhere between Bozeman and Columbus, for he killed one of the Keeney brothers in a saloon in Bozeman, too. At the time he was riding for the "79," and the owner, John T. Murphy, got him off—or at least out of the Gallatin country. I never knew Sim, but when he died in Butte in the late twenties I remember that his passing was the occasion for several glorious benders, both in relief and celebration, among the older element hereabouts.

Charlie Brown also headquartered in Melville for a while. He, too, was impulsive with a six-shooter, and, though he winged a few people, most must have been running shots, for I never heard of him killing anybody. I do know, however, that in a fit of pique he hunted a man through town, gun in hand, and the guy only escaped by seeking sanctuary under a schoolma'am's bed in the Melville Hotel.

Charlie's real reputation was as a horse thief, and he was a dandy! Trouble was, though I can understand a man stealing a good horse, he stole them in bunches, and besides, as I know from bitter experience, he inspired a number of copy cats that were around long after he had gone.

Speaking of horse thieves, while there's a creek over on the south end of the Crazies named after him, I don't believe "Kid" Royals could actually be called a Melvilleite. He should have been, for he'd have fit in! In jail in Big Timber for borrowing a horse unbeknownst to its owner, "Kid" escaped and hid under some bunched hay in a field within a hundred yards of the jail. After spending the day there he got clean away that night. Another time he stole the sheriff's top horse out of the sheriff's own barn. Left a nice note thanking him, though. I'd like to have known the man, damned if I wouldn't, even if I *am* in the horse business. He had sand!

At that, I'm glad Tinch Hannon wasn't around when Barbara and I moved to the Melville ranch in '37. He was another cut out of the same leather as Charlie Brown and had been shot in 1930 in a bickering out in front of the Melville Hotel. If he'd been alive, with his usual tally of sycophants, I don't see how I could have kept anything around my barn—from horses to a worn-out halter rope— without standing guard twenty-four hours a day. As a matter of fact, during most of the twenties, the town was pretty damn raunchy. There was a lot of moonshining going on up at the heads of the creeks, and some of the men making it were bad medicine. It was only when Hannon got killed in a squabble over some stolen whiskey, and a couple of those responsible for the killing had left for parts unknown, that the general tone of Melville sort of cleared up and got decent again, but I remember a so-called "joke" of that sorry era.

A woman in town gave a big party. She went all out and had everything fixed up nice, plenty of good food, and had even gone to the trouble of making a couple of freezers of ice cream, which she had packed in ice down in the springhouse. Well, after dark, when the party was in full swing, some of the trash from around town slipped down and put cow manure in the ice cream. However, they either got spooked off early, or the manure was a little dry, because it wasn't too thoroughly mixed in. I guess the people that served it just figured it was some new sort of strawberry ice cream. Dad was there, and he said it had him stumped—it sure as hell looked like manure, but it was hard to tell with strawberry ice cream on it, but what the devil would manure be doing in ice cream anyhow—but he played safe and sort of ate around the edges, avoiding the questionable lumps and colors. Said it was good ice cream too, as much as he ate, and that a big, newcomer Norsk from the "Settlement" who sat beside him must have thought so for sure; the guy cleaned his up, lumps and all, and asked for another helping!

As far as I know there were no ill effects, but such squalid actions damn sure weren't typical of Melville, and the reaction of the town and general area got pretty warlike. So much so that the humorists in question sure kept quiet, nor was there recurrence.

Jack Winsborough was quite a figure in the Melville Country during the '90s and early nineteen hundreds. He was an Englishman and his outfit lay northeast of town in the piney hills under the Fish Creek rims. He loved fast horses, always had a few, and would run them any time, anywhere, for anything. Bad man to match, too, for he was a good jockey as well as having good horses. Jack's silks were sort of unorthodox and always the same—socks, bright red long handle drawers and a sash. That and nothing more. There was some speculation in the countryside, too, as to whether it was always the same set of drawers. One of his best horses was "Blizzard," and old-timers still get wrought up about the time he took the measure of Bill Besley's "Nox All" at the Musselshell Crossing in '91.

Jack was a natural for Melville in other ways, too. He and his wife split up on account of something or other, and he got himself another one a while later. I guess the first wife got lonesome, for directly she moved back in and the three of them lived together. Got along fine, too. Friendly as Shepherd pups.

Seems like Melville has always played host to a branch of the YMCA; at least, in my time, it was affectionately spoken of as the "Y." The original headquarters were down just under the bench below town, and whenever a live one hit town there'd be a glorious, howling drunk. Since it all was within sight and easy earshot of town the better element got sort of tired of it, and one morning, when the celebrants were sleeping off a particularly gaudy party, did something about it.

The town fathers gathered at the "Y" with an array of jacks, teams and running gears. Quietly it was lifted, set on two logs on the wagons, chained down solid, and the teams hooked up. Bob Brownlee, the town blacksmith at the time, took the lines, crawled up and straddled the roof, and away they went.

Some two miles down the creek, on the edge of a rim that dropped about thirty feet down to the water, they stopped. Carefully they reversed their earlier procedure, set the building down on the very edge of the cliff—with the door to the landward side, since they didn't want anybody to get crippled or killed—and drove off. Not an occupant came to during the whole operation!

I'd have loved to have seen the expression on the old boy

who first staggered to the door and opened it. Must have been unsettling! I guess it took the better part of a week for everybody to straggle back to town, and eventually the building was brought back, too. But a point had been made; and it was put a good deal further away than before.

It would be hard to pick the dirtiest person I have ever known, but there were three in Melville that were up near the lead! Jim McQuillan was one. God knows how old he was when I knew him in the twenties, but he had come to Montana with a trail herd from Texas in eighteen eighty something or other, had stayed and finally ended up in Melville. The old saloon he lived in, and bootlegged out of, looked and smelled like a wolf den. Fortunately for his patrons the moonshine he sold, when he had any to spare, pretty well stood off the germs. I'm certain, from the dirt caked in the wrinkles of his neck, that he hadn't had a bath for years, maybe never, and I imagine he'd 'a had to been soaked a day or two before even lye soap and a scrubbing brush would have touched it.

A couple of men came in one day and asked if he had any whiskey. "Damned little," said Jim, and produced a pint bottle with a couple of drinks in it.

The sneaky sons of guns were revenue men and took him to Big Timber to jail, but he was so damned dirty neither the county nor the city jail would let him in. The barbershop wouldn't let its bath be used to clean him up either, and the upshot was that he was turned loose. The revenuers had to haul him back to Melville, too, for the stage driver said, by God, he didn't want him in his rig! The law left the old booger alone, pretty carefully, from then on.

Funny old fellow, though, Jim. Somebody came in for a drink one day, noticed blood on the floor and on Jim's hands when he was being served, got curious, and was told, "Killed me a rabbit."

Seeing a kettle on the old potbellied stove back by Jim's

bed, he wandered over and peered into it. Stuck up out of the stew were the hind legs of a jack rabbit, the skin still on from paws to hocks! "Godamighty, McQuillan," he exploded. "Don't you even cut off the damn feet!"

Jim looked up from where he was smearing the few glasses on the back bar, "Ah, they make a domned fine handholt to stir wit'. Ye don't burrn yer fingers."

It was in McQuillan's saloon that a classic remark was made one Saturday night. There'd been some fisticuffs, and, like a bunch of pups watching a dog fight, everybody was getting pretty bristly around the shoulders. Old Halvor Sandsness from the Norwegian "Settlement" west of town was taking it all in quietly, leaning back with his elbows on the bar. Somebody walked up, got him by the whiskers, shook him gently and announced, "Sandsness, I can whip you, and your whole damn family to boot."

"Hm, vell," replied the old man seriously, "dere are t'irteen of us, jou know."

The Weatherman brothers, Fletch and Cris, came awful close to putting Jim in the shade when it came to dirty, though. Missourians, they had prospected and trapped every canyon in the Crazies, but when I first knew them they had retired, in Melville. They raised a garden, trapped some or worked out once in a while and got by. As a matter of fact they had a later version of the original "Y," and the story goes that one time they gave asylum to a herder and his paycheck, tied on a beauty, and finally all rolled into bed, the visitor in the middle.

The first to come out of it was Fletch. He fumbled on the floor for the jug, found it and took a pull at it, poked the man beside him and asked, "Want a drink?"

No answer. But Cris, who was awake by now, collared the booze with, "By God, I do," took a pull and poked the visitor again. "Better have a snort," he offered politely.

Nary a word, so Fletch hoisted the jug again. When he lowered it he shook the man hard. "Have a drink, goddammit. You dead or somethin'?"

No response forthcoming, he leaned over, looked a minute and decided, "By God, he is," and he was! But be damned if those two old devils didn't finish the booze and go back to sleep. Didn't get up until the next day when, as one of them put it, "He was gettin' too damn cold to sleep good with!"

Like any ranch kid under the Crazies I figured I was a sure enough trapper. I never did catch but one coyote—probably he was weak minded—but I was sure hell on skunks, weasels, muskrat and mink, and once in a while, a beaver. The latter by mistake of course, since they were illegal, in a muskrat drowning set.

One day this mink showed up, and was a pretty cute proposition, too, for he got to making a habit of robbing my rat sets when I caught anything in them. Since he seemed to be smarter than I was, I saddled up one morning and rode down to Melville to see if I could get any pointers from Fletch.

He and Cris were still in bed when I arrived. It was sure some kind of a camp, and since I knew it was so bed buggy that even they couldn't stand it in warm weather and always summered in an old barn down on the creek bottom, I was careful not to sit down or take anything off. Not even my gloves. So I just stood while I told him my troubles, and ended by asking what I should do.

When I finished, Fletch mumbled something to me, and then to his brother.

" 'S lost his goddam teeth," the latter told me, and the two proceeded to root through the bed sougans and tarp. No luck.

"Try th' goddam spitoon," suggested Cris, so Fletch reached under the bed and came out with a gallon can. It looked to be about half full, but he pawed around in it and came up with some false teeth which he inspected closely. Then, apparently satisfied that they were indeed his, he wiped them off on the leg of his long johns, slipped them into place and clicked them a time or two. "Well, hell, set a trap an' bait it an' ketch th' sonofabitch," he told me.

I've forgotten whether I ever caught the mink or not, but I damn sure haven't forgotten that episode! I told Barbara about it after we moved to the Melville ranch, for, though Fletch was dead by then, Cris was our neighbor. He was a good neighbor, too, and raised a big garden which he insisted on sharing with us. Said fresh vegetables were good for the kids. Dirty or not, he was a nice old man and we liked him, though I must admit that we never invited him in.

# Gramp

## 2

MY GRANDDAD was quite a guy! When he came west he was just going along with a family penchant for following the frontier. The first Van Cleve came to America in 1653. His descendants split into several groups. One moved down into the Carolinas on the Yadkin River. Squire Boone, Jr., Daniel's kid brother, married a Van Cleve girl, the family went to Kentucky with the Boones and are still there. Another branch crossed to New Jersey, and the first president of Princeton University also married a Van Cleve. The graveyards around Princeton and Lawrenceville are loaded with Van Cleves. Gramp's granddad married a Houston, and in light of subsequent events, I think she was some kin or other to Sam Houston.

Gramp's dad went to Princeton, then to West Point and graduated in 1831. He was posted to duty on the frontier and there met Gramp's mother, Charlotte Ouisconsin Clark. She had been born at Fort Crawford in 1819, the first white child, so the story goes, born in Wisconsin Territory, and her middle name was the French spelling of the word. She was raised at Fort Snelling, Minnesota Territory, met Lt. Van Cleve, and they were married at Fort Winnebago in 1836.

Her brother, Malcolm Clark, was born at Fort Wayne in 1817, was raised at the frontier spots where his father, Capt. Nathan Clark, was posted, and entered West Point in 1834. Thrown out for challenging another cadet to a duel

15

and stomping him when he wouldn't accept, he went down to Texas and served under Sam Houston as lieutenant in the Lone Star Militia.

He didn't particularly like the country, and when the war ended he went to the upper Missouri in 1839 with Alexander Culbertson, head man of the American Fur Company. Before long he was handling the Company's operations on the upper Marias River. There he married a Piegan girl and was known as "White Lodge Pole." This was changed to "Four Bears" in honor of his killing four grizzly bears in one day! The Bloods, Piegan, and Blackfeet must have liked Malcolm at a time when they weren't exactly famed for their friendliness toward whites. As Calf Shirt, a chief of the Blackfeet, told him, "Clark, I hate all white men, but you I hate less than any white man I know!"

When the fur business petered out Clark settled on one of the first ranches recorded in Montana on the Little Prickley Pear, in 1865. In 1869 he was killed on his ranch by some renegades led by his wife's cousin, Ne-Tus-Che-O. I gather Malcolm had some killings to his credit himself during his thirty years in the country. He must have been a hard customer, and I wish I had known him.

But to get back to Gramp, he was a lovely, gentle person, with a great sense of humor, though to call it earthy would be a definite understatement. He was easy on horses and a favorite of all kids, family or otherwise. As I grew up, though, I began to appreciate the fact that he must have run with some pretty salty characters and heard the owl hoot in a lot of places. I liked to get him to talking, to reminiscing. For while he thought the present was fine and enjoyed it, he had a great affection for the past. The measure of the man, too, was that I can't recall ever hearing him say anything plumb mean about anybody. He might, and frequently did, refer to them as sons of bitches, but there was something good in everybody he'd ever known, and no matter how rough things had been he could always find a chuckle in them. It's a shame that tape recorders weren't in common use before he died, but I'm sure glad at least three of my children knew him, even if they were pretty small!

As a little bitty guy he lived in Long Prairie, Minnesota, where his dad was ranching after he resigned his commission, and he told of the grasshoppers wiping out their crops. Or of the family sitting around the table in the evenings picking over wheat for bits of glass from granary windows broken by Indians. Said he never cared a hell of a lot for wheat since, for their diet was mainly that grain cooked whole, with occasional bread made from wheat ground in a coffee grinder. As a kid he was raised in St. Anthony, Minnesota, which was a logging town and a hard proposition, and he had two stories from that time that tickled him.

Seems they had trouble keeping school teachers, for the girls kept getting married, and the men kept getting run off by the loggers' tough kids. So everybody was surprised one fall day when into the schoolroom came a slim young fellow in a claw hammer coat. He was a good deal smaller than some of the boys in the room, but he quietly looked them over for a minute and then remarked, "I understand there's been a lot of trouble in this school. Well, I'm equipped for a lot of trouble," and from under his coattails he produced two Navy Colts which he laid on the desk in front of him! Gramp said there damn sure wasn't any trouble; not then, nor during the two years the man taught!

In the parlor of his folks' home was a large picture entitled "Christus Consoler." Of course the kids didn't get into the parlor often—that was reserved for grownups, especially the minister—but they were much impressed by the picture and its title had a fine ring to it, to boot. He and his brothers—he had four of them—used to swim in the mill ponds among the saw timber, and naturally they swam bare. This day Gramp's brother, Mort, clambered onto a big saw log, carefully stood up, struck a commanding pose with his right hand extended in a gesture of benediction, and proclaimed in ringing tones, "Christus Consoler! Of the Horse Marines!"

Shortly after he was married, Gramp went out to have a look at Colorado Springs. Gen. W. J. Palmer, who founded the town, was a cousin—Army families all seemed to be pretty well related back then—so Gramp paid him a visit. Didn't like the looks of the country, and didn't stay, thank God. He used to chuckle about an incident that occurred the day he got into town, though. Happened it was the day they were voting to see whether Colorado Springs or Denver would be the capital of the state, and when Gramp got off the stage he was greeted with a drink and an invitation to come vote. He demurred, saying he wasn't a Coloradan, and was told, "Hell, you're as good as a nigger, ain't you? One o' them just voted!"

Gramp said he guessed he was, and cast his vote. I gathered, too, that he cast a couple more before the day was over. He used to say it sort of got him in shape for Montana Territory!

He was a fine swearing man. Not conversationally, but when he was stirred up he had the most flexible, vivid, blistering vocabulary I ever listened to. It's a cinch he must have hobnobbed with more than a few bull whackers and mule skinners in his time. There is a family story about how, when they lived in Coulson—that's where Billings is now—in the early eighties my Aunt Agnes, then a little girl and she must have been a mealy mouthed little Goody Two Shoes, told her mother she'd heard her father swear. Granny called Gramp to an accounting, and he, poor guy, said Agnes must be mistaken.

"Oh, no, Papa," she insisted, "you said Mr. Finch was a son of a -----."

Gramp had stiffened at the man's name, and now interrupted with, "So I did, my dear, so I did. And so he is!"

He was polite about his swearing, though. When he settled on his outfit under Porcupine Butte below the Crazies, he dealt with a man about a windmill, and the man came out to set it up. He put it together on the ground and was tipping it up into place with a couple of deadmen and block and tackles when the two legs with all the weight on them buckled, and there was a terrible wreck. Gramp said he looked at the mess, got his mouth open to cuss and then realized he didn't have to pay until the rigging was up, and so, very thoughtfully, deferred to the other man's cussing rights. That individual surveyed the havoc and said philosophically, "Oh, sugar!"

Gramp said the remark unnerved him so badly *he* couldn't cuss then!

He must have had quite a time in Coulson—he arrived there in 1880—and it must have been a going concern! He knew Calamity Jane right well, and told of meeting her on the street one day with a nice-looking young man in tow. She informed Gramp that she'd just gotten married, and introduced the young fellow as her husband. Gramp naturally invited them to have a drink in celebration of the occasion, and they headed for the nearest saloon. As they started in the door Calamity turned to her new husband and cautioned him, "Albert, you stay outside. You're too young to come in here," and she meant it! That tickled Gramp.

There were some rollicky individuals in Coulson, and he knew and liked nearly all of them. Liver Eating Johnston was, "as big and rough an old devil as I've ever known," and then he'd go to chuckling about an incident that involved the Liver Eater.

Seems Johnston went down on the line one time, got a girl in one of the houses and took her upstairs. When they got to bed the old rascal was so drunk that he promptly went to sleep. When he woke up he found that his girl was gone—had snuck out and gone back downstairs to the other patrons—and it made the old frontiersman mad. So he scouted around the room and found the girl's pot de chambre. One of those big ones with a bail handle and a lid. It was about half full. So he got what clothes the girl had hung up in a corner, stuffed them down into the thing with a broom handle and stirred them in thoroughly. Then he dressed and went downstairs where he was greeted with much merriment and hoorawing, particularly by the girl. "Never mind, honey," he told her, "you got better screwed than you know."

A sequel to the affair, which Gramp recalled with great gusto, was that the editor of the Coulson paper heard the story and printed an abridged version of it under the headline, "A Scout's Revenge, or Stirring Times in the Old West"!

There were a lot more old-timers he knew well. I can remember him telling about Muggins Taylor, Yellowstone Kelley, X. Biedler and one who has always intrigued me, "Sandbar" Brown. As Gramp told it, Brown was a mountain man who was cut off by a war party and run out onto a sand bar in the river without even any driftwood to fort up in. The Indians sized up the deal, saw there was no chance of making a sneak on him and must have finally decided that if they all charged him he might get one of them, but it was a cinch they'd get to him and raise his hair. So here they came, whipping over and under and yipping. Brown held fire until they were pretty close, for he had what was probably the first repeating rifle in the territory. Then he turned loose, and after the fourth shot, and the fourth buck down, they gave him the fight and quit the country. From then on out he was known among the whites as "Sandbar." I don't know what the Indians called him, but they sure figured his medicine was strong. What tickled Gramp most was that "Sandbar" always claimed, "Ever' damn one o' them bucks had a s'prised look on his face when I went to peel their foretops."

After the family had moved up the river to Big Timber in 1887, a Crow girl who was living with them tipped Granny off about the coming Swordbearer uprising. Gramp spread the word, people forted up in the little towns along the Yellowstone, troops came out from Fort Custer, and after about one volley hit the hostile Crows they quit the fight and the trouble was over. As far as I know there was only one white killed, and a friend of Gramp's was a casualty, more or less. Gramp said he saw the man a few days after the excitement was over with a hand bandaged and in a sling, so he asked what had happened. "Oh," answered the friend, "I got crippled in the uprisin'."

Pressed for details, he elaborated, "Well, I was on sentry duty, leanin' on my rifle an' keepin' an eye out for trouble when m' least child crawled up, pulled th' trigger, an' blowed off m' thumb."

Gramp used to chuckle, too, about a few of the things that happened when he started ranching on the Sweet Grass. The buildings were just below a good spring on Porcupine Butte, and the Blackfeet and Crows were accustomed to using it as camp while raiding one another. Consequently, the first few years on the place they had lots of visitors, mostly Crows. Plenty Coups, principal chief of the Crow nation, was a good friend, so there never was any trouble. One morning, though, after a war party had camped at the spring, Gramp went up to get a bucket of water and found the scalped head of a Blackfoot comfortably ensconced in the spring box! Didn't faze him much, but Granny took a dim view of the proceedings.

Gramp never was what you could call a mechanically minded man, and any contraption that didn't have a bullwheel or a pitman stick had him whipped. Far as I know he only tackled driving a car once, a Model T, when I was a kid. He got it into the wrong gear and drove it through the garage wall up to the windshield. Then, brushing off most of the odds and ends that had been hanging on nails on the wall and had showered down on him, he strode up to the house and informed my dad, "That misbegotten, stinking sonofabitch is trying to get out of the garage, and you better go down and take care of things before it does."

So Dad went down, and there was the Ford chugging happily along, rear wheels spinning and smoking on the floor. Speaking of cars, Gramp claimed that the ideal garment for a car trip was a fur-lined linen duster that'd shed water!

He served in the legislature and was the secretary for both the 1884 and 1889 constitutional conventions. When he was pretty old, he ran for treasurer of Sweet Grass County and was defeated. Somebody asked how he felt about it. Gramp thought a minute, then answered, "Well, there are a terrible lot of liars in this county." Asked why so, he replied, "Everybody I talked to before the election said they'd vote for me, and everybody I've talked to since the election said they had voted for me; and I talked to damn near everybody, either before or since!"

Ranchers paid their bills once a year back in those days, after they'd sold their livestock. Gramp used to tell of getting a bill from Kellogg's, the main store in Big Timber, and included in it was a charge for an ice cream freezer. Well, he couldn't remember buying one, so he asked Granny, "Alice, did you get an ice cream freezer from Kellogg?"

She disclaimed all knowledge of the affair, so when he went in to pay his bill that fall Gramp said, "By the way, there's an ice cream freezer on my bill," and the old store keeper interrupted with, "Hell, Paul, forget it. I sold somebody an ice cream freezer and couldn't remember who it was. So I put it on the bills of twelve of my best customers, an' three of 'em have already paid for it!"

# Wolves

## 3

I IMAGINE that pretty nearly everyone, thinking back to when they were real young, has some particular thing that made a special impression on them; that they remember vividly from way, way back. Maybe some toy; or their first ice cream. Perhaps the smell of blown out coal oil lamp; the sound and scent of a wood stove; a train whistle. Something, anyhow, that depends on how and where a youngster lived. For me, from the time I became really aware of what was going on around me, over sixty years ago, it has been wolves. Their sound, their smell, their looks. Even now, once in a while I dream about them and wake up listening. A well-meaning friend sent me a phonograph record of wolf calls some time ago, but I damn sure don't enjoy it. Makes me restless and uneasy. At first I thought I might slip it on to the player when Dad was dozing after supper some evening, but decided I better not, for I was leary of the results it might have had.

Wolves were bad when I was little. They ranged from the Missouri River south across the foothills of the Highwoods, over the Little Belts and along the breaks under the Crazies to the Yellowstone—a distance north and south in central Montana of better than a hundred miles. The livestock on the ranches in that whole scope of country suffered badly.

Colts were a favorite tidbit, but they sure wouldn't pass up cattle or sheep. We lost eighteen head of grown cows one

23

night to wolves, scattered across a couple of sections on the head of the American Fork of the Musselshell. They weren't all dead when we found them, but they were all down, hamstrung, with their bags, flanks or part of their quarters eaten out. I was with Dad when he killed the poor devils with the 32-40 he always carried on his saddle; most everybody packed a rifle in those days, particularly in the winter. He finally got rid of his holding on the American Fork and it was on account of the damn wolves.

We weren't short of them over south on the home ranch on Billy Creek either. Anything but. Dad had a string of greyhounds with him wherever he rode, and they were sure death on coyotes. Wolves, though, they weren't really keen on tackling, but if they could hold one up a time or two until a rider could get up close enough for a good shot, they'd done their part. Incidentally, Dad had a sister, Helen—she died before I arrived on the scene—who must have been something. When the dogs bayed up a lobo she'd ride in and club the animal with a loaded, four-foot billiard cue butt she carried on a thong at her saddle horn! She was a top rider, rode good horses and sure must have had nerve. More than he did, Dad claimed, and he was as gritty as flypaper rolled in sand. I wish I'd known her. Wolves had nothing to do with her death, either.

Sometimes the dogs didn't want any part of a wolf. I remember a day over on the head of Fish Creek, north of Porcupine Butte. Dad spotted a wolf headed toward the butte, and we built to him. It wasn't over half a mile to the timber, so we didn't have much time, but it was a big dog wolf, and I guess the dogs figured they hadn't lost anything quite that salty. He was in plain sight, but when Dad gave the yell he used to tell the hounds he saw something, they were careful to look busily everywhere except towards Mr. Wolf. Just couldn't seem to spot him, and the upshot was that he reached the butte and got away.

The day wasn't over by a long shot, even so. Within a

mile, as we rode down Fish Creek, we jumped a coyote. The dogs were eager to get their reputations back after what Dad had had to say about them apropos the wolf, so we had a fine run. The country was open then, except for line fences and pastures near ranch buildings, so running with hounds was a lot of exciting fun.

In the excitement of the run I must have used some words I'd picked up from hanging around the bunkhouse. Besides, I imagine Dad was still pretty ouchy about the wolf escaping. Anyhow, as we rode up to where the dogs had pulled down the coyote, he promised me a working over if he heard me cuss again. Being well acquainted with the caliber of his spankings, I said I sure wouldn't. So he backed the hounds off the dead coyote, got out his pocket knife and straightened out the carcass to skin it. Just then I saw another coyote come out of the sagebrush down the coulee and, perfectly naturally, yelled, "Look, look. There's another of the sonsabitches," or something along those lines. Dad said, "Why, damn you," looked up, saw what was going on, tossed the carcass behind his cantle and tied it down with the saddle strings. I, realizing what I'd done, made a run for my mare, Panama, hoping I could get under way and that he'd forget by the time we had caught the coyote. I didn't and he didn't.

I was doing my damndest to get aboard, but I was so rattled that I kept losing the knotted saddle strings under the fork, and I needed them to pull myself up to where I could get my foot in the stirrup. Besides, I had a quirt on my wrist that kept getting in the way; my Aunt Allie had given it to me for Christmas, and it was a dandy; braided rawhide and fringed, and I sure was proud of it.

Finally I slipped the quirt off to hang it on my saddle horn. As I did, Dad took it away, cut me a couple of licks across the seat of my britches hard, and I was in my saddle, plumb afire. I don't know whether Dad put me there, or the quirt, but there I was, and hurting. He growled, "I warned you," swung up, and away we went, the dogs in the lead.

I was a little behind everyone, riding as high as I could, and I felt gingerly to see if I was bleeding. I wasn't, but right then and there I decided that I'd be damned if *I* was going to be whipped with *my* quirt again, and as Panny jumped a sage bush I dropped the thing in the middle of it. I hated to do it, but the alternative was worse. Incidentally, I've never carried a quirt since.

We had another good run, but as Dad got off at the second kill there was a sharp snapping sound from the off side of his horse. He walked around to that side, said, "I be damned." So I went around, too, and there, tied behind his saddle, was probably the maddest coyote I've ever seen!

He was pretty far gone, but his eyes were green slits of hate, and as Dad swung his hand in front of him he strained to reach it, his jaws snapping loudly. What we'd heard were those teeth reaching for Dad's leg as he dismounted!

When Lazarus was taken care of and the two coyotes were skinned, we tied the hides behind our saddles and started home. Panny took a real dim view of our hide, and sure enough pretty soon she bucked me off and headed for home trying to buck off the skin as well. I lit right square on my tender bottom, so while Dad was off gathering in my mare I indulged in a good cry. Velvet, my particular friend among the hounds, hadn't joined Dad, so she came over to comfort me. By the time the horses were back she'd licked the tears off my face, I had gotten in pretty good shape again, and the two of us were sitting together waiting.

"Here's your horse," said Dad. "Dammit, I wish you'd learn to stay on top of her." Sizing me up, he added, "At that, she got pretty rough, so I'll carry both hides."

When the transfer had been made he asked casually, "Where's your quirt?"

"Lost it," was all I could manage.

"Want to go back and look for it?" with a glint deep in his eye.

"Nope." So we rode on home.

Years later he told me he had the quirt deal pretty well figured out, and that it had bothered him when he rode back and found a kid sitting forlornly with his arm around a hound for comfort, and we chuckled together about it. I've wondered if there are any remains of the quirt left. Surely not, for long ago the mice and gophers must have figured it manna from on high, though they must have earned their bacon working on that rawhide. But be damned if I don't think I could ride back to that very sage bush today.

We not only had wolves in the hills, we had them right at home, for Dad had a high old time in the spring hunting up dens and digging out the pups. If they weren't too big he'd bring them home to raise, and when I was too little to get around much, he had about fifteen in a pen back of the house. They used to howl at night sometimes, and I'd lie quaking in my bed. No wonder I had nightmares! Only one ever got gentle, old Lobo, and he used to lie around the porch and yard like a big dog. He *was* big, too, and when he stood up with his paws on Dad's chest, the two of them were eyeball to eyeball. Probably his size was the reason the hounds never tackled him, though there was plainly no love lost. When he lifted a lip and those yellow eyes got cold, they sure walked 'way around him. So did visitors who dropped in and people got so they left their dogs at home when they came calling. Actually, after one trip I think it was the dogs themselves that decided to stay home. If they survived the first visit, that is. I was always warned not to mess with the big son of a gun, and the threat of a licking wasn't in the least bit necessary.

Digging out a wolf den could sometimes be a touchy operation, so I never got to go on those trips, even when I grew up a little. From what I'd heard about it I wasn't very eager anyhow. Usually the old folks would be gone, but the bitch would be home often enough to make it an interesting proposition to crawl in with a lighted candle in one hand and a six-shooter in the other, which was Dad's long suit. He sure boiled things down to the fundamentals! Of course there were no flashlights back then, and a lantern was hard to carry ahorseback. Besides, if coal oil got spilled on a horse it could blister the hair off. But, being Dad, I don't believe he really gave a whoop whether there was a wolf inside or not, except that if there was it would just make things more exciting.

Once, though, it did get a little juicy. Maw was home and not neighborly. When she snarled and charged, the candle blew out, and as Dad threw up his pistol she chopped down on it at an angle so he couldn't shoot her. He backed out like a pup from a beehive, with her clamped to the gun. When they hit daylight she tried to change holds, and he was able to kill her.

Another time, one windy March day, he shed the sheepskin coat he was wearing and laid it on the ledge over the den mouth before he started in. He'd seen two wolves slip off down the draw as he rode up, so he nonchalantly crawled in, got the pups into a gunny sack and backed out. The pups were making quite a fuss, and about the time he cleared the den mouth something heavy lit on his back, and for a little he would have put the rankest bucking horse to shame. When the smoke cleared he found that it had just been his coat which had blown off the ledge. The only damage was that his horse, spooked by the gymnastic display, had run off, and Dad had to walk home carrying the pups. He claimed that from then on out he never worried about his heart; if it hadn't quit him that day it damn sure never would.

Pop went out of the wolf business in a hurry one night when his pets somehow escaped from their pen and got into a band of sheep he was running for Gramp a couple of miles up the creek. The herder downed one or two before they wised up to the fact that a man could be dangerous. One of them was Lobo, who had enthusiastically joined in the massacre. By then, though, the sheep had scattered, as had the wolves, killing as they went. When morning came, everybody on the outfit, plus the nearest neighbors, went wolf hunting and by evening all the renegades had been run down ahorseback and shot. I didn't get to go along.

It was a wild deal. January, below zero, and about a foot to sixteen inches of new snow on ground that was frozen iron hard; conditions which aren't exactly ideal for real fast riding. Of course a good horse can run up on a wolf if the terrain is reasonably level and there's enough of it, and these wolves were so full of mutton that they couldn't run too fast nor too far. Even so there were some wrecks, but none bad enough to do more than make a horse, or a rider, pack a leg for a day or two, and Dad often chuckled about one of the day's incidents.

Seems he, Aunt Phyllis and Mr. Jack Hart, a lovely old English sportsman, friend and neighbor, were laid straight after two wolves on the flat above Battleship Butte. They knew there was a ditch about three feet deep somewhere in their vicinity and were watching pretty closely for it, but the deep new snow and a frost haze in the air made it hard to spot things on the ground until they got right to them. Mr. Jack was slightly in the lead and was warning them, "Mind now, mind. Theah's a bally ditch heah somewheah," when his old pony picked it up with both front feet. The two disappeared in a billowing cloud of snow, out of which came the grunt of Mr. Jack's horse and a strangled, "Gad!" Then, "And I seem to have jolly well found the blightah, by Jove."

I have read that wolves run only in family packs, or at least in packs of no more than eight or ten animals. Perhaps they do, now, or further north, but it certainly wasn't true in this region when Dad was a youngster, or even when I was little.

Aunt Allie, when she was small, had a mutt dog. It was

useless, as kids' dogs are, except to the kids, and, true to form, was always getting into jackpots of some sort or other and having to be bailed out. So it wasn't unusual when one snowy January day, Aunt Allie came weeping to Gramp and told him her pup was missing. He, well acquainted with the dog's propensities, immediately thought of a set he'd made the day before for coyotes, about a mile east of the house. It was almost a dead cinch that the truant was there, and in trouble, or trap. Same difference.

There was close to a foot of snow on the ground, the temperature was right around zero, and although it was getting towards evening Gramp decided he'd better go have a look at the set right away. If he didn't, the odds were that by morning there'd be a three-legged pet or, very probably, a dead one. The latter for sure, if a wolf happened by. He was getting into his outdoor clothes when Aunt Allie appeared again and raised such a fuss that he finally dressed her, too, and off they went afoot.

Sure enough, when they got to the traps they found the dog. Not only had he stepped into one, but had sat down in another as well. He greeted their arrival with enthusiasm, there was a great reunion scene with Aunt Allie, and by the time Gramp had gotten the traps open it was dark and had begun to snow. On top of that, the pup didn't seem to be able to walk, so Gramp wound up carrying him with Aunt Allie trudging alongside holding onto his coat.

Gramp said they had gone perhaps a quarter of a mile when he heard what he took to be wind starting, up on Porcupine Butte. As it increased he realized it wasn't wind, but wolves, a lot of them, howling. From the sounds, they were dropping off the flanks of the butte toward him, and he speeded up to as fast as the little girl beside him could travel, which, he said, seemed almighty slow. It must have been bad. There was the queer, light darkness of a moonless winter night, but the falling snow limited his vision to around twenty feet, and the wolves kept getting closer. He was backtracking his trail, so there was no chance of missing the buildings, but he'd have felt 'way better if only he could have seen the lights of the ranch, no matter how far there still was to go. They had perhaps three-eighths of a mile left when the wolves arrived. The howling stopped, except for a few stragglers still on the butte, and all of a sudden he could feel them all around him. He couldn't see them, though he halfway thought he caught movement in the murk on either side and ahead. He told me years later that he, by God, just wouldn't look behind him; guessed that if they were on three sides it didn't matter a hell of a lot if they were on a fourth as well. Besides, he might see one if he looked back. Gramp said he'd never heard of wolves bothering humans, outside of the windies the old-timers told. But still, especially with that little girl—he had her by the hand now—there was always a chance that these wolves might have heard differently. The damn dog kept slipping in his one arm so he started to put him down. Immediately Aunt Allie began to wail that the "woofs" would eat him. "Good God, child," he hastily reassured her. "Hush. I'll carry him," and kept walking, fresh wolf tracks crossing their path every few yards.

It was a long trip. Silent except for the whimpering of the dog and an occasional snarl as their escorts bickered or played among themselves. Finally the lights of the house showed dimly through the snow, and in short order they were in the warm and friendly kitchen. Gramp put his burden down, collapsed into a chair, leaned back and relaxed, played out. Aunt Allie was excitedly telling her mother about the trip when it suddenly registered on him that the pet was frisking around the room. "And you know," he told me, "if Alice (that was Granny) hadn't stopped me I'd have put the little sonofabitch outside. With the wolves, damn him!"

Right after they got to the house the howling commenced again, and kept on pretty steadily for most of the night. Nobody slept real well, and Gramp was up before daylight to build the kitchen fire and put the coffee on. When he went up to tend the stock everything was quiet, and the snow had stopped. It was full daylight when he finished, and he could see, down the hill back of the barn, across the swale by the spring and up the hill beyond, a beaten trail in the snow. A trail at least a foot wide, made by wolves. He would never venture a guess as to how many it had taken to make it, but the snow had been beaten into solid ice. If just eight or ten head made it they must have been traveling boogers and awful heavy on their feet.

When I was a little kid, Dad and Mr. Jack Hart were riding up on Otter Creek. Where the two main forks of the creek join, a scant four miles above my present house, the ridge between them drops back toward the upper country as a wide, grassy hill with timber along each edge. At the bottom is a sage brush pocket of perhaps ten acres, and to the west, facing the open hill and overlooking the pocket, is a rocky ridge with a scattering of bull pine.

The two riders topped this ridge and stopped for a minute for Mr. Jack to light his pipe. He was pottering about getting it ready, when he suddenly stiffened. "I say, look theyah," and pointed with his pipe stem at a wolf that had gotten up out of the sage and was sauntering toward the timber. They both were packing rifles, and Mr. Jack jerked his old 303 out of the scabbard, pulled down and dropped the animal in its tracks. He was always a fine rifle shot. At the gunshot two more got up, Dad joined the excitement and the more shooting that went on, the more wolves appeared until it looked like the pocket was boiling with them. When their rifles were empty and their targets had quit the country, they found that they between them had downed eight. "Eight beautehs," the old Englishman told me years later, and they set to skinning the carcasses. Mr. Jack seemed preoccupied and suddenly burst out with,

"By gad, Paul, how many of the bally beasts were theyah?"

Dad had been wondering the same thing, so they exchanged notes and finally came up with a total of thirty-eight different wolves that had come out of the brush.

"Jolly well a Council Rock gathering from Kipling's Mowgli," said the old gentleman. " 'Strordinareh."

Sometimes wolves acted like they had a sense of humor. A rancher who lived up on the head of Dry Creek was coming home from Melville when two wolves showed up out of a coulee. He wasn't carrying a gun, and when they figured out that fact they moved in, ran his dog under the wagon and kept pace with the rig as it moved along. Finally the man stopped and loaded the dog onto the seat with him, much to the animal's relief. The wolves backed off a little and sat comfortably with tongues lolling while he did, and he swore they were grinning. Then they loafed along on either side until he was almost home. He said it didn't seem to bother his team. Maybe they sensed that the wolves weren't gunning for them. The dog took a different point of view.

We had a colored couple working for us for a while when I was a weaner, part of a crew of darkies Aunt Phyllis and her husband had brought out from Virginia. Tom worked around the yard and garden, chored and milked, while his wife did the cooking. They were happy and doing fine until one afternoon he went out over the hill for his milk cows and was gone for such an inordinate amount of time that Dad began to think perhaps one of the cows had come in heat and had gone traveling to see if she could find a bull, and was at the barn saddling a horse when they appeared.

It must have been quite a sight. The cows were ambling along happily, Tom and the dog behind them, and about thirty yards back of the man paced a big old wolf. In front actually, for Tom was walking backwards, carrying an arm load of rocks. To add to his woes, the dog was keeping as close to his heels as possible, practically in amongst his legs, and the old fellow kept tripping over him every few steps. The wolf spotted Dad when he made a run to the house for his rifle, stopped, and then trotted back the way they'd come. When Dad came out with the gun he was just disappearing over the hill and got clean away. Tom arrived, still clutching his rocks, pretty badly shaken, his face plumb grey. When Dad told him that there hadn't really been any danger and that the wolf had just been curious the old darkey told him, "Didn' look cur'us to me, Mister Paul. Jes' look mean. Animal that kill a cow sho' can kill a man, an' we purely like to go on back home." They did go, too, as soon as Dad could take them into Big Timber.

An occurrence at Gramp's lambing camp down on White Beaver, when Dad was a youngster, wasn't so innocuous. One night a wolf got into the shed through a hole in the siding and went on a killing spree. The night man—he had charge of the lambing during the night—went to investigate the ensuing uproar. He was a big, stout newcomer Norsk, descended, I feel sure, from a long line of Vikings, for he immediately charged the animal barehanded. The sheep in the shed slowed the wolf in getting to the hole, and it was just partly through when the man managed to grab it by the tail, get a foot braced on either side of the hole and hold it. Then, by God, he got out the sheath knife that newcomers invariably carried and killed it! When the rest of the crew, wakened by all the racket, got to the shed he was pretty hard to understand, especially in English. Hell, in his shoes I'd have been hard to understand in anything! But he damn sure had a big wolf, stabbed to death, and a bloody knife. For a wonder, he didn't have a scratch on him, either.

The last time I heard a wolf howl was in the late '20s, and in a way it was sort of funny; peculiar, that is. I was alone, headed to the dude ranch from the home place and aboard a colt that had his shingle out as being some pumpkins. Not real bad, just nasty to get on and off; he always tried to spook by and kick, and I wasn't riding him by choice, but because Dad had told me to take him up where we could show him a lot of country. I had gotten away a little late, there was quite a go-round every time we went through a fence, so it was toward dusk by the time we hit the gate tucked under the bluff back of Lookout Mountain. I was shutting the gate, when from the timber a couple of hundred yards above us, a wolf threw back his head and tuned up. The hide between my shoulder blades and up the back of my neck crawled and turned chilly. I was pretty well grown up, and I knew there wasn't anything to be afraid of, but, by God, I *was* afraid. Then there was that ouchy horse. Would I be able to get on him now? God knows he was rank enough normally, and I tightened my hold on the reins so he couldn't jerk away, for I *damn* sure didn't want to be put afoot. I needn't have worried. He was scareder than I was and stood like a rock, shivering, until I was in the saddle. Then we made tracks. Far apart and fast. From then on that colt and I got along real well. Mutual sympathy, I suppose.

That same year, or the next, I was tending camp for a band of sheep Dad had back in the head of Sweet Grass canyon. I was out after my horses one morning just below North Fork Lake when I spotted what at first I took to be a coyote across the pocket from me. As I watched it, I realized it was way bigger than a coyote, and though it saw me, it didn't act a bit worried. In fact it seemed pretty nonchalant as it worked up through the slide rock and limber pine, and finally crossed over the ridge onto American Fork. I figured it was a wolf. Perhaps not, for nothing bothered the band while we were at that camp. If it was, it was the last wild wolf I've ever seen. I'm not a damn bit sad about it, either.

# Shipping Time

## 4

By the mid-thirties most of the dryland farmers had starved out in our part of the country, and the county commissioners abandoned a lot of the roads they had been forced to maintain since the influx of homesteaders. As a result they could do a lot better job of taking care of the remaining roads. That fact, coupled with the advent of sizeable trucks and stock racks gradually put an end to the early day practice of trailing cattle to market under their own power. The establishment of sales rings in the larger towns throughout Montana finished the job, and today practically all the cattle are loaded on semis at the ranches and trucked directly to feeders, or to Billings, Great Falls, Butte or some other good-sized town, and sold. It's handier, faster, easier on stock, and I suppose you could call it progress, but in my estimation it's a damn sorry substitute for the way we used to do it; no excitement or fun.

We said "shipping time" the same way the average person says "autumn," and I imagine I always will; the same way a refrigerator will always be an "icebox"; and it covered roughly from the last week in September through the first week of November. It was during this period that nearly all the ranches gathered their fat cattle, trailed them to the nearest railroad stockyards and loaded them for shipment to a major market. The Northern Pacific, along the Yellowstone, was our nearest rail line, so we trailed to Big Timber and loaded out for Chicago. Of course

I never got to make a trip with a cattle train back then, though in the late thirties I came up from the Mexican border on one with a thousand head for the ranch. Shipping time, with all its associate excitement, was about the high point of the year in my estimation, and I made the trip with the stock to Big Timber each year from the time I learned to ride by myself until I was sent away to school.

The trip usually took us about five days all told. Three days to Big Timber, or just across the river from it where we could hold the stock overnight in a pasture, and a day to load ours and those of the other ranches which were making up the shipment. Sometimes, if a lot of outfits were on their way in to the shipping pens with stock, we might load cattle most of the night to make room in the yards. Then, the next day we'd ride home.

On the way to town, when we got down to where the country was pretty well fenced, we usually could deal with a rancher for a pasture or trap where we could throw our cattle overnight. The first night's bedground, though, up under the Crazies, usually was out in some handy hollow or open creek bottom, and could cause problems. Gentle stock gave no trouble, but though the old-time, open range practice of night herding cattle was pretty much a thing of the past by the time I came along, once in a while we had to do it. I remember the first time I ever stood night guard. We had gathered a string of big steers to ship; three- and four-year-olds; and they were a rank, boogery outfit. The first day out, before we hit the county lanes, Dad decided we'd better hold them together a little and keep an eye on them during the night, for some of the cattle were restless and kept trying to head back for their home range. So he paired off riders to take their shifts together, and then turned to me, "You and I'll take the last go-round," and I bet I grew a couple of inches right then. I was all of five years old, or maybe just six, and here I was a good enough hand to stand guard! I was so excited I couldn't get to sleep for a while, and as I lay there in our bedroll I heard one of the riders singing as he circled the steers. For some reason, though I have never heard it since, I remember the song. Sort of sad, really, but damn sure pure quill cowboy.

*Oh the Indians an' the cowboys*
*They used to live in peace,*
*'Til the goddamned dryland farmers*
*Come adriftin' from the east.*

*Oh down along the coulees*
*Where we used to run our steers*
*They're raisin' big potatoes now,*
*An' little roastin' ears.*

*Oh where once was chaps an' saddles,*
*Spurs, boots an' Stetson hats,*
*The big steam plows are rollin'*
*An' tearin' up the flats.*

*So we'll have to sell our ponies,*
*We'll throw away our twine,*
*An' eat the old sow bosom*
*Right close up to the rind.*

The guard I stood that night actually wasn't so much. Darker than hell with the fires out, my mare looking for spooks, the cattle blowing or grunting occasionally from the darkness, and a wolf howling 'way off. I was glad Dad was with me and gladder yet when light began to outline the hills to the east. But by full daylight, I was riding tall in the saddle; a sure enough hand!

Lots of things happened on those trips that I remember well, like when a rider joined us the next day before we hit the fenced country. He and Dad were talking on the yon side of a deep draw, so, being curious, I poured my mare off into it and up the other side at a run, and pulled up with a flourish beside them. Pop swung around in the saddle with, "What the hell's the idea of running a horse across ground like that for no reason?"

"I'm a member of the Royal Canadian Northwest Mounted Police," I returned proudly; Gramp had read me all about them in the *Youth's Companion.*

"Well, by God, you'll be a member of the Royal Canadian Northwest *Dis*-mounted Police if I ever see you do that again. Get back to the cattle." I went; at a circumspect gait.

My mare, Panama, was a pretty classy mount for a youngster. She was a paint, with the continent of South America in white on her off side, four stockings, and her head was white to above her eyes. Her off eye was blue, what we call a glass eye, and I was very proud of it, even if the white hairs around it caused it to run quite a bit. All in all a flashy mount for a budding hand. She was a funny mare, though, with a lot of personality, even if most of it was cross-grained. She didn't like men, and if one rode her, she bucked. She couldn't buck a wet saddle blanket off, but she'd stay with it as long as her wind lasted. Then, as soon as she got enough air again, she'd have another go at it. Consequently I fell heir to her, and being as I was a kid, she tolerated me. With reservations, of course, for she regularly bedded me down whenever she happened to think of it. Usually once a day, anyhow. Naturally, with the practice, coupled with Dad's occasional exasperated advice, I got so I could ride her pretty well, which, I realized years later, was the reason I had been given her in the first place. She was a hell of a fine ladies' horse, though. Never turned a hair with them, and that was why, one shipping time, she was taken away from me and lent to a friend of my mother.

Her name was Marge Smith, and her dad was the superintendent of the smelter in East Helena, and she and mother had gone to school together in Helena. I didn't like her; she was bossy and always wanted to ride Panny when she visited. Normally it would only be for a ride or two, but this time she was going to make the trip to town with the beef, which meant I'd be set afoot for several days and couldn't go along. So I raised quite a fuss, being careful, however, not to annoy Dad enough so he'd decide I *couldn't* make the trip, and finally he said, "All right, you can come along. Ride Nutsy Fagen."

I wasn't plumb happy about the deal, but I kept my mouth shut. To look at her, Nutsy filled the bill; a grey, pretty, well-bred mare. Trouble was, she'd run up against a shot of loco when she was a yearling or two-year-old, the age when a horse is especially susceptible to loco weed, and, while she was gentle and easy gaited, she had the disconcerting habit of suddenly running backwards with her rider for anywhere from a frog's jump to as far as the spirit moved her. Usually it wasn't too far, thank God, for it sure was unsettling. No rhyme nor reason, and she couldn't help it, just every now and then away she'd go. The hell of it was that a guy not only had to watch where he was going, but had to remember where he'd been to boot, and I didn't like to ride her. But it was a question of her or stay home, so ride her I did.

Well, we strung the cattle out for Big Timber and things rocked along in good shape. Except for me, that is. Three or four times during the morning Nutsy threw it in reverse and away we'd go. When I'd finally get her straightened out, or rather she'd straighten herself out, I'd catch up with the others. Nobody seemed to give a damn about our fits either; just went on moving cattle and talking to one another; so by the time we nooned up at a good spring in a draw west of Wheeler Creek I was working on a real good mad, and pulled off and ate by myself.

We watered the cattle, let them bed down for a while, and after an hour or so headed down the draw for the Wheeler flats. We trailed across them, and just before we hit Ten Mile, as I rode by after one of Nutsy's spasms, Dad asked idly, "How you doing?"

I thought to myself, why you old bastard, you can see how things are doing if you aren't blind, it's your fault, and damned if I'll answer, so I rode on without a word. He called out something else, and once again I paid no attention. There was an exclamation from behind me, and suddenly Dad loped up alongside. He stopped Nutsy, picked me out of the saddle by the front of my shirt, shook me and said in a level tone, "Damn you, when I speak to you, answer me. Even if it's only 'go to hell'."

Well, I was fed to the gills with things, sullen mad and spooked by Nutsy's reverse antics, and as a result my judgment blew sky high. So, as I dangled there by my shirt front, I looked him right in the eye and said, "Go to hell!"

Years later I told Dad I figured it had been a dirty trick to give me a licking; that, what the hell, he'd asked for it; and we chuckled together. But at the time, he was blind to the justice of my answer, and I rode pretty high out of the saddle the rest of the day, no matter in what direction Nutsy happened to be going.

That was a memorable trip, even discounting my mare, for just as we got to the loading pens at Big Timber the next day, we ran into troubles. The yards were on the east edge of town on a bench between the railroad tracks and the edge of a bluff that dropped almost straight off to the Yellowstone about a hundred yards below. The town dump was along the edge of and over the dropoff for a distance of maybe a hundred yards, to boot, and in order to pen cattle they had to be driven up the bench between the tracks and the dump, which ordinarily wasn't too bad.

However, these big country-boy steers of ours, touchy at best, had gotten plumb owly, what with the people, rigs, dogs and other trappings of civilization which had increased steadily as we got closer to town, and were plainly doing a lot of thinking about the beauties of home. As a matter of fact, they were on the verge of just quitting us and heading back en masse. We hadn't met any automobiles, thank God, for there weren't many back then. If we had, it would have been a case of Katy-bar-the-door.

We had to cross the bridge over the river to the town side, and getting the lead started was tricky. When it did, a couple of riders fell in behind them, and at the far end swung around and held them until the rest could cross. The latter started gingerly, but by the time they were halfway across were in a hard run, and they poured off the end, in a clatter of planks and thrumming of iron struts, like water out of a headgate. We got them held, just barely; Nutsy, for a wonder, was operating sanely and seemed to thrive on excitement; but it was a goosey string of cattle that we eased up on to the bench a couple of hundred yards from the stockyards. It sure took kid-glove handling as we worked them along, for they were trying to mill, crowding one another, snorting, and boogering at every shadow. The goodies in the dump alongside weren't helping us either, and if it hadn't been for the tracks on the other side holding them, on the strength of sheer suspicion—the cattle didn't like their looks and wouldn't get near them—we'd have probably spilt the works. At last, though, the point was between the wings that ran out at an angle from each side of the opening into the pens, and we were within probably a minute of slamming the gate behind the last steer when a train whistled at the far end of town. It was coming fast, with its attendant rising roar, and the lead doubled back. Just possibly we might have still held them, but the matter was taken out of our hands and made completely academic when, at the near edge of town, and just beyond the yards, the engineer rared back on his whistle again! Why no riders got run down I don't know, except that the fast freight was alongside the cattle so quickly that they didn't break the way they'd come. Instead they turned inside out, veered away from the tracks, and over the bluff to the river they went, the clatter of tin cans and the popping of bottles audible even through the roar of the train.

There was no use in God's world trying to do anything, so we lined up on the edge of the bluff and watched one of the damndest brouhahas I've ever seen.

There were cattle up, down, or rolling ass over teakettle, the length of the slope, each one doing his level best to get long gone. The lead hit the river, which was swimming water, though the season being early October, not dangerous, on about a thirty-yard front as hard as they could run and disappeared in a cloud of spray. They came up swimming; well, really not swimming, more like each had a high-power propeller; I didn't know cattle could swim that fast! At the yon shore they didn't even bother to shake themselves to get rid of the water, just took up where they'd left off, and hit a barbed wire fence between the river and a hay field on the bottom beyond, wide open. We could hear the wires creak and sing before they popped like .22 rifle shots. Funny thing, they weren't making a sound except for the rattle of their dewclaws. Looked like they were too terrified to bawl; or maybe were saving their wind for running. There was one poor devil, though, who'd rolled in amongst a spring wagon running gear in the dump on our side of the river and was bellowing frantically for his friends to wait for him as he fought feverishly to get loose. He did, in a shower of spring wagon shards and tin cans, hit the river in overdrive and tried to jump it. Being as how he was hampered by a wagon wheel hanging on his horns he tripped and somersaulted in with a roar of fear. He'd shed the wheel when he reappeared, and he boiled across the Yellowstone like a moth-miller in a toilet bowl. If a beaver had started even with him he'd have jerked its head off with a forty-foot rope! He hit the bank with his neck stretched out and his mouth open, and caught the others before they swung around the point of the hill and on up Big Timber Creek for home.

We watched them go, with me just busting to laugh, but, warned by the heat waves coming off the back of Dad's neck, I kept quiet. Finally his tight jaw eased off. "Damn that engineer to hell," he said, "and there's no way we can whip him either. At that it was almost worth it to watch that last steer swim the river. I couldn't figure whether he was in the water or on it. Well, hell, let's mosey on up town and leave our horses at the West Side Livery, and get something to eat at the Chinaman's." So we did.

By evening we were getting reports of steers stirring up cattle, milk cows, Hollander farmers, drylanders and Norwegian herders and their bands all the way to Ten Mile and beyond, and in the morning mother called up from the ranch to report that some steers were already back. We gathered them all the way home, though it took three days and a lot of broken fences to do it, and, surprisingly, none was badly hurt. Skinned up a little, and gant as gutted snakes was all, and one had a can on a front foot. We stretched him out and cut it off with a pocket knife, and he'd lost the hitch in his getalong by the time we got home. There were a few, of course, that we never located until a couple of months later, and they went the next year.

After they'd had a couple of weeks to quiet down and put a little tallow back on, Dad and about a dozen good cowhands, well mounted, headed them for Big Timber again, and this time got them penned, loaded and on their way to Chicago. I didn't get to go along, but consoled myself with the thought that it couldn't possibly be as exciting as the first trip had been. I believe, too, that the railroad was warned as to what would happen if another freight came by at a crucial moment, and the station agent, being right handy and open to suggestions, saw that none did.

Another trip during shipping time comes to mind; in '32 it was. Dad, for very probably the first time, had decided to sell his calves rather than to run them over to yearlings, twos, or more, in the old style. He'd made a deal with a buyer and was to deliver the calves at the railroad pens for shipment to a middlewestern feeder. No money had changed hands; just a normal handshake agreement.

Anyhow, Dad decided we'd trail the calves in, still on the cows, and cut them off in the yards. That way they'd have their moms, and milk, up until they were weighed.

There were six of us with around three hundred head of cows and their calves, they handled well, and the trip in was uneventful. However, after we got the cattle into the stockyards the buyer must have decided we were a long ways from home and figured he'd pull a fast one. So he reneged on the price he had offered for the calves. Probably thought he had Dad under the gun, but he damn sure misjudged his man.

"You sniveling bastard," Dad told him. "A man whose word isn't as good as his bond is a sorry specimen. Hell, I'll trail my stock home again; that doesn't matter; but if I see you around when we start tomorrow I'll drop a loop on you and break you to lead. Or maybe you'd like to get down off of the fence into the pen here, and I'll educate you right now," and he stepped off his horse.

The buyer wanted no part of it. He got off the fence in a hurry, but on the outside, climbed in his car and went yonder. He wasn't in evidence in town that night; and damn sure not the next morning when we headed the cattle for the ranch.

We were strung out moving fine about eight miles out of town when an old truck, with sideboards, came up from behind us. Leslie Browne, known as "Grizzly," and I were in the drag, and I idly noticed that the license plate wasn't from Montana, but it was too dirty to tell where it was from. Dad dropped back and started opening a lane through the stock for the outfit, and suddenly Grizzly spurred his old pony and made a run for the truck just after it passed him.

Well, I thought, maybe the guy nicked his horse and Les is figuring on snatching him out of the rigging and stomping him, and I got interested all of a sudden; we were all still sort of ouchy about the calf deal, anyhow. But when he got to the side of the truck, which was easing along in low gear behind Dad, he climbed onto it from his saddle and waved to me to come on, come on! I did, and he leaned down, came up with a watermelon, handed it to me, then another one, said, "Keep an eye on my horse," and waved to the next rider as they went by him. By the time the poor driver had worked through the stock all four of us were carefully balancing two watermelons apiece, and Griz dropped off with two more cradled against his chest.

The truck cleared the last cattle and disappeared up the lane. Dad rode back to us, looking more and more surprised the nearer he got. "I be damned, where'd those come from?" and we all grinned at Leslie.

"That old boy had a load of 'em on," he explained. "Peeked in an' saw 'em when he went by me, an' figured a melon or so'd go good. Thought Spike'd never catch on. Time the others seen him an' me, though, she went fine."

"Well," said Dad, "He's long gone now, and we sure can't catch him. The cattle are moving fine, so how about us stopping a while and trying those out for size before somebody drops one. There are too many to handle ahorseback, except inside us."

We did exactly that, and there were puzzled looks from the few outfits that went down the road by us at the spectacle of six guys sitting in the sage brush eating watermelon in October. Some of our friends even got so curious they whoaed up and came back to find out about things, and they got their share of melon, too. I've wondered what the poor fellow with the truck thought when he looked in his outfit; must have figured his load had settled considerably.

The last time we trailed cattle into town to ship was about '38. During the trip we ran into problems that, as far as we were concerned, put an end to shipping time as I'd always known it; good roads and lots of cars. The D-Y Trail, from Canada to Yellowstone Park, ran north from

Big Timber, and the old dirt road now was paved for eight miles out of town and a lot of travelers through the state used it. We had cows and calves again, and they weren't too well acquainted, nor wanted to be, with anything but a man ahorseback or teams and wagons, so the trip was hard on our dispositions, horse flesh, lane fences and tallow; and the latter is what the cow business is all about.

We'd made it within some three miles of the stockyards by evening. As a matter of fact, to the ranch where we had always penned the stock for the night if it were late, but it had changed hands and we didn't know the new owner, so we kept on. It had gotten pretty dark and there was no moon, but the cattle had been spooked so often during the day that they were getting tired. Which was all to the good; for pavement is not the ideal footing for jumping a horse out and turning a runaway calf, particularly a shod horse.

We were almost to the Big Timber Creek bridge, which is at the end of a half-mile straightaway, when a car came down the stretch. The driver evidently figured he was late for whatever he was going to, though from the way he was traveling it was a pretty good bet that he was going to one hell of a surprise. Barbara had ridden back up the road a hundred yards or so, and had been slowing the cars down, and I could see her in his lights waving a warning, but he just kept firing up the boilers.

Two things went through my mind; the damn fool was going to kill my wife; and he was going to be early in hell shortly thereafter. If the cows didn't see to that, I would.

I saw Barbara rein off, the lights glinted on her inside spur as it hit her horse's shoulder, he jumped sideways, and the car went by. Close enough, it seemed, that you couldn't have slipped a cigarette paper between them. The near miss must have registered on the driver, for he hit the brakes and came lurching down the road with a squeal of rubber, and riders scattered into the borrow pit. He was still moving pretty briskly when he plowed into the cattle.

The car came to a jarring stop, the hind legs of a big calf sticking out from underneath. As we converged on it like ants on a grasshopper, the whitefaced driver met us, apologizing profusely. Mayhem was imminent, but just as I reached for his neck someone said, "Look!" and out from under the vehicle a wet, steaming stain spread across the pavement in the glow of the one remaining headlight.

Gently we pulled out the carcass, and as we stretched it out in the light Barbara pulled up, stepped down, gritted, "Damn you, *damn* you," and the guy backed away apprehensively. As he did, an eye opened, a startled bovine stare appraised the surroundings, and with a rattle of hooves the calf scrambled to his feet and galloped off to his compatriots with nary a sign of injury.

As we blankly watched him go you could see the man sort of let his weight down a little. Dad dipped a finger in the liquid on the road, smelled it and said, "What do you know, it's water." Inspection brought the discovery that the radiator was magnificently squashed and completely drained. How the car could have hit the cattle hard enough to break a headlight and smash the radiator without doing any damage, barring the calf's nerves, is beyond me. But all's well that ends well, so we gathered our stock and started them again.

Just before we left the man, he asked plaintively, "What am I going to do?" and I imagine our suggestions were of small comfort. "I don't give a hoot in hell," contributed Dad; "Learn to drive," Barbara suggested; and, "Thank God," was my advice. I meant it wholeheartedly!

We reached the stockyards without further incident. The buyer was waiting to receive the cattle and asked if we could help him shape them up, as he intended to load just as soon as he could, so we cut the calves off their mothers. Then the man, for some obscure reason, asked if we'd help him cut the calves by sex, steers and heifers. This was going to be no cinch, for the yards were poorly lit, and we were going to have to find a spot where we could see the belly line of each animal as it came up the alley to the cutting gate in the semi-darkness. We were discussing the best way to do it when a girl came over to us. She had been a guest at the dude ranch, had stayed on for shipping time and had made the trip in with us. She was plainly worried by the job at hand and asked, "Uncle Paul"—that was Dad—"How in the world can we tell the difference between them in the dark?" Then she brightened, "Though I suppose we *could* use the touch system."

Another shipping time happenstance comes to mind from away back. I think it was the year after I had my short-lived tour in the Canadian constabulary. We were strung out across the basin south of Wolf Butte, Dad, myself and another rider in the drag. One steer had been lagging all morning, for something was plainly wrong with him. It might have been loco or a touch of tall larkspur—delphinium to a gardener, poison to a cattleman—that he'd picked up early some summer and hadn't quite died of; or maybe Nature, as she sometimes does, was careless, or just working for the hell of it, when she made him. In any event, the poor devil was in sorry shape; tottery, sunken-eyed and rough-haired. As he wobbled into a shallow draw Dad glanced at him and remarked to the other rider, "Looks like I might get that poor damn steer gone. Bothers me to see something like that and not be able to help them. I'll be glad to get rid of him."

By the time he had finished speaking the steer had stopped, sort of all spraddled out. I, wanting to get into things, said, "I'll get him," rode up alongside, and popped him with the ends of my bridle reins. The result chilled me, for the steer shivered, collapsed, gave a strangled cough and died. Dead as a door nail!

My hindquarters tightened in anticipation of coming events, but Dad was philosophical. "Well, it looks like I'm sure rid of him," and I relaxed. It was quite a while, though, before I rode up and swatted an animal again.

Then there was the time Dad drove the pigs to town. He was a great hog fancier; claimed they'd raise three litters a year instead of just one calf. The drawback was that he just ran them loose, much to the dismay, and annoyance, of our neighbors, but finally, when Mom's garden and the potato patch showed up missing one morning, he decided to get rid of all but a few breeding sows he could keep penned. So there was a hog gathering.

I was pretty little, so I missed it, but I sure heard it. Hogs at best are vocal, and since these were to all practical purposes, feral, their clashes with dogs and riders were full-mouthed, to say the least. Dogs like to work hogs anyhow because they make such lovely and exciting noises. But finally the gather was complete, and the hogs safely in a tight pen.

The next day, Dad, all the men on the ranch except the chore boy, and several extremely willing neighbors, among whom was Mr. Jack Hart, headed them for town. They were ahorseback for the first part of the trip while the hogs would still be spooky. Then, when they hit fenced country, where horses would be a drawback, and their charges hopefully more tractable, they would finish the trip afoot.

They must have gotten to town, but everyone who made the trip was curiously reticent whenever the subject arose later on. It was at least thirty years later that Barbara and I had Mr. Jack down for dinner at our Melville ranch, and after a few drinks and a good meal I broached the subject to the old gentleman.

"Jove, yes. I do indeed recall it." I am sure he shuddered slightly. "Frightful! Absolutely! Jolly well a mahvel that no murdeh occurred among us. I dahsay, also, one could have beaten any bush within a mile of our pawth from the rawnch to the Yellowstone and flushed a bally hog from it for months thereawfteh. Gad!"

That was all, but I got the idea.

# Ranch Hands

## 5

THE OLD-TIME RANCH HAND was a different breed of cat than today's "agricultural employee." Nowadays they all have cars, go to town at least every weekend, and spend their wages. The first time I noticed the trend was better than twenty years ago. I had a couple of good young fellows working for me during haying. They had an old car and went to town almost every night, drawing their day's wages each time. At the end of six weeks' steady work I paid them off; one had one day's wages coming and the other broke even. It put me in mind of the old song, "I went to the boss to draw my roll and he had me figured out ten dollars in the hole," but they were plumb happy; said, hell, they'd spent it.

The men we used to have seldom got to town. Maybe two or three times a year was all. As a matter of fact, in view of the fun and frolic involved, that probably was about all they could stand.

When a man did go to town the first thing on the agenda was to buy clothes and things he'd need for the next six months or so. Then he'd put on a new outfit and send everything else back to the ranch on the stage. The latter was to cut down the odds that he might hock something, or trade it for booze later on. Then would come the drunk, and by night every denizen of the bars would know, and take advantage of the fact, that a live one had hit town. I'm not including the bartenders in that; they were almost

51

without exception damn good men. As one once told me, "Hell, I get 'em drunk, so I figure I better keep an eye on 'em so's the law won't bother 'em too bad."

Years ago one saloon owner had a big back room in his establishment with sawdust on the floor and ringbolts along the walls maybe three feet above the floor, each with about two feet of cotton rope tied to it. When a customer'd get too drunk to navigate, one of the bartenders would take him back, bed him down in the sawdust, and tie a foot up pretty close to the ringbolt. When the guy was sober enough to sit up and get his foot untied he could come back and do some more drinking. Meanwhile he was reasonably comfortable with no chance of getting into trouble. I might add that the sawdust was changed right frequently. Needless to say, that saloon keeper was a respected and well-liked man, especially by his patrons, and he deserved it.

Anyhow, when the average man was sick, sober and sorry enough, and usually broke to boot, he'd get word to the boss to come get him. Actually, if a man had worked for an outfit long enough, the boss would know about when to come get him anyway. Then it would be six months or so till it was repeated.

There were some, particularly the younger men, who never drew much cash but took their wages in livestock, usually heifers, with the right to run them on the outfit. So we had quite a few who, when they left after a number of years, had a start in the cow business. I might add that today the cow business is a luxury damn few ranchers can afford, but in those days when a boy of that caliber married the local schoolma'am, or whatever, he usually was in pretty good shape.

The ranch hands, back when Dad was a youngster, damn sure had the bark on! Charley Bennett, a New Mexican and a popping good cowhand, came calling on my Aunt Allie. Her younger sister, Aunt Phyllis, figured she'd have a little fun one time and spook him. So she hid behind the back door, jumped out and said "Boo!" as he was leaving. Only it didn't work out the way she'd planned. She found herself looking down the barrel of his gun. "Gawd, girl," he told her, "Don't never do that. I like to shot you." She says she's never tried to spook anybody since then.

Nate Young was another of the same ilk. He'd come north with a trail herd, and must have left some trouble back home. He was a real good man, made a first class hand for Gramp, but as long as he worked for him he'd never sit with his back to a window or door, and when he ate he always laid his gun on the table right handy. He and Sim Roberts, another touchy customer, didn't see eye to eye, and the upshot was that Sim killed Nate on the main street of Big Timber in '99.

Gramp had a cook, too, an ex-buffalo hunter and scout whose uniform in the kitchen consisted of a big hat much the worse for wear, buckskin shirt, pants, moccasins, a flour sack apron and a big six-shooter. I gather he was a good cook and that he was also a good shot, for whenever he'd open a can of anything he'd take the empty to the back door, throw it in the air and put a hole in it before it hit ground. Gramp said everybody got used to it in time, except possibly Granny, and the kids sure liked the man's gaudy stories.

Granny had a strapping Norsk girl, Tina, from the "Settlement" helping her around the house. Dad always chuckled about one time when a milk cow had just calved and he and his sisters were having trouble getting her in and the calf off her. Pretty juicy old cow, half Shorthorn and the rest range stock. She was horned, knew how to use them, and was eager to demonstrate. The kids were ahorseback but even so, it took quite a while to work her over to the buildings, and she finally sulled up on the hill about thirty yards above the corral. Tina saw the commotion and up from the house she came. Picking up a stick she

strode up the hill toward the cow and calf. Of course the
kids all yelled that the cow was on the fight, look out and
get back, but the girl just kept coming, telling them, "Ay
vill gat her." She did! Up to the tail end she came, swatted
it with the stick and said loudly, "Coom now," and the cow,
who had been eyeing the riders in front of her, swapped
ends with a bawl of rage. The girl took in those horns, red
eyes and slobber, and turned this would-be cattle drive into
a footrace. "Yeesus!" she said, gathered her skirt up to her
waist and headed down the hill for the corral at a high lope.
Dad said she was a long-legged girl and was making a good
ten or twelve feet to a stride, so the cow, who had started
with her horns tickling a pair of drawers, lost ground
though she was digging like a champion. As the girl got to
the corral, she put one foot about halfway up and swung up
and astride the top pole. The cow hit the corral with a
crash, knocking herself silly. As she staggered back, sway-
ing, the kids swarmed down and snaggled the calf, while
the girl ran the back of her arm along her forehead, flipped
it in the air, and said, "Oofdah! Ay svat!"

Dad told me, too, as a warning when I deviled any of the
men working for us, about how, when he was a kid, he and
his sisters slipped up to a sheep wagon and smeared
molasses on the inside of the window in the back. About
then the herder showed up and took a jaundiced view of the
goings on. The upshot was that he set his dog to watching
them while they licked the window clean. Most herders
don't waste much time in housekeeping so a camp window
isn't plumb appetizing and the herder had said, "Not yust
de molass' but ever'ting," and that's what they did. Dad
said the fly specks were the worst, and that in short order
his tongue felt like it was a yard long. His mouth kept
watering, too, he damn sure didn't want to swallow, and
every time he'd back off for a breath of air the herder'd say,
"Vatch dem, Vooley," and the dog would growl and show
his teeth. Finally the man decided it was clean enough,

after making them redo the corners, and let them go. When they got home and complained to Gramp, he chuckled and said it served them right. They never did tell Granny for fear of what measures she'd have taken to counteract the germs. Anyhow, they learned a lesson, and from then on whenever they got into devilment they'd put a sentry out on the nearest hill. Even so, Dad said, they were pretty damn careful what they did.

Later, when I was a kid, the men Dad had weren't as raunchy maybe, but they nonetheless qualified as individualists. Table manners weren't their long suit by and large, and the hearty eating habits of two in particular are still fresh in my memory. Of one I heard somebody in the bunkhouse make a remark that just about covered things. "If he'd only keep his damn front feet outa th' trough a man wouldn't mind so bad." The other standout had a big mustache, and, when he especially liked something, he'd corral the platter in the crook of one arm while he ate with the other, dispensing with a knife for fear of letting go of the platter. Anybody wanting whatever he had gathered in almost had to take it away by main strength. Naturally he came into a good deal of hard feelings, engendered in part, I feel sure, by yet another endearing habit. As a final fillip to a meal he would comb his mustache with his fork and carefully lick off the gleanings. Neat, tidy, and damn sure not wasteful, but I noticed everybody tried to be all done with the meal before he went into his final act. Fortunately he was only there for haying, for by the time he left the crew was gobbling their food like a bunch of coyotes.

We had a man with a peg leg, too, and he sure made a hand as a rider or roper, or anything else. He was a good skinner and he broke work colts when he was feeding in the winter, and claimed they learned to stand well when he was loading at the stack. He'd put a hobnail in the end of his peg so he'd have a purchase on the hayrack floor when he set back on the lines. He could even stack hay. Just nailed a tomato can on the peg so he wouldn't bog down. Said he liked the winter best because, "Feet's what gets th' coldest. I only got one, so I stay warmer than most folks."

Melville had a salty baseball team back then, and a bitter rivalry with Two Dot over on the Musselshell, and Big Timber down on the Yellowstone. Every ranch in the community contributed members, and Dad always seemed to have two or three men working for him during the summer, who, while they were no great shucks on a hay crew or building fence, damn sure could play ball. Some of them came from quite a way off, too. "Chicago Bill" was one of those imports, and he liked the country so well that, after the baseball season was over, he asked if he could stay on. He was a good man, so Dad said sure, and one suppertime Mother asked him if he'd come around the next day and help her put down some sauerkraut. Later that evening he came to the house and asked if he could have a couple of old, clean dish towels, and disappeared back to the bunkhouse with them.

The next morning he showed up after breakfast all slicked up, in a new pair of Levis, with the legs rolled up so far and tight that the veins in his legs throbbed like blue snakes, with his bare feet carefully wrapped in the dish-towels. Mother, in some surprise, finally said, "My but you look nice this morning, Bill."

He proudly replied, "Thanks, Ma'am. I hauled water and bathed real good last night, an' I washed hell outa my feet again after breakfast, so I'm ready to tromp that 'kraut for you soon as I get these towels off."

Mother told him she appreciated all the trouble he'd gone to, and learned that he'd been assured in the bunk-house that he'd have to get in the barrel to tramp the sauerkraut bare footed. Bill was pretty quiet during the rest of the day. There were broad grins around the table in the men's dining room that evening, and roars of glee once they were outside the house. There was a fight or two in the bunkhouse later, and the next morning Bill asked for his time. A shame, too; he was a good man, but lacking a cow country sense of humor.

A man who stammered worked for us for a long time. He loved to talk, but when he got excited, which was just a frog's hair from his normal self, he stuttered up to where he sounded like a stationary engine at top speed. His name was Otto, but he went by "Stampede." He was also strong on windies, and for years there was an old wood-slat manure spreader on the outfit with "Stampede" lettered boldly on the side. Some joker with a paintbrush!

Otto was hard to buck off, if you could get him on a bronc, that is. Every now and then we'd make the match, and even if nothing happened at the corrals Stampede would always ask, when we got back from a circle, "D-d-dya see him t-t-turn it on when I g-g-got over th' hill?" Of course nobody had been able to see through the hill, and he damn sure knew it. We saw him once, though. During shipping time we were trailing a string of steers to Big Timber to load for Chicago. Part of the county lane ran along the edge of a cut bank that dropped off into a creek about a hundred feet below. We'd talked Otto onto a bronc that morning and he'd ridden him. But I guess the old pony had been carrying a grudge, for right above the bank he let out a bawl, threw a fit, bucked through the steers, into the lane fence and over the cut bank. He was two-thirds or more over the edge when the wire stopped him and there they hung with Stampede, still in the saddle, looking down between the horse's ears at the creek below. "Wh-wh-what'll I do n-n-now?" he croaked. It looked a little raspy for sure, but we finally got some ropes on the horse and got the two of them back on solid ground. It was awfully hard from then on out to get him on anything that wasn't dog gentle.

We once had a guest at the dude ranch named Charley. He was a nice young fellow but had trouble talking when he got stirred up. He'd sort of hang fire and keep repeating ah-ah-ah, with his right elbow getting higher and higher. We were at the home ranch one day and Stampede was handy, so I introduced the two. I wasn't being ornery, I was just curious.

"Pup-pup-pleased t-t-to meetcha," said Otto, and stuck out his hand. Charley reached for it, opened his mouth and said, "Ah-ah-ah," and his hand came back as his elbow went up. From then on it was bad. There they stood, nose to nose, each figuring he was being mocked. Stampede sounding like a string of firecrackers, and Charley plumb high centered, his mouth open and his elbow pointed straight up. I was ashamed of myself, so I explained to them that it was for real. In maybe fifteen minutes they were talking together in good shape, and being nice guys, neither blamed me.

Back in the late forties I had a man with a cleft palate working for me during haying; a nice fellow and a good hand. He went by the name of "Otay" because he used the expression "Okay" a lot, and that was about as close as he could come to it. Anyhow, he was raking hay and was probably half a mile from where we were stacking. Even so, we occasionally could hear him yell something at the gentle old team he was using. At lunch one of the bullrake men who had been bucking hay to the stack from quite a bit closer to where the raking was going on, said, "Say, Otay."

"Hnuh?" and he looked up from his plate.

"What's the name of your near horse? I know you call the off one 'Muhmuhmuhmits,' but how about the other?"

Years ago, on Billy Creek, Dad had a chore boy who quit. It was just before shipping time and everybody was too busy to take him to Melville to the stage that day, so he decided to walk, it being a matter of only about five miles. His forty years' gatherin's didn't include a bedroll, so he sacked all his plunder in a salt bag, got his check, and pulled out. To get to the county road he had to cross a pasture below the place, a full section, a mile across. A string of big steers that had been gathered to ship were being held in the pasture, and that was the poor devil's undoing.

Big steers, especially when they are fat and feeling good, are terrible gunsels. Curious, excitable, silly as school girls, and arrant cowards who can frighten themselves by merely thinking about it. They are harmless unless you crowd one enough to get him on the prod, but they can look pretty scary. Especially when they are horned, full of vinegar, and there are enough of them to act as brave-makers for each other. There were a couple of hundred in the pasture when the kid started through it. He was from back east somewhere, too, and didn't savvy cattle; leastways that kind of cattle.

He was pretty well out in the field when a steer spotted him, and not having seen a man afoot before, except in a corral, let out a bellow of excitement, and here he came at a lope for a closer look, bucking, kicking, and hooking at his shadow every now and then. The boy's powder began to dampen, and he speeded up his gait to a brisk walk. Of course every steer within earshot of the first immediately began to sound off as they came on high to find out what was going on, and when they saw this strange object their interest exploded. Steers are a mouthy outfit at best, so in short order every animal in the section was converging on the poor guy, talking excitedly about what they were going to do about whatever the hell it was. Naturally the man picked up to a long trot, and then a run. This was right down the steers' alley. Glorious! Something that would run for them, and they enthusiastically joined in the fun. Better, even, than chasing a coyote.

Nobody saw the actual proceedings, but any cowman knows what happened. The old kid lost his head, for which he couldn't be blamed, seeing as how he was green when it came to cattle, sacrificed his possible sack in the interests of speed and headed for the yon side of the pasture as hard as he could run. The steers, except those who stayed to booger themselves with the sack, were hard on his heels and having just a hell of a time. I don't imagine he ran wide open for much more than half a mile, but that's aplenty. When he reached the fence he fell through it, crawled a little way beyond, was violently sick, and passed out.

Somebody spotted the body a while later, investigated, and took him to Melville. There he got a ride to Big Timber, and we heard that he took the first train that was headed east. They said he was pretty jumpy while he waited for it, and when somebody's old milk cow bawled from a back yard in town he practically barricaded himself in the waiting room. Poor devil, if he'd just taken a run at the steers they'd have probably crippled one another trying to get away from him; certainly they wouldn't have hurt him. They were just playing.

Sort of like the Frenchman at a cow camp years ago; they slipped him a bronc, he bucked off, and when he complained he was told the horse had just been playing with him.

"Playing?" said he. "If zees ees zee case, I would rahzer zee game to make myself."

Those steers and the chore boy remind me of Gramp's story of the buffalo and the railroads in the early days. Seems the animals kept rubbing the telegraph poles down. Perfectly naturally, since there weren't many trees in the plains country. That was why, until they were plowed up, there were so many buffalo wallows in the region; because a buffalo rolls, like a horse, to scratch and dust himself, and their humps eventually dig out a depression in the soil which in time and with lots of use gets to be permanent. There are still wallows in the native grass country under the Crazies. Anyhow, some hot shot in an office back east came up with the idea of driving long sharp spikes through the poles, up to a height of five or six feet, to stand the animals off. From a buffalo's point of view this transformed the smooth poles into magnificent scratching places, word got around among them, and, where previously one animal had come to rub, now dozens came to tend to their itches. Consequently the new poles were laid down in veritable windrows. So the railroads had to go back to the original variety again until the herds were wiped out. Hell, anyone that knows bovine habits could have foreseen the result of those spikes.

I grew up alongside the Norwegian settlement on the Sweet Grass above Melville, and we had Norsks working for us as far back as I can remember. I learned to swear in Norwegian just as early as I learned to in English, and I am still bilingual when it comes to cussing. Trilingual, actually, because I can handle Spanish pretty well, too. A "newcomer" was fresh out of the old country, and a lot of the earlier ones worked for Gramp at one time and another. He claimed the first English they learned was, "Goddam," and, "T'irty dollars a mont'," but they were popping good men and nice guys, and in many cases their third and fourth generation descendants are still living on the places where they originally settled, and they, too, are hard workers and good neighbors. The original settlers established the Melville Lutheran church in 1885, the first church of the denomination in Montana Territory, and it is still going strong. God fearing people.

One of the newcomers working for Gramp was quite a go-getter, and was always working on his English, and his accent, and bugging other people about theirs, as well. He and another man from the ranch were down at the Melville store one day, and he asked the clerk for some ginger snaps. His partner, a German, figured he'd do a little bugging himself, and took him to task, in all seriousness. "Ha, Ole, you are so damn schmart and you say 'yinyer snaps'! Vy not say it der American vay like I do, 'chincha sneps'!"

In the line of self improvement this same Norsk was always borrowing books from Gramp. One evening he brought one down to the house, and when asked what he wanted to read next inquired as to whether a copy of "The Traveling Ute" was available. When asked who it was by, he said, "Some big yeneral." Well, Gramp sifted through every Indian book he had, Army books, and Indian Campaign books, but came up empty. His curiosity aroused by now, he settled down to lengthy and devious questioning, and at long last discovered what Ole was after; "The Wandering Jew" by General Lew Wallace!

A number of years later, after Ole had married and homesteaded, he arrived at the ranch all stirred up. It developed that he'd been having trouble with two drylander neighbors, brothers, and had decided to "vip dem," and he wanted Dad along to keep the two from doubling up on him. Pop, always one for any excitement, said sure, and away to the two drylanders' place they rode.

When they arrived, Ole stepped down, handed his reins to Dad, swaggered up to the brothers—they'd come to the door to say howdy—and announced his intentions. One of the two answered that he hated to see a good man waste a druther, and that Ole could build to it when he had a mind to. They tangled, and the brother proved to be damn hard to "vip." So much so that before long he was doing most of the "vipping," so Ole called for Dad to help.

"Hell, no," was Dad's response. "You asked me to come along so they wouldn't both jump you. They haven't needed to, looks like, so if you can't finish what you started maybe you better call things off."

Ole did, and the brothers got a bucket of water from the well and helped clean him up. Then they had a shot of moonshine all around and went home. I don't believe there was any more trouble from then on until the brothers finally starved out in the '20s.

A couple of years ago an old fellow and his wife drove in

to the dude ranch and asked for Dad. He expressed regret when I told him Dad had died the year before, said that he lived in Illinois now, but had homesteaded below Melville and had known Dad. He wanted to talk about those times, fifty-odd years before, and since I knew a lot of the people from back then, or about them anyhow, I asked him in and we had quite a talk. When he happened to mention that he'd had a brother with him on the homestead, I got curious and asked him if he'd ever whipped one of his neighbors.

"Hell yes, once," he said with a grin. "That's when I met your dad," and he told me the story just the way Dad had told it. He wasn't a very big man, and must have been, as the fellow says, "Little for big, but hell for stout," for Ole was right sizeable. He was a nice guy and I hope he had as good a time with us as we did listening to him remembering.

I graduated from Berkshire School back in Massachusetts the spring of 1932. Times were awful tough, so, though I had a scholarship to Harvard, I wrote to see if they'd hold it for a year for me. Their response was that they would, and so the winter of '32 and '33 I stayed home on the ranch and worked. Mother and Dad went east right after Christmas to drum up dude business, and I was left alone, with a couple of Norsks, to tend to things. Dad believed in responsibility, and I was a kid just out of prep school; but, what the hell, I'd learn. We had a big old girl, Norsk naturally, doing the cooking. Dad had told me he wanted us to butcher about a half dozen hogs as soon as he was gone, and put them up for the summer. We did, but it got ungodly cold—forty below and more—so we hung them where the magpies couldn't get at them and waited for a good chinook to thaw them so we could finish the job. The hogs were what started the trouble.

The girl, as soon as the family left, had gone to cooking primarily for the other men. I like most Norwegian food, hell, I was raised around it; fattigman, krumkakken, chudballer, remmagrut, lefse—one of the finest things ever concocted—and even lutefisk can sometimes be passable; but these three went on a Scandinavian gourmet spree. Maybe, if I'd been weaned on it I wouldn't have found it so tough, but it flat overwhelmed me. The thing was that these two, when the hogs were stuck, caught the blood in kettles, stirred salt into it so it wouldn't clabber, and, practically licking their chops, carried it carefully down to the house to the girl. She, immediately and happily, embarked on a sanguinary culinary kick. Her idea of dessert was blood pudding, a Norsk delicacy I can damn sure take or leave, preferably the latter. Blood pancakes, which are, in my considered opinion, pieces of old inner tubes which have been impregnated with hog blood. The latter tastes about like a hog smells anyway, which doesn't exactly excite me gastronomically. There was a juicy blood sausage she'd fry for breakfast, and unless a guy washed his teeth immediately, and before the grease got cool, he'd resemble the eminent Count Dracula for the rest of the day. Or blood "dumples," made of a mixture of grated raw potatoes, flour, pepper, and blood, with each dumpling having a thimble sized chunk of hog fat in its center, and the whole boiled in water of a becoming pink hue. Incidentally, when a piece of blood dumple hit the bottom of a man's stomach it hit like a chunk of lead and stayed, resulting in coppery belches for hours; hell, for days! I stayed away from the house as much as possible so I wouldn't have to watch her, or smell her, mixing and cooking, and I'd hold off until way late at night so I could sneak in after she was done with the food. I got to be a reasonably steady customer at McQuillan's saloon at Melville, too, even though the weather was damn brisk and it necessitated a ride of five miles each way. Meanwhile, the other two men went around with broad, satisfied grins, and took to arriving ten to fifteen minutes early for meals.

Finally we ran out of hog blood, and my hopes skyrocketed, but I soon found that her long suit was now fried fresh side pork. Three times a day; occasionally gussied up with a white gravy that resembled nothing so much as runny library paste. I have never been really ecstatic about fresh side pork, even when it's fried crisp. This wasn't. Unfailingly it was limp, pallid and slick, and the platter was usually cool enough so the slices nestled cozily in partly solidified lard. Not only were mealtimes pretty nauseating, but there was a fringe benefit, if you can call it that, to the girl's preoccupation with side pork, that became a problem.

I was feeding the cattle, so I had several loads of loose hay to pitch each day. A pitchfork handle is one of the greatest heat generating propositions ever invented, and when I use one I sweat, no matter what the weather. The trouble· was, that due to my diet, what I got to sweating was practically pure leaf lard, and it made me so slick I had trouble keeping my clothes on. Which isn't real shiny in below zero weather. I thought seriously of taking a pick down to the creek and breaking loose a chunk of sand to take to the house to thaw and dry. Then I planned on carrying a small sack of it on the rack standard and scattering a handful down my neck when I felt things start to go. Figured it would give my clothes traction and they'd stay put. However, it didn't come to that, for the family got back from New York, and the food underwent a drastic change. I still like Norwegian cooking, but thanks to that winter, I draw the line at the more exotic varieties. Side pork I won't eat.

Even so, I remember those Norsks who worked for us, in one instance from before I was born until well after I was married, with a good deal of affection. Good men. Men who took pride in their work; men who put the welfare of the livestock in their care ahead of their own. They helped raise me, and many's the time it must have been a pretty thankless proposition. I overheard one; he was celebrating in the Melville saloon at the time; asked why he had worked for us so long. His answer still warms me. "Ay like dem. De old yentleman Wan Cleve is a fine man. Paul Yunior is a good man, too." A pause, "An' den dat damn Spike!"

azy Mountains—head of Big Timber Creek

e Melville Country

*Butte Ranch, 1885 (original house on right)*

*Gramp, 1880*

*Gramp, 1945*

*tte Ranch, 1900*

*ing room*

*On a Sunday afternoon—at Melville*

*Forefooted*

*aded for the corrals*

*ipping time*

*Frank*

*Aunt Allie*

*Crew and cook*

*ey had the bark on.*

*ming to the fire*

*Dad, 1900*

*Ranch visitors*

*Near the stillhouse*

*Lobo*

*en I was a kid*

*Wolf hunters: me, Dad—Billy Creek Ranch, 1917*

*Starting the gather: (left to right) me, Jim Bowman, Dad, Aunt Phyllis, Aunt Allie, Bill Hunt*

*Dad on "Lady"*

*Waiting for the irons to heat*

ady for the iron

Dad working out the kinks

*Ready for the show—Big Timber, 1930*

*Melville Rodeo, 1940*

rse race—Melville, 1904

Bucking contest—Melville, 1900

b Langston

Fringe benefits—Livingston Roundup

ROSS MADDEN

Tracy fitting a ride—Big Timber, 1925

*vder horses*

*mwinder Tunnel, Belle Mining Company*

*d rock man, Belle Mining Company*

*Saloon where we lived in 1937—later the ''YMCA''*

*Urner Store, Melville*

# Cody and Terry

## 6

I AM A HORSE MAN. I was raised with them, have lived with them all my life, and I hope I'll die with them. I've known a lot of good ones and a few bad ones. But looking back, while I've ridden—and still do—some popping fine saddle horses, it seems to me that I've known more really great work horses than I have riding horses. Maybe it's because none of the work stock bucked me off when I was breaking them—I never was a bronc rider by any stretch of the imagination—but I can well remember some real juicy go-rounds the first time I hooked up a stout old colt, so I guess the bucking off hasn't anything to do with it! It wasn't that we had more work horses, or that I was around them more, because we didn't and I wasn't. It was, I have finally decided, because while the saddle stock were individuals sufficient unto themselves, the work teams were just that, teams. Two individuals who, in the course of time, became almost one individual; two horses which were one unit. To this day I can't mention a work horse without thinking of the teammate, too! Somehow or other I got closer to them, with a few glaring exceptions, than I did saddle horses, and it is an interesting fact that I have heard the same thing from other ranchers. Funny—and I mean that peculiar, not ha, ha—but true.

Lord, but I've known some fine teams! They were mostly Percheron, and the first I can recall was Tex and Mex. Iron grey geldings and perfectly matched, with Tex a quiet

83

gentleman and Mex a boogery, dangerous son of a gun. I remember them mostly because of the time when I, a little guy, toddled into the stall between them—something a grown man did pretty gingerly—and while Mex stood humped and quivering, old Tex blew his warm breath down the back of my neck and nosed me under his broad belly as he sidled over and braced himself against Mex until Dad could talk me into coming out on his off side. I might add that I got the living hell paddled out of me, too, when I got within Dad's reach. I did the same to Buckshot years later, come to think of it, when she was about five and wandered into the stall where I had a bronc tied up. The bronc was bay, and so was her mare, Mickey!

Another of the old teams was Fitz and Sharkey. Dad loaned Fitz to a rancher over on the Musselshell, and every time they turned him loose he came home to his sidekick. A matter of thirty-odd miles, too. After about the third trip over for him the rancher gave Fitz the fight, and he and Sharkey looked positively smug about it for a month at least.

There were others, and I'm not just naming names, I'm naming friends I knew well: Jack and Dinah; Margaret and Jessie; Toodles and Tacho—Toodles was out of Margaret, and Margaret was out of Dinah; Jack and Kelly; Sigurd and Sharkey—Young Sharkey; Betty and Babe— Babe was Toodles' colt; Modoc and Thunder—the latter another of Toodles'; and what I think was the finest team I ever broke, and one of the best I ever threw a line over, Bullet and Young Babe. She was out of Babe, and Bullet out of a grey Percheron we got from Frank Mackey of Billings. Only colt the grey ever had, worse luck. And, of course, the only team I have left on the place now, Chief, he was out of Bullet by a Belgian stud and so damn big I had to buy a Belgian gelding to match him. I named the newcomer Bill, though I am certain that for the first month he didn't know for sure that it wasn't "You big sonofabitch!" Good team, the big gunsels, but I haven't enough work to keep them toned down, so we have some rapid feeding circles, and I'd sure hate to try and put them up alongside a threshing rig!

There were lots of others, but names don't mean much to anybody who didn't know them, and what I am getting at anyhow is Cody and Terry. I won't forget them.

I couldn't have been very old when they were foaled, for I remember coming in from school one winter evening and hearing Dad remark to my granddad, "Those two colts I drove today are sure going to be a fine pair. Both are geldings, and what'll we name them?" From the vintage of the names I suspect Gramp came up with them. Anyhow, it was Cody and Terry, and a team, from then on for better than twenty years. Still is, really.

Funny how unalike they were, and yet how perfectly matched. Cody was black, pretty chunky, and operated on a hair trigger. Terry was bay, rawboned and levelheaded. Both were gentle and good natured. Terry was absolutely honest and accepted things as they came, while Cody was wise, suspicious and put in a lot of time trying to make things happen the way he figured they should. Neither ever scotched his share of the work, but Cody had a sneaky, grain-thieving bent that would preclude calling him plumb honest. In fact we had to devise such an intricate rigging on the oat box to keep Cody out that a human had trouble getting in, and the best way to run the son of a gun through a gate was to try and head him off from it, and swear as he thundered by. Funny he never wised up, either. I guess because he had a devious mind. We all loved Terry, for his heart and dependability. We loved Cody, for he had a great heart, and his rapscallion ways were something you could depend on, too. Often I've heard a teamster remark, "Ol' Terry," even when he was a green colt, followed by, "That damn Cody," but always with a grin. They were a pair to draw to!

There was a bad alkali bog out north of the buildings about a mile, an innocent white crust covering a soupy blue muck, and before we finally got it well fenced we lost an animal in it from time to time. Anyhow, one morning Cody showed up alone, more fidgety than usual, wouldn't let himself be caught, and he kept heading off north, stopping to see if we were coming, and then thundering back to fuss around and get in our way. Making a general nuisance of himself. "He's trying to tell us something," Dad said. Terry's in trouble. Get Jack and Kelly, all the chains we've got, and let's go. I'll bet it's that damn bog hole, and I sure hope we aren't too late."

We weren't, but Terry was sure enough in trouble. He was in so deep that only his head and fore quarters showed above the muck, but he wasn't fighting. Too smart, and he never moved while we shoved a plank out and got a log chain around his chest and the grab hook fastened. Then ever so carefully the team eased him towards the edge, and finally the old fellow lurched to his feet on comparatively solid ground. Naturally by that time he was pretty well covered with blue slime. Cody, who had been messing around, worrying and bothering us and the team, took one look at this great blue monster that had emerged from the bog, let out a snort and headed for the barn as hard as he could go, Terry right behind and calling for him to wait. How the old horse did dig—this horrible thing had his partner's voice, maybe had eaten him even, and was trying to trick him to where it could catch him, too. By the time we got to the barn with our very interested team Cody was backed into a corner of the corral, in a state of near collapse, desperately threatening his mate, and it was only after we had taken Terry down to the trough and washed him off that his partner would have anything to do with him. But then Cody fussed around like a mare with her first colt—sniffing, nuzzling, nickering and reassuring himself that everything was in good shape, and all with a puzzled, disbelieving look. We laughed, but our eyes were misty.

Another time, along in January, Dad and I were feeding down on the Sweet Grass some six miles from home. We drove down in a little sleigh and then hooked the old team to a bobsleigh and rack to feed. We had quite a string of cattle, and it took most of the day to haul the six or seven loads of loose hay we needed, and it was cold! There are no thermometers on a hay rack, but it must have been thirty-five or forty below, with at least four sun dogs glaring balefully through the frost haze. About the time we'd finished the last load a stiff breeze sprang up, right square in our faces, and the snow started moving, whispering wickedly across the crust. By the time we'd changed sleighs it was shoulder high, and after we'd gotten the dog in and on our feet, the lines tied up and the lap robe pulled up over our heads, all we could see were two powerful rumps ahead of us. We spoke to them, and those two fine gentlemen took us home. Twice they stopped and one of us would get out, fumble up to their heads and open the gate they'd stopped for. They'd go through, wait until they felt somebody get into the sleigh and then head doggedly into the ground blizzard again. I wouldn't have believed anything could have faced it alone, and I still don't believe anything could have, except that old team. And after they'd brought us home—I can still see it, smell it and hear it—side by side in their stall in the warm barn, harness marks in the frost on their broad backs, the sweet scent of hay, the regular munching as they contentedly ate their oats and the tinkle of the icicles on their fetlocks as they shifted their weight from time to time. Fine friends in rough going, those two!

Years passed, and the two got pretty grey around the heads, but whatever they were asked to do they still did in a workmanlike fashion. There were younger teams for the hard work, and finally we only used them for getting out a little timber in the winter, mainly really so we'd have an excuse to see to it that they had plenty of grain in the rough weather. Right down Cody's alley, since it was all light, downhill work, but that didn't keep the smart son of a gun from talking Terry into slipping off to the barn with him any time they were left alone in the timber. It got so a man automatically took a hitch around the nearest stump with the log chain before dropping them, and it was worth it to slip back quietly to where you could watch Cody stealthily test out the hitch first one way and then the other to see if it was solid.

By the time the snow melted off the skid trails and the soft haze of a Montana spring crept into the air, they were fat and slick. A good time to end their work, so one bright day in late May I saddled up and led them over to the high benches on Otter Creek and turned them loose. There was plenty of grass; only a few fences broke the miles of rolling foothills, and they had it all to themselves. Come fall, before the weather got rough, I'd come up and take them down home for the winter.

Spring seemed to have gotten into the old devils' blood, for they tore away like two overgrown colts, circling, neighing, bucking ponderously and ripping up the tender grass with their joyous hooves. Then they swung back to me, touched noses with my saddle horse, scowled and nipped at him like they'd never seen him before, and turned to the serious business of feeding. As I rode home I could see them grazing shoulder to shoulder, outlined against the sky on a distant rise, partners.

It was maybe three months later that I happened to be in the vicinity again, and though several times during the summer I had caught distant sight of two black spots close together on some grassy ridge, for some reason I decided to see how they were getting along. I located them without any trouble, but as I rode down the green draw where they were feeding I could feel that something was wrong. Cody

met us half way, eyeing us suspiciously, with the distrust
and wildness of an old horse long on the range, his ears
pricked inquiringly. He was fat and shiny as a two-year-
old, but Terry, down the draw a little, barely lifted his
head, and as I got closer I could see that he was pitifully
thin and that a festering barb-wire cut slashed to the bone
on one hind leg from hock to hoof. I hurriedly got down,
and while Cody was scorning the friendly advances of my
saddle horse I carefully examined the leg. No chance; the
foot was almost off, flies and hot weather had done the rest.
There was one thing to be done, and I looked up at the old
fellow who was watching me so trustfully and hopefully.
The partners would have to be split up. I straightened and
slapped the old horse reassuringly, "Terry, old friend, I
guess I've got to." I stood there rubbing the soft nose that
nuzzled me in hopes of some oats, while Cody, his wildness
forgotten at the possible prospect of a handout, crowded in
on my other side. I stayed quite a while talking to those
two, and petting them, and I cried a little, too. Finally I
swung into the saddle and headed home, cursing barbed
wire, and myself.

The next day when I got back to them, with rifle under
my leg and grain in the sack tied behind my cantle, Terry
was down. This made things a must, and after making
friends with a very worried Cody, who was all ready to fight
for his sidekick, I got down and poured them the grain and
knelt with my arm over Terry's neck while they ate. At last
the oats were nearly finished, so, sneaking the halter I'd
brought over Cody's head, I led him to some aspens on the
side of the draw and tied him back in them. He knew
something was wrong, and he fumed and pawed as I left.
Terry was just cleaning up the grain, and for just a minute
I fondled the greying head. Then, hating myself, I jacked a
shell into the chamber. The grand old fellow was just
getting the last oat munched; he was happy, happier than
he'd been for quite a while; as fine a gentleman as I'd ever

known. I didn't look at his great soft eyes, I couldn't—and the rifle barrel crept up to the base of a silky ear—.

As the last trembling echo died slowly away there came a soft, frightened nicker from the aspens. A silence. Then a call, a lonely, lost call, followed the gunshot out through the evening twilight over the quiet hills. A heartbroken call. Cody knew.

It was a broken old horse that I led home that evening. The sparkle was gone from his eyes; his head, usually so alert, drooped; even his flanks looked gaunt and thin. He looked terribly old and lonesome, paying no attention to anything, plodding along beside my saddle horse and occasionally trying to turn back up country. It was a slow, sad trip. Even my horse was subdued, and the only sound was the slow beat of hooves through the grass and a coyote crying in the distance. When we got to the ranch, however, a change came over the old gelding which brought tears to my eyes. At the sight of the barn he brightened—for twenty years and better Terry had always been around the barn, and Cody plainly thought that there might be a chance that his partner was still there, somehow. He looked eagerly toward the open door when we arrived at the corral gate, and the minute I turned him loose he hurried to the barn whickering anxiously. In a moment he thundered out the door and around to the hay corral behind; perhaps Terry was there. Then down to the watering trough— perhaps—. But no, as I turned my pony loose I saw him come up from the waterway, head low, tail drooping, feet dragging. Hay, grain, cake; he showed not the least interest in any of my offerings, and as I went down to the house I could see him standing there, old and alone.

Time seemed to help a little. The old fellow slicked up again after a month or so, but he wasn't the same. Something was gone, and though once in a while he perked up and acted a little like himself, I believe it was just that, like any old person, he got to remembering and imagined that he and his partner were together again. Such times were few, though, so figuring it might cheer him up, toward spring I put him in with the weaner colts. I don't think he ever really noticed them; not even scowling when one of the little pests would slip in and steal a bite of his grain! So I was sort of glad one lovely May morning, with the red winged blackbirds trilling in the willows and the white collars of the killdees bobbing as they prospected the banks of the spring, to find him sleeping when I went down at daylight to feed the stock. Or so I thought, at first. Just about a year from the time I'd turned the two of them out in the upper country.

Betty and Babe and I took a slip and opened a spot under the cottonwoods on the creek bank in the colt pasture and put the old horse in it. Then I saddled Smoky Joe, put a pack outfit on Snip, and we brought Terry down and laid him beside Cody. When the spot was covered and smoothed I hunted up a small slab of sandstone, chiseled their names on it and put it there.

The willows and chokecherries have pretty well covered the spot by now, and the stone is hard to find. The birds and the cottontails know where it is, though, and I hope all the colts that have grazed the pasture since then, and those that will do so in the future, know too. For I am horseman enough to believe that it has been, is, and will be, good for the little colts; for where those two great horses lie, there too, certainly, will be gentleness, honesty, courage, loyalty and love. *Cody and Terry.*

# Rule Britannia

## 7

I'VE ALWAYS LIKED the English. I suppose it's because we had several of them in the Melville Country, and all of them were good men. The Hart brothers, Mr. Harry and Mr. Jack, originally from Coventry—Lady Godiva's stamping ground—came to Canada first, and then in the early '80s moved down here and started a horse ranch. Dad put in a lot of time with them when he was a youngster and showed it all his life. He acquired a taste for "gamey" meat from them and, though he was right-handed, always used his fork with his left hand. He would impale a piece of meat, with the fork tines turned down rather than up like most people do, and get more food piled between the meat and the top of the tines than the average person can put in a tablespoon. It's an English custom and fascinates me even now. The gamey meat doesn't, and I have another name for it which is a good deal more realistic.

The brothers were "terribleh, terribleh" British, and Mr. Jack was a favorite of mine. He was stocky, red-faced, with a walrus mustache and a belly laugh that made everybody within a half mile grin. I've heard it said that English don't have a sense of humor, but that's wrong—they have a fine sense of humor, only it sort of hangs fire a little. Mr. Jack was a dandy guy, and he had some great tales about the early days, especially the terrible winter of '86 and '87 which broke so many stockmen. I could see it and smell it, when he told me seriously, "In the spring of '87 one could walk up the Sweet Grass from Melville to the Mydland crossing and nevah step off a carcass. Poor beasts had sought shelteh in the brush of the bottom and died in absolute windrows!" He was talking about a stretch of creek at least twelve miles long!

Then he continued, "On Otter Creek, almost exactly where your father has built his shed, a bally range bull wandered into a snow drift and froze to death. On his feet, snow so deep he couldn't topple. In December, and he stood until May. 'Strorinareh! Like a veritable statue."

He was the sort of man who stood hitched until the smoke had cleared, too. He was called on to identify an animal in a rustling case, did so and cleared the suspect. Later he confided, "Of course I knew the beast, but if I hadn't I should have said I had. The man is my friend, by gad!"

By the time I came along both brothers had married and had families. Mr. Jack went home and brought back a wife who was supposed to have been a dressmaker for Queen Victoria. She was nice, I thought, for it was fun to try to figure out what she said. She was sort of eccentric, excitable and could talk a blue streak when she got wound up—which was damn near any old time. She was to give a short patriotic speech at a Liberty Bond rally held at the Melville church one "Fourth," and Dad suggested to Mr. Jack that perhaps she could stand a short one before the festivities commenced. "By Jove, yes," was his response. "A jolly good thought." Then he cautioned, "A wee nip, mind now, just a wee nip. Else she'll be off."

Riley Doore, who was working for the outfit when I was born and who was still with us when he died just a few years ago, had come out from town with a wagon load of supplies and happened to mention that he had seen Mrs. Hart in Big Timber. Mother asked how she was, and Riley replied, "All right, I guess. She was goin' down the street with her head in the air an' her tail over the dashboard."

She traveled just that way, too!

During threshing time Hillman Gunderson with his steamer and separator went from ranch to ranch, we all helped one another, and everybody got their grain cleaned up. It was a good deal; neighborly, and with fringe benefits, to boot. We looked forward to it because each cook tried to outdo her peers when it came to setting a good table for threshing, so the crew lived high off the hog.

This one year Mr. Jack had a patch of oats to thresh, and Mrs. Hart was as busy as a bird dog for at least a week in anticipation of the big event. It just happened that we cleaned up at home, had an early lunch, pulled over to Hart's and went to work. We had a good crew, finished his oats, pulled to the next place and set up the rig before supper, so not a man showed up for a meal. The poor woman was quite put out. The Hart children didn't complain—they sure were on the front tit until they worked through all that food she'd gotten ready and they went around with wide, satisfied smiles for at least a week.

During the tough times in the twenties, Dad talked Mr. Jack into tackling the milk cow business. I know for a fact that he didn't peddle him any cows, either, for I had the job as Dad's milkmaid and I'd have sure noticed, and appreciated, any that had turned up missing! About the time the old gentleman got his herd together and his kids broken in to milking, the price of cream went 'way down. Dad happened to meet him one day and inquired as to how the dairy business was doing.

"By Jove, Paul," said Mr. Jack earnestly, "the price of the bally cream is so low, that, by gad, it barely pays foh the wear and tear on the animal's teats."

Both the brothers were great hunters. Mr. Harry was deadly with his old ten gauge double on birds, and he hung them "unplucked" and "undrawn" by their necks until the bodies dropped loose. Then they were ready to be cooked. Gamey! Why, Godamighty, those damn things backed me off to such an extent that I can't eat a pin tail grouse even today!

Mr. Jack favored big game, and he could sure use his old 303 rifle like an expert. The fact that he could kill deer so far away that the meat came close to spoiling before he could get to it didn't faze him a lick; just a good start toward the gamey deal. He and Dad were boon companions during the hunting season, so it sort of surprised Dad when, 'way before daylight one morning, Mr. Jack called up and announced, "I say, Paul, I cawn't go with you today as we had planned. Frightfully sorry."

Pressed for an explanation, he elaborated, "Nellie is going to town and leaving me to mind the children." Then with utmost seriousness, "And by gad, Paul, I'd rawtheh be left in the house with a bear than with those three kiddies!"

A nephew, or some sort of a relative, lived with Mr. Jack's family. A grown man, extremely well-educated, he hadn't exactly been in the lead when the smarts were given out. I learned "Rule Britannia" at an early age. It was Artie's favorite song, the only one he knew as far as I could figure, for everybody on our outfit, including those in the house and very possibly even in the root cellar, could hear him a couple of miles away over the hill as he sang and used his buck saw at the wood pile on chilly winter days. Nevertheless, though he damn sure was missing a button or two, he wasn't stupid. Reading a paper that told of still another defeat for the Germans during the first world war, he suddenly exploded. "I say, don't the blightehs evah win? They *do* have guns, don't they?"

The tables were turned on him one time, though. The old-time Norwegians always celebrated two special days: May 17th—Norwegian Independence Day or the "Seventeenth of Norway," as it was commonly known—and the Fourth of July. Both were pretty gaudy affairs—the Lutheran minister was about the only Norsk that stayed sober during them—and it usually took the participants a while to heal up afterwards. Anyway, Artie got all stirred up and indignant about the Norsks celebrating what, in essence, was a defeat for the British "Empiah," and—he was in the Melville Post Office at the time of his tirade—concluded with "What do these bally Scandinavians know of the Fourth of July, anyhow?"

John Hoff, one of the original pioneers in the Norsk "Settlement" and a good old guy, had been listening quietly and agreed, "Not a t'ing, Art'ur, not a t'ing. Until de fift' or maybe sometimes de sixt'," and grinned broadly.

The last time I saw Mr. Jack was nearly twenty-five years ago, shortly before he died. He had dinner with us, steak and kidney pie Barbara had made especially for him, and he got to reminiscing, talked through dinner, the evening and most of the night. His chuckle was catching, as was his laugh. His stories were magnificent and he loved telling them, interrupting himself at intervals with "I say, may I have another wee nip? Theh's a good fellow."

I got sort of worried about the late hours, but each time I asked if he were ready for me to drive him home his reply was the same, "Shank of the evening, old fellow. Meah shank of the evening."

Finally about daylight his hired man got worried, too, and came looking for him. We were as reluctant for him to leave as he was to go, and the last thing he said was, "I say, a ripping evening. Simply ripping, by Jove!"

I think of the grand old gentleman often—every time I ride the short grass country across the heads of Wheeler and Horse Creeks where he and his brother ran horses in the '80s. The range where he asked that his ashes be scattered. They were, and it's a fine place for a good man to rest!

Rivers Browne was another popping good man. He was pretty old when I knew him and went by the name of "B." A quiet, courtly, spare English gentleman who, before my time, was known from the Judith Gap all across the head of the Musselshell and the Melville Country as "Slick Saddle" Browne, or "Wild Horse Charlie." He earned the names fair and square, too, for he never rode anything but an English saddle and the wilder the stock the better he liked it. The remark, "If the beast is too frolicsome to drive, p'r'aps you should bring him to me to ride," was attributed to him. He, by God, did exactly that, many times. I've done it the other way around, but to ride one that is too salty to drive—!

"B" was born in Murree, India—he spoke of it as "Inja"—and his dad commanded a regiment of native infantry. An uncle is supposed to have invented the "Sam Browne" belt used by officers in so many armies, too. Traditionally the family had attended Sandhurst, England's West Point, but they turned "B" down on account of poor eyesight and he went to Oxford University instead.

After graduation he came to America: first to Mexico, then to Texas, and to Montana with a trail herd. He liked the country, went home and married an English girl, then came back, took up a homestead and raised a family. His two sons, John and Leslie—the latter known as "Grizzly"—were horse hands, but not of their dad's caliber.

When the World War broke out, though he was almost fifty years old, "B" hurried home to England, joined the Twentieth London Regiment and spent four years in the trenches. No wonder the English are so damn hard to whip!

When I knew him the old fellow lived with the Harry Harts, took care of their garden, pottered around their yard and raised the loveliest flowers in the country. I don't think he owned a thing, but he arrived at the charivari the Melville Country gave Barbara and me with a single magnificent red rose as a gift for my bride. I believe it touched her more than any other gift, for right today, more than forty years later, when charivaris are mentioned Barbara will invariably get a soft glow in her eyes and ask, "Remember "B" Browne and the rose he brought me at ours?"

He also, having been raised in India, taught her the secret of making a curry that is one of the finest dishes I have ever eaten. Hotter than a bandit's pistol, but magnificent!

Poor, gallant, chivalric "B." He left Hart's when he got too old to work and went to Big Timber where the county took care of him. This must have galled his pride and self respect, for he finally killed himself. Being a product of the Victorian age, he couldn't do something as mundane as just pulling a trigger. Nope, he had to "open his veins," so a nice old man died slow, messily and hard; a gentleman all the way.

Heywood Daly was a Manxman, having been born on the Isle of Man, and he damn sure said so when someone spoke of him as an Englishman. The breed strikes me as being about the same, for Heywood was an all right guy; easy going, a sense of humor and a good hand with horses. He had ranched for years in eastern Montana, had quite a string of cattle at one time and also ran some good saddle stock. He must have done fine, for he sold out down there before the second war, moved up under the Crazies and bought a little outfit on the very head of Spring Creek where he ran a few cows.

Towards the end of the '40s he got plumb out of the cow business, but he and his Canadian wife, Belle, stayed on the ranch. They lived up there alone, having even gotten rid of their hired man when they sold their cattle. Didn't even have a saddle horse. They kept a milk cow, and a calf to turn on her when they were on one of the trips they invariably made visiting around the state and Canada. They were a friendly, hospitable pair, got along with everybody, and he was a damn good old style stockman. Since I've always tried to run my stock just as close as I could to the way my granddad had run his, Heywood and I got along fine—we both figured the more a man fiddles with his cattle, the more things seem to go wrong with them. It's vital to vaccinate against Blackleg, Bangs and Vibriosis, but those are about all that has ever bothered my cattle, and Heywood felt the same way.

The winter of '48-'49 was rank, and we didn't get our usual wind to clear the grass and put the snow in the coulees. By February things were pretty tough, so the government sent 'dozers out to help the ranchers. Heywood and Belle, 'way up under the mountains, were in the rockiest shape—had run out of everything, including whiskey—and were getting by on biscuits, canned chicken and coffee. "I had gotten to the point where I felt that I was about to lay an egg," he told me later, "though I daresay it would have been a biscuit."

Luckily they had gotten a 'phone in during the fall, so we knew their troubles, and as soon as the cats got up into the Melville Country we pointed one for the Daly place. When it got there they had their car all warmed up and ready, and immediately headed down the 'dozer track for Big Timber—Melville wouldn't do, for the state liquor store was in town.

For a wonder the wind stayed away long enough for them to make the round trip, and they got home with enough grub to feed the Chinese army for at least a month. While Belle had been buying it, Heywood took care of the essentials, so they had six cases of booze in addition to the food. That night they drifted in solid, even worse than before, but it didn't matter any longer. They now had everything they needed "to make it to green grass," which in this country means that you've got a strong hold, a downhill pull and the skids greased!

Heywood and Belle are long gone now. I run a stud and his mares on part of their old place. A string of yearlings and twos are in another pasture over the hill, so I have to go up there pretty often. When I do I always think of them. They were good people.

# Southdowns

## 8

THERE USED TO BE a lot of mountainy people from Tennessee, Georgia and the Carolinas in the Melville Country. They were known as "Southdowns," for whenever they were asked where they came from their reply was invariably, "Down South." In general they weren't plumb in the lead when ambition was given out so most of them lived pretty hard, but happy. In general, too, they were pretty rollicky, tended to get mean when they were drunk, which was frequent, and a few were damn dangerous—had left down home a jump ahead of the "High Sheriff." As a rule when one of that ilk arrived he'd move in with somebody and use their last name, which was a fair lick since they were probably kin of some sort anyhow. They were always strong on using initials in place of given names, or nicknames, and I had an uncle, "Long Jesse," a dandy guy. He had a half brother, "Squinteye Jesse," and I have a cousin "Jesse," and he a son, "Young Jesse." And it was always pronounced "Jess"! Back then none of the Southdowns had much, except children, but the girls were as pretty as any I've ever seen and most of the boys about halfway ornery. Most of them made whiskey back in the brush and sold a little, but by and large they minded their own business—except when they got to bickering amongst themselves. The end result of which would usually be someone badly stomped, a still burnt or a shot taken at somebody, and once in a while a killing. They had a way of thinking and talking though, and a slaunch-wise humor that was magnificent, and a lot of them, particularly the old folks, were as fine people as I've ever known!

One of them tried drylanding over on Fish Creek. My granddad happened to ride by one nice spring day where he was plowing. Of course they both whoaed up to say howdy. After passing the time of day, Gramp, who had noticed that there seemed to be quite a bit of the shellrock showing in the plowing, remarked, "Doesn't look to me like you've got much top soil, Rufus."

"Nope, ain't much," was the reply.

"How much you figure there is?" asked Gramp.

"Wul," after a moment of deliberation, " 'bout a' inch, inch an' a half."

So it was no wonder Rufus lost interest in farming right quick and went to making and peddling a little moonshine, and playing pitch in the Two Dot bar. His wife took care of the place, cut the firewood for the still and milked the cow, for he claimed, "Bothers me to take them liberties with a cow." Anyway, he was sitting in a game one day when a neighbor poked his head through the door and excitedly reported, "Rufe, yore ol' cow got on clover, bloated herse'f, an' up an' died!"

Rufe looked up, shrugged, and replied philosophically, "Them as has kin lose. Them as hasn't, cain't," and went back to his cards.

Long Jesse's brother, Grady, and a friend were coming out of Harlowton one time in a Model T 'way before daylight. Grady was driving and the friend was taking care of their jug, a gallon earthenware one. There'd been a thaw and the road had quite a few mudholes, their lights were sorry, and so they eventually ended upside down in about three or four inches of sloppy mud. The friend jumped, saving himself and the moonshine, but Grady was caught under the car. Efforts to get him out were to no avail, so the friend headed for the nearest ranch to get help, carrying the jug, of course. It took a while to get there, so it was past sunup and the rancher was just hooking up a team to start work.

Well, they had a short one, visited a little, discussed the weather, and the team was admired. Then the friend asked courteously, "You busy?"

The rancher wanted to know why he asked.

"Wul, ol' Grade's under th' T model down the road a ways in a mudhole. Reckon you could come he'p me to get him loose?"

When they got there Grady had smothered, probably within a few minutes of the wreck. At that the friend was quite an old boy—he took Grady's two orphaned sons home with him to his little place on the head of American Fork, and he and his wife raised them until they were in their teens. One of those boys retired a couple of years ago as senior pilot for Pan Am!

This wife swapping I read about now isn't anything new, for years ago a couple of these old boys decided they'd make a trade. One of them lived on the head of Dry Creek, and *his* wife was all for the deal. The other wife, though, sat back like a borrowed dog, so the Dry Creek man went over to try and convince her. The piéce de rèsistance of his convincing was, "Wul, Christ, honey, I jest wanted you fer packin' water to the stillhouse."

There was another old fellow who lived "way back up yonder" under the Crazies. It wasn't much of a place, and about his only crop was children. As a neighbor put it, "Slip up to th' house an' th'ow a chunk on th' roof an' it looks like school'd let out." Anyhow, word finally reached Doctor O'Leary in Big Timber that the man's wife was sick, so he rode the stage to Melville, borrowed a rig and drove on up to the outfit. The man allowed as his wife "don't feel so peart," so Doc went in and had a look at her. When he came out the old fellow was sitting on the gallery that ran along one side of the cabin, rocking and looking out over two hundred-odd miles to the Big Horns. Doc took a small one from the proffered jug and said, "Burt, your wife's going to have another baby."

There was a moment of silence as Burt considered. "Wul," he spit thoughtfully over the railing, "she's had ever' oppertunity."

Mister Henry Reynolds was a fine old Southern gentleman. A graduate of the University of Tennessee, he'd come west and finally starved out over on the "Tennessee Bench" on the Musselshell—my granddad always said, "The government bet you the land against your filing fee that you'd starve out before you proved up, and the government usually won"—and had moved over into Melville where he did a little harness work, and "made a little honey."

He kept himself clean as a hound's tooth, and what with his white hair, mustache, courtly manners and quiet gentlemanliness, he was quite a figure and a grand old man, to boot. Never a man, particularly a "Southdown," hit town that couldn't get a place to sleep and to eat with Mister Henry. Some of those boys from down south were pretty juicy, but except for a few times, like when Tinch Hannon got killed, the old fellow kept them pretty well in line. He lived in the old hotel, which I owned, and every winter he'd gather all my harness and give it a good going over. It was a lot of work for the old gentleman, but he said he didn't want to be "beholdin' " to me, since I never charged him any rent. He did a good job, and I wouldn't have hurt his pride for anything anyhow, so we were both as happy as a couple of kittens on a hot rug.

His son, Cliff, lived with him, trapped and worked around at different ranches. He was a good hand at anything and one of the nicest people I've ever met. His humor, always totally unconscious, and his way of putting things was magnificent. I imagine he was in his late fifties when I first knew him, and he was slow talking and deliberate. A wonderful guy and a crying example of the breed of Melville neighbors of the time!

I remember running into him up town one summer evening. He was packing a leg, so I asked what the trouble was.

"Wul, I'm workin' up at Green's, hayin'. Had quite a little run wranglin' th' work stock this mornin'. Was ridin' ol' Baldy, an' he picked up a badger hole an' couldn't shake it off. Didn't hurt us bad, though. Just put a hitch in m' getalong."

He was a better than average drinking man, even by Melville standards. He happened by one day shortly after the end of the war when Hanson was cleaning out his sorry old wartime booze in the saloon and was invited to have a snort.

" 'D 'mire to," said Cliff.

Hanson put a big, tall glass down out of sight behind the bar and filled it to the brim with a mixture of everything he had, from whiskey to vodka and what's in between. Then he handed it over the bar and said, "Try that on."

Cliff took a slug, rolled it around, swallowed, and asked, "Jest hut d'you call it?"

"Three star special," said Hanson.

So they sat and chatted while Cliff worked on that big drink, and the bartender waited for it to show some effect. Directly someone else came in, ordered a drink and asked Cliff to join him.

" 'D 'mire to," came the reply.

Hanson asked, "What'll you have?"

Cliff deliberated a minute, "Wul, I'd sorta like another of them three star specials."

He got it, downed it and walked back to the hotel straight as a string!

When Mister Henry died along in the early forties Cliff carried on with the honey business. I'd see him pottering around the eight or nine hives he had, with a screen proposition hung on his hat, puffing smoke at the bees from a sort of little bellows. But I really got an understanding of his honey business one afternoon when I dropped into the hotel during the war. It was in the fall, and he was sitting scraping honeycombs, wrapping them in paper and then sealing the paper with a chunk of beeswax which he heated at a candle he had burning beside him. I remarked that, what with sugar rationing, the honey business must be real good.

"Nope," returned Cliff, peering over the top of his spectacles, " 'Pears ever'body wants it rectified. My 'quipment's all for th' other kind."

That sure tickled me—honey combs, paper, wax and a candle. 'Quipment! And, being a good whiskey maker, "rectified" was the word.

A son, Bud, was "a might pretty little bronc rider," as Cliff put it, and would have been a great one if he'd laid off the booze. Bud finally got to where he had to have a mickey or better before he got down on a bucking horse. A bronc he drew at the White Sulphur Springs show killed him along about '50. Before that, though, Cliff put a little mill together, set up on Amelong Creek under the Crazies where there was some good lodgepole pine, and off and on he'd get Bud to "hep" him get out some shingles. He made good shingles, too.

Happened one day he asked me if I had time to take him and some groceries up to camp. On the way he mentioned that, "Me an' Bud got out a square or two, nuff for th' ol' truck anyways, an' he tuk off. Ain't seen hide nor ha'r of him sence. 'Spect he sold 'em an' got drunk. I run out o' grub an' had to walk out. Got to get back, 'cause I got a team up to camp an' I 'magine they're gettin' pretty shad gutted by now."

I remarked that I didn't think much of Bud. "Wul," replied Cliff. "Can't say as I do, neither."

We got to camp, and he insisted I take a few bundles for

my trouble. So we harnessed up, hooked the team to a little sleigh and headed for the mill up the creek. The snow was pretty deep, and the horses weren't plumb ambitious—can't say I blamed them after the short rations they'd been on in the little corral—and one of them in particular sat on the evener pretty steadily. Every now and then Cliff would slap the line along the old horse's back and talk to him. It was *"Dy*namite! Git in thar, Dyna*mite!* Damn you any-ways, Dynamite," without the slightest effect. Finally he looked over to me and said philosophically, "Christ! Hut a team!"

He had a long involved story we used to love to hear him tell after he'd had a few drinks. About how he and Bud started out for a hunting trip in the Little Belts north of the Musselshell.

"Ol' T Model I had, bad in th' off front tar. Tuk some time to get all our traps packed, so's 'twas night time we left Melville. Had a cookstove in th' back. Bud was adrivin' an' I was holdin' a lantern so's he could see. He mistuk one o' them drifty spots, got in th' borrer pit, th' bad tar blowed, an' over she goes. I th'owed th' lantern far's I could an' jumped. Got free, but she caught Bud, an' I says, you all right, Bud? An' he says ' 'M all right, Dad, but I wisht you'd git this thing off'n me.' "

He finally did, after hunting up and down the road, asking Bud the same question and getting the same answer each time he went by the wreck, until he found a fence post that was rotted off and that he could kick loose from the wires. But, "We never did get to th' Belts huntin' that year, dad burn it."

One night in the saloon somebody asked him for the story. Cliff looked along the bar and demurred, "Ol' Bob Langston's down yonder. Get him. He can tell it better'n me!"

He finally moved over to the Two Dot country and "did a little sawmillin.' " He always made the rodeos and had a few with his friends, and to me it was a high point of a show to see Cliff again and he always wanted to know how "Miz Barbara an' th' younguns" were. After a few years he got so stove up he couldn't work in the timber, moved into Harlowton and retired. I ran into him there on the Fourth, a few years ago. He had a Sunday-go-to-meeting hat he wore only to special events. It was a damn expensive hat, a pretty blue color, and he wore it pulled down to his ears so far he had to lift his chin to see. When I met him that last time he had a ragged, blackened hole in the brim and a burned place on the side of the crown next to it. Naturally I asked what'd happened.

"Wul, I was standin' by th' beer window 't th' end o' th' stands an' some kid th'owed one o' them damn bomb crackers down. Lit on my hat brim an' blowed. Like to deefened me. Sent one o' Tiny's boys up to whup th' kid that done it, but he couldn't find th' critter."

A friend of mine that was having a drink with him when the firecracker went off told me Cliff didn't so much as drop his bottle of beer. Didn't even blink. Just said, "Christ! Hut uz that?"

I went to Cliff's funeral two years ago, and most of us there grinned at one another because we all knew the old fellow would have had some remark to make if he'd been able to.

When he quit Melville he'd given me Mister Henry's sewing horse, and it's in my harness room in the basement, where I use it pretty steadily. Last winter I built a new bunkhouse, and I put those shingles he'd given me, up on Amelong at least twenty-five years ago, on the roof.

I guess maybe I'd been saving them up in the loft of the barn for something special. Every time I look at the bunkhouse, I grin, for I can hear him saying, "Mighty pretty little bunkhouse, Spike." I'm glad I had the privilege of knowing Cliff, and I am proud he called me his friend. A lovely, gentle person!

# Rodeo Ramblings

## 9

WHEN I WAS A KID there weren't any rodeos as such, but it was a poor "Fourth" on the Sweet Grass when there wasn't a bucking contest sometime during the day. Local riders using their own saddles on salty horses from around the neighborhood. Most Sunday afternoons at Melville there'd be a bucking contest and a steer roping out on the flat back of the hotel, and horse races always.

The first celebration I ever saw that was like a rodeo was the old Bozeman Roundup in 1921. I was too little to remember much about it except that Dad's horse fell with him, and that Lloyd Coleman won the bronc riding. The only reason I know the latter is that Don Davison, who was one of the first persons I can remember as having to do with rodeos when I was little, told me years later that Coleman came into Bozeman on a freight. He said that he'd staked Lloyd to some food and his entry fee, and that he won the riding over such hands as Yakima Canutt, Jess Coates and Howard Tegland.

Dad went up there a couple of years later to take a sitting at a grey horse Ringling and Work had. Fifty dollars if you rode him, but Dad didn't get the chance. Lester Work told me several years ago, "Hell, I was afraid Paul would ride him and spoil the horse's reputation, so I slipped him a hundred not to make the try."

Dad agreed when I asked him about it, "Sure did. Easy money and no chance of getting scarred up, but damn I'd have liked to tackled him. I sure needed that hundred, though."

Several years later, at Two Dot, he and Jess Coates drew straws to see who'd have a lick at another grey horse named Grey Dick that Gib MacFarland had. Jess won, tied up the stirrups and rode him to a fare-you-well.

Jess was one of the first outside bronc riders I can remember, and the last time I saw him was at the Big Timber Rodeo in about '27, and he was stove up badly.

Another of the old-timers was Cheyenne Kaiser. I ran into him after bulldogging got to be an event, and he was a wild one. He'd jump at a steer further than the average man would rope at him!

The first version of modern rodeo that I ever saw was put on by the McDowell brothers, and as far as I am concerned they started sure enough rodeo up in this region. There were the twins, Aubry and Mabry; Snyd; Marion; and "Sarpy" Sam—all transplanted Texans and all good hands. Two of their bucking horses were rank—Butterfly and Cricket, if I remember right—and for the first time I saw bulldogging and calf roping. Also, the outside hands began to show up at the McDowell rodeos: Paddy Ryan, Tegland, Bob Askins and youngsters like Turk Greenough and Cecil Henly. The 'doggers were a hard bitten crew: Jack Coates, Mike Hastings, Chey Kaiser, Booger Red Allen, Dad—he had to try this new event as well as bronc riding—and a loud, real good young hand named Oral Zumwalt. The calf ropers were Zumwalt, Rufe Ingersoll, Dad, of course, and Mabry and Sam McDowell. I'm not sure whether Irby Mundy, Dick Merchant and Johnny Mullins were at that show, but if not they sure were by the next year or two, for they were the first southwestern hands to get up into this region. I'm here to tell you, too, that all the contestants at that show were *cowboys* first and foremost.

It wasn't so much the money in those days—it was to see

who was the best, the champ. Maybe he'd be the chump at the next show, but right then he was *it*, and the purse was pure gravy. Something to spend—and they damn sure did—or something to stake an unlucky friend with so he could make the next show. They were a rollicky bunch, but I liked them, though I imagine there are still little towns around that would disagree with me. The boys were a raunchy bunch at times, most times.

The first entry fee I ever paid was at Big Timber, in 1925, in the calf roping. I caught my calf in a hurry and then got the living hell tromped out of me. It tickled Zumwalt, and I remember him advising me, "Gunsel, you better put an anvil in the seat of your britches so you got weight enough to handle those cattle."

From then until the '60s I rodeo'd around quite a bit. A few big shows, lots of little ones and over quite a scope of country. I never was any hell of a hand, but I made enough money to make it interesting, especially during the war when the good boys were gone. And it sure was fun! Sometimes that money, during the early thirties when we were first married, helped Barbara and me. One time at an early spring show I roped up a storm and ended up with enough winnings to buy a new plow. Incongruous maybe, but I needed that plow. I won a few trophies, too, over the years, but as they say, you can't eat belt buckles!

What I enjoyed the most and remember the best were the funny things, and there were lots of them. Like that first show in 1925. Snyd McDowell, and he was a good rider, came out on a saddle bronc scratching high and handsome. About the fourth jump his latigo broke and down he came, rigging and all. He was pretty much on the fight when he stomped back to the chutes, and his temper wasn't improved when somebody snickered and said, "What's the trouble, couldn't you ride him?"

My first rodeo sort of set the pattern for a lot more, for Snyd snorted, "Ride 'im, hell, I could ride 'im in my shirttail before breakfast, an' never show my ass!"

It was at that same show that a big old bronc with Miller Pederson aboard got out of the arena and headed for the Yellowstone, which runs deep, fast and close to the grounds. The old pony was running and bucking and bellowing through the cottonwood timber, with Miller yelling, "Git him, Paul. Christ' sake git him!"

Dad was the hazer—they called pickup men that in those days—and he got the rein and his dallies just before they hit the edge of the river bank. Miller grinned and said, "Thanks, Paul. Damn if I didn't think I was in for a bath, an' hell, it ain't Saturday."

Lots of incidents from those years of rodeoing stick in my mind: Frosty Johnson on a bay mare at Melville in '41, both of them one-eyed and wild; Doff Aber on a sorrel mare by the name of Wildfire at La Fiesta de los Vacqueros in Tucson the same year; Alvin Gordon on Big Enough in Billings in the late '30s; Jake McClure tieing a calf in 12 flat at the same show, and never taking the cigar out of his mouth; Ray Mavity on Will James in Livingston when he made the first qualifying ride ever made on the horse; Oral Zumwalt 'dogging a steer at Palm Springs in 2.2, a time that still stands!

There were many others; some comic, some tragic. Things that went on in the arena, behind the chutes or in the bars—the fun, the excitement. I wouldn't swap the memories for a lot; and Zumwalt's show in Augusta, Montana, back during the war is right up towards the lead when I start to recall typical, rodeo-related happenings. It wasn't a big show, but it drew the top hands, and I'll remember it for a long time, and with pleasure. For fun, frolic and just general, good-natured hell-raising, it was sure in the lead.

Bob Langston was breaking colts for me that spring, and he and I left home early enough so we could get there by noon—which was pretty early, since it was better than two hundred miles to Augusta, and we had some stock to tend to before we left. I was roping calves, and he was riding barebacks. Barbara stayed home with the kids. Lucky she wasn't with us, too. Oral had been down to my place a few days earlier to pick up a stud and had told me I could use his rope horse, old Rainbow, so I was damn sure mounted. Since we weren't carrying a horse with us we made good time and got to the grounds a little while before the show commenced.

It was a good rodeo, and when the smoke had cleared I had split second and third with Floyd Peters behind Pagett Berry, and Bob had won the bareback. Ray Mavity came out looking ten years younger than he was, spurred over his buck rein and got homesteaded, and Bob Olson won the saddle bronc. Jay Overman was just back from a German prison camp and so weak that, though he got down fine, he never could throw his steer, and I forget who won the 'dogging. Probably Zumwalt. Anyhow, Bob and I drew our checks, cashed them and were in business.

Augusta isn't very big, there were a lot of people in town, and food got hard to come by right quick. But not booze—the bars must have been stockpiling it for the last couple of months, looked like. There were a whole gob of soldiers around from some base or other, for the show featured a soldier's wild cow milking—looked like ants on a grasshopper when they manhandled those old mamas down without ropes. But the cowboys, since there was a war on and we figured they were needed, ignored the congenital boorishness of the military and confined most of our bickering to those of our own ilk. Duffy Crabtree, as usual, got to pestering an old rancher in a bar, and was told, "Sonny, cut it out, or I'm going to just plumb smother you with cleverness."

Duff poked out his chin and said, "Hit me, Dad. Go ahead, hit me."

Dad did, plumb from the cellar, and Duff upended. He

was pretty warlike when he got up, but we told him, hell, he'd asked for it, and that he'd have to whip all of us if he bothered the old fellow again, so he cooled off. Ran into "Dad" later in the night and by that time he was pretty well fixed and ready to fight a buzz saw and give it ten turns head start. Told us all to line up and he'd whip the whole passel of us pups. Good old guy!

Langston and I'd left home that morning about three, so after a while we decided to try and find a place to sleep. There was one hotel in town and it was a cinch it'd be plumb full, but we went over to give it a try anyhow. The night clerk was asleep, either that or drunk, behind the desk. There wasn't a key in sight on the board, so we started trying doors. Finally we found one unlocked, peered in, and there was a fine double bed with an Indian passed out on it. Just the ticket! I took his head and Bob his feet, and we packed him out into the hall and laid him gently along the wall. Made him comfortable as we could, too, with his hat over his face and his hands nicely crossed on his chest. Then we shucked our boots and pants and rolled in, congratulating ourselves. Tickled as a couple of pups with a hoof paring.

It was a little hard to sleep, what with the excitement along the street outside. Shortly it reached a crescendo, so we peered out the window hopefully. No fight worth our time resulted, so I, using a thick Norsk accent picked up in the "Settlement" above Melville, called down and told them profanely what I'd do if they didn't hush up. There was a moment of stunned silence. Then, differences forgot-ten—or at least sighted in on "that Swede bastard"—I was threatened with everything up to and above mayhem. Chit chat back and forth led from one thing to another, and into the hotel they came, breathing fire. Up the stairs and along the hall they came, our door crashed open and a crowd of drunk cowboys crowded through it like spooky cattle through a narrow corral gate. Bob sat up rubbing his eyes,

"What goes on anyhow? Waking an old boy up."

"Hell, it's Spike and Langston! Say, there's some mouthy Swede up here that's going to get his comeuppance. Know where he's at?"

I allowed as how, being only about half awake I couldn't be sure, but that I thought he was in the next room. Thanking us, out they trooped, hammered on the next door, and then on the one on the other side of us. Somebody fell over our Indian, mistook him for the Swede, and it sounded like a real good brawl was brewing. Things got sorted out, though. The Indian got the idea and enthusiastically joined forces with the palefaces to give the Swede his just desserts, and finally they quit attacking the doors, agreed that it had been dry work and milled off downstairs into the street. There were a few bellowed insults to the Swede, but with no reply forthcoming they wandered off for the nearest saloon. Bob and I grinned at one another and went to sleep.

The next morning we scouted for some breakfast. The cafe had nothing to eat but eggs and bread, on which they were realizing a handsome profit in the form of fried egg sandwiches, which, not having had much solid nourishment of late, we ordered. Shortly we were joined by Pagett Berry and his wife. Pagett had won the roping, had celebrated the fact and was hurting. So he sat extolling the virtues of his current rope horse, wolfing fried egg sandwiches and tossing the crusts over his shoulder out the window behind him, while his wife plaintively described to us what a miserable bastard he was to live with. Margie Greenough came in, grinned and said, "They ever find that Swede? I was in the room next to you two jokers and had a damn good mind to tell that outfit the truth. Time I got the bureau moved over against the door, though, they'd found the Indian and got side tracked."

Bob and I remembered some of the language used the night before and grinned sheepishly.

About then Pagett, surfeit with fried egg sandwiches, invited us down to the barn with him while he tended his horse, to see the animal. Of course, we'd seen him the day before, but Pagett was insistent, we had nothing better to do until the saloons opened, so we went on down with him. The barns in Augusta are down on the creek bottom in the timber and sort of dark. Besides Pagett wasn't seeing too well, I guess. Anyhow, out he came leading Floyd Peters' rope horse, climbed on him bareback and went to reining him around with the halter, sitting up there proud as an old gelding with the first spring colt. Directly he looked down, shook his head, squinted again closely and told the pony, "Why, you ol' sonofabitch, this ain't you!"

Bob and I kept straight faces until they had disappeared back into the barn, then we collapsed. Pagett came out with the right horse, asked us, "What the hell you two so tickled about?", gave us another exhibition of riding with a bad hangover and, after the horse had been fed and watered, we wandered back up town.

As we got to the bar a car pulling a trailer boiled up. Floyd Monroe got out, called something through the saloon door and went around to undo the tailgate. Naturally we followed, and as he dropped the ramp we got a look at the load he was pulling—drunks stacked about waist deep, and God only knows how many of them. As they started to unsort themselves and crawl towards the opening he kept pushing them back and saying, "Stay in there, dammit. There's beer on the way."

Just then the bartender staggered out carrying a couple of cases of Great Falls Select, took a look into the trailer, said "Christ!", and deposited his load on top of the bodies.

Floyd turned to us and asked, "You guys mind shutting her up for me while I pay the man?"

We did, careful not to catch fingers, feet or heads, and as Floyd came out and climbed into the car Bob asked, "Where you headed?"

"Browning," was the reply. "I beat the town an' the brush an' believe I got 'em all. Hell, they'll do fine unless somebody gets smothered. They'll be drunker right quick, so they'll lay good. I got the mirror set so's I can keep an eye on the window, an' if anybody makes it to their feet I'll just jam on the brakes hard. That'll keep 'em down."

He slammed the door, pulled by us, and I got one last peek into the trailer. There, in the off corner, stuck up out of the tangle, was our Indian's head. Wearing a bottle of beer and a glassy grin. Bob looked at me, "Maybe we better get started, too."

I've found that while getting to a rodeo could sometimes be a problem, getting home again could be a lot worse. Especially if a man had won and had a gregarious cuss for a partner. Bob was sure that, and we both felt rich, to boot. Of course I'd learned long ago that the first thing a man should do when he gets to a rodeo is to fill his gas tank so he's sure of getting home. We had, but, between the two of us, it proved to be quite a trip back to the ranch. When we made it to Wolf Creek, between Augusta and Helena, we stopped at Frenchy's to cut the dust. Some of our friends were already there, others kept dropping in, one thing led to another, and before we knew it, it was too damn late to go any farther that night. Besides, it was too interesting to up and leave, anyhow. There was a dandy fiddler, until he got too drunk to fiddle, sporadic fisticuffs, and a lot of cattle got roped and broncs ridden at the bar. Bob progressed to where he looked sober, serious and sanctimonious—all of which he damn sure wasn't—and when an old stove up guy started to tell us how he'd had a sitting at Five Minutes to Midnight in Cheyenne in nineteen and twenty, or along about then, Bob put on a blank expression, cupped an ear, and asked, "Hey?"

I stepped in and explained that my partner was "deef," the result of having been kicked in the head by a bronc at the Calgary Stampede a few years back. The old fellow nodded understandingly and went through it again, loud. Another "Hey?" and a bovine look from Langston. This happened a half dozen times, the story getting shorter each trip. Finally the old guy rared back, filled up his paunch and let out a roar, "I said Five Minutes to Midnight!"

Understanding dawned on Bob's blank face, "Oh." Then surprise. "Damn, I didn't know it was so late," he remarked.

"To hell with it," said the guy, and wandered off where people could hear better.

To make a long story short, we bid a fond farewell to everybody late the next morning and headed for Helena. On the way we decided to drop in and say howdy to Ray Mavity at Clancy, so, for the moment, bypassed Helena. Besides, we'd been short of solid food, and Edna Mavity was a good cook! When we arrived, though, she was on the fight. Seems Ray had celebrated, or drowned his sorrow, over getting homesteaded in the Augusta arena. He was now at the sick, semi-sober and sorry stage. "Crudo," the Mexicans describe it—a magnificent word, that! He wanted a drink bad, and Edna figured he'd get one, and his second wind to boot, if Bob and I were around. She had a point, too. Anyhow, she told us to get and stay the hell off the place. There was some small discussion concerning frontier hospitality, unneighborliness, feminine vapors, and the like, but when she snarled, "Why, you two—," choked up and fumbled for the rifle on the antlers over the doorway, we got! Ray was calling pitifully from the bedroom, and I don't believe she'd 'a shot us, but we didn't stay to find out. No sir! So we headed back to Helena, hungry.

For years the Weiss Cafe had been the finest place to eat in Montana. It was pretty old-timey, and besides a large, varied and magnificent menu it had a string of funny little old waiters that had been there as long as I can remember. So it was with great anticipation that we followed one of them to the small rooms in the back—the only places where they had tables. We sat down and had an appetizer from our jug. Our little man came in with the menus and set the table as we studied them. The first surprise was a small sticker on the menu which, in essence, meant that since it was Tuesday no meat would be served. The second surprise, though it shouldn't have been, was that damn Bob. Before I could even complain about the meat he pointed to the highest priced steak on the card and announced, "I'll have this. Rare." I realized he was back on his deaf deal.

The waiter went into a long explanation about the war, how Weiss's was doing its bit and so on while Bob sat watching blankly. Then, "Well, then this un'll do," and he pointed at the next steak on the list.

The explanation started again, and I interrupted, as usual, to say that my partner was deaf, and the little guy raised his voice half a dozen notches. Bob shrugged and pointed at a T-Bone, and away we went again. Time he ran down I could see the old fellow was getting annoyed, but he was hiding it pretty well, for after all, this poor man was deaf. About then Bob growled to me, "Thought you said this place was good. Strikes me as a sorry sonofabitchin' outfit. Got nothin' a man wants. Hell, I've ate better in jail!" and he pointed again. He'd gotten down to about the prime ribs by now.

Well, it must have taken the best part of an hour before he worked through all the meat. Short ribs, stew, heart, brisket, liver, tongue, kidneys, tripe, and God knows what else, plumb down through sweetbreads and brains. Weiss's was a first-class outfit! Early in the game the old guy was shouting at the top of his lungs, but he had sand and stayed with it, while I buried myself in my menu, tried not to grin and ignored the din. During this, too, every customer in the place had to go to the rest rooms so they could look in our door on the way and find out, maybe, what the uproar was all about. At one time or other every waiter in the place peered in, even the chef. I guess the manager wasn't on the premises, probably not even in town, for we never did see him.

Finally Bob rasped, "Hell, I hate fish, puny damn stuff!" and ordered some fine seafood dish, and a shaken little man turned to me and bellowed, "And you, Sir?"

Carefully, and not daring to look up, I said, "The same for me," and added, "Bring me a fried egg sandwich on the side, too."

"Yes, Sir!" was the answer, at a level that would have carried a quarter of a mile easy, and he stumbled out, sweating pretty badly.

Bob, just busting with curiosity, whispered, "What in hell you going to do with that fried egg sandwich?"

"Ignore it," said I.

We did exactly that as we ate a magnificent meal, except, of course, when one or the other of us would salt or pepper the hell out of the sandwich. Or pour on Worcestershire, Durkees, or sugar, or something. Bothered the hell out of our waiter, and he swelled up like a toad with curiosity. But he damn sure wasn't about to start any more conversations with us, so we ate in silence. The whole cafe did, seemed like.

It sort of surprised us what we'd done with our winnings when we went to settle up, but we got her done and left a good tip for our little guy. The rest, except for a little change, we spent at a filling station, hoping it would get us home. It didn't quite. Our outfit quit just above Two Dot about a half mile. We pushed it in to the only station, finally woke the man up and, between our change and the last bit of our current jug, talked him out of a couple of gallons of gas.

We took the old road to Melville—it was the shortest—driving carefully and slowly, coasting where we could, and got home about sunrise with the needle on "empty." Barbara was cooking breakfast for the children and remarked, "The show was Sunday, and today's Wednesday.

Mind telling me——. On second thought, I'd rather not know. Sit down and eat."

One of the funniest deals I ever saw at a rodeo, and for a wonder I wasn't directly involved in it, took place over at Harlowton, Montana. It's crowding thirty years now since it happened, but I'll never forget it! Joe Orr and Alice Greenough had the show, and while I wasn't contesting—I wasn't an RCA member—they had rented my half-Mexican calves for the roping, so I saw the whole lovely affair.

They had some rank bulls in their string, and somehow one of the rankest got out of the arena during the bull riding. He was itching for trouble and in short order had everybody treed up in the stands or on the fence. He sure had the place to himself as he stood glaring, head up and ears cocked, looking for something, anything, to take a bust at.

The Harlow grounds are down on the Musselshell River bottom right alongside a sort of tourist park. It's a pretty place with nice camp grounds scattered among the big cottonwoods, and lots of people had been using them before the show commenced. To this day I don't know whether the participants were tourists or not. If so, they damn sure had a tale to tell back home, and very probably a jaundiced opinion of Montana from then on out.

Anyhow, as the bull stood tossing slobber back onto his shoulders, out from the cottonwoods came this little man at a leisurely walk. The Brahma spotted him, reacted like a teased snake, and here he came sort of slaunchwise back of the guy's shoulder, not making a sound except for the rattle of dew claws. Of course everything took place in plain sight of the grandstand, and as they saw hell and high water headed for the man, everybody as one drew in their wind and let out a warning yell.

He looked up to see what was going on, saw, and his head and his feet must have been well-coordinated, for in one jump he's doing his damndest. If a man had a calf horse

that was geared to come uncorked like that guy did he'd
have it made. He was out pretty well away from the timber
and the nearest refuge from impending doom was a little
white house with "women" lettered on the door. The man
didn't hesitate—nor would have I, in his boots—he was
seeking sanctuary!

Lord but that old boy did run! His head was thrown back
like the lid on a coffeepot, and the stride on him would have
put a jumping horse plumb in the shade. So he had maybe
fifteen or twenty feet the best of the bull when he blasted
through the outhouse door and slammed it behind him. He
had enough leeway anyhow so the bull had room to stop
before he, too, followed his quarry inside. Then he bawled
in disappointment, backed off, still keeping an eye on the
door, and began pawing dust over himself. It hadn't settled
when be damned if the door didn't open and the man poked
his head out.

There was a snort, the man got taken again, ducked back
like a gopher into his hole, and this time the bull didn't
have room to stop before he jarred against the house. Then
he backed off and stood watching the door like a cat at a
mouse hole.

Sure enough, out popped the head, and the bull bellowed
and charged again. The pickup men were on the way by
then, but twice more before they got there that damn fool
poked his head out, and the bull ran him back in. Matter of
fact, Mister Bull seemed to be enjoying the game and
wising up, to boot, for the last time he never backed off a
step; just stood there with an ear and a horn cocked, eyeing
the door expectantly. If things had stayed quiet likely the
animal would have gone away, but the guy was either a
little weedy or he was bound and determined to get the hell
out of that ladies' john, and right now! Luckily the pickup
men arrived, roped the bull and headed back for the arena.
They hadn't gone twenty yards when out popped Old
Gopher again, sized things up, stepped out and headed

back for the timber he'd come from before the fracas began. He wasn't alone; a solid roar of glee followed him as long as he was in sight, and then some.

As things quieted, though, that same johnny door opened slowly once more. Two girls slipped furtively out and tried to make it to the timber unobtrusively before they were spotted. They didn't, and the roar that had greeted the man was a pale facsimile of the howl that went up at the sight of those two poor damn girls! I still laugh when I visualize the inside of that little house, the poor guy bursting frantically in and just as feverishly trying to get out. Lordy!

I had a funny thing happen to me over towards that same Missouri country along in the early '50s, too. Funny peculiar, that is. Though looking back it turned out to be funny funny besides. It was a jackpot roping at Judith Gap, and my partner and I got hotter than a two dollar pistol and wound up winning the four steer average in the team tieing—forty percent of the pot—plus ten percent for the fastest run made. So we pocketed fifty percent of the whole team tieing shebang. It was worth having, too.

Naturally some of the other ropers were itching to relieve us of some of our, as we put it, "well-deserved" winnings. The rancher supplying the cattle had no objections, as long as he got a couple of bucks out of each head run, so we kept on jackpotting after the formal events were over. We kept on winning and insisted to the rest of the ropers that it was simply a question of sheer ability on our part, coupled with outstanding horse flesh—I'd raised the two horses we were using. We rode our streak high and handsome until the other boys decided maybe a calf roping jackpot might be the way to get some of their money back, so it was agreed we'd have one run at calves and then quit.

I hadn't roped a calf for several years, but hell, the way I'd been roping I might just make a good run. My partner, being smarter, begged off on account of "chores" back home, loaded up and pulled out. But not me. I paid my money and discovered—not with any great surprise—that the calf that had been drawn for me was the biggest in the pen. To boot, I was the last roper; back where I could stall walk a little.

Anyhow, when I backed into the score box and the flag man asked, "Ready?" I told him, "Hell, I *came* ready! Let's have him."

I was riding a big Hancock who had a lot of gas and a hell of a whoa. He put me there right now, and I felt like Mansfield the way I whacked it on. So much so that I tried for a little trimming, and as I jerked my slack I whipped it over my mount's head to the near side—something I never did ordinarily—he died, and I quit him, figuring Skipworth had nothing on me when it came to getting down. I'm afraid he did though, for something went wrong—damn wrong; as my off boot cleared my pony's rump my near foot was jerked ahead and up, and I thought, "What the hell?" as I saw it over my head against the evening sky.

When I opened my eyes I was lying under a sougan on a bed in a room I'd never seen before! I tried everything out, found it all worked, carefully got up and peeked out the window. No help at all; just flats running off to the horizon. Might have been anywhere. Where the hell was I, and how come the sun said it must be damn near noon?

I could hear noises from below, so I pulled on my boots, buckled on the spur that was lying by them, the right, and scouted around for the left. No luck, so, feeling a little apprehensive, I opened the door, went down the stairs, headed for the sounds, and damn but I was glad to recognize a rancher and his wife from over under the Snowies. I was at their ranch, and the story came out.

Seems I'd had some sort of a wreck quitting my horse, had gotten up and tied the calf, but not fast enough. It had been the last go-round, so I loaded my horse, pulled up to the bar, had a beer or two, said so long and left. When the rancher and his wife came out an hour or so later, there I sat in my rigging. He asked what I was doing, and I told him I was trying to go home, but didn't know which way it was.

Well, he knew I couldn't be drunk, so he sized me up a little more carefully, decided my eyes looked sort of funny, climbed in, moved me over and drove my outfit to his place, while his wife drove their car. They took me in, pulled off my boots and put me to bed. He'd tended my horse last night and again this morning. I asked about my missing spur, for I've had them since I was thirteen, but I'd only been wearing one when they found me.

To make it short, we ate, I loaded up, thanked them for all they'd done and pulled out for home. Just for good luck I decided to go back to the arena, and on the way I discovered that my wallet, with all my winnings, was missing. I knew that if it happened to be at the ranch my friends would get it back to me, but I stopped at the bar on the chance I'd lost it there. The owner hadn't seen it, and the few remaining patrons from the night before were either so drunk or hung over that I didn't bother to ask them, so I drove down and prospected the grounds. Sure enough, out a hundred feet from the calf chute and off to one side I spotted my spur, and when I picked it up I saw that the strap was broken. A good stout strap, too. About twenty feet away, and almost covered with dirt, lay my wallet, my winnings still intact. Better than a hundred dollars!

As I drove home I figured out what must have happened—when I had popped my slack back over my horse's head he had been making so many knots that the loop had hooked back over my near spur. When my mount threw his stop and that big calf hit the end of the rope it had jerked my leg straight in the air, broken the spur strap doing it, and the wreck was on. I'd probably spilled my wallet when I was standing on my head, and the jar had knocked me silly, though I could still operate. All's well that ends well is my motto, and outside of having an ungodly stiff neck for a few days I was fine. Nothing lost, but, by God, I've never thrown my slack over a horse's neck since.

Then there was the time at Bozeman just before the war. It was the last night and Fritz Truan had drawn "Dim Out," Rich Richter's top saddle bronc, as his finals horse. As he got ready the announcer gave a long song and dance, the lights all dimmed for a minute, and Richter rode along in front of the stands looking for all the world like a pouter pigeon. There was a hush as Carr belted Truan down, and that screwball of a Fritz looked up at him, grinned and asked, "How'd you like to come along for the trip, Clay?"

"Why not?" was the answer, and Carr dropped down behind the cantle. Truan said, "Give him to us." The gate opened and out they came, Fritz spurring from hell to breakfast in front and Clay fanning the old pony with his hat from the rumble seat.

I thought Richter would have a stroke, especially since they both rode the horse to a finish while the crowd roared approval. Hell of a thing, actually, to do to a man's top bucking horse, but it was a sight! That damn Truan; he was a dandy! He joined the Marines after Pearl Harbor and was one of those that never came back from the South Pacific; Iwo Jima, I believe. We sure missed him!

Art Orser died a few years ago. I was snowed in and couldn't get to the funeral. I was sorry, for I liked the son of a gun, and it'll be a long time before another like him shows up, if ever. Orser was—well, he was Orser!

A bucking horse man, if one ever lived, and he wasn't what you'd call bashful about saying so. "Askins invented bronc riding," he claimed, "but Orser perfected it!" I wouldn't go along with that completely, but Art was one hell of a bronc rider. He was wild when the chute opened, but hell, he was wild everywhere, and I still hump up a little when I think of some of the parties we had together.

Art was a good guy, though a little raunchy at times, and he sure had a great sense of humor.

I was away at school one spring, either '29 or '30 I believe it was, when he was working for the Donald outfit down on the Sweet Grass, and Walt Heacock, the current bronc riding champion was breaking horses for my Dad. A rodeo champion in those days could be a first class horseman, cowman, cowboy and good ranch hand, to boot.

Anyhow, as Artie told it, he was out setting fence posts along the "Settlement" lane one morning when he saw some sort of rigging coming down it from the west. After a while he could make out that it was a sheep wagon, with an old boy standing in the doorway driving. It was pretty early in the morning, the wagon was headed into the sun, and there was something in or on it that reflected back into Orser's eyes something terrible, so he just turned his back and went on building his post hole.

Finally the outfit got to where he was, whoaed up, and there was Walt Heacock handling the lines. The reflection had come from the big "World's Champion Bronc Rider" buckle on his belt!

They chatted a while, then Walt picked up his lines and said, "Art, I won't tell if you don't," clucked to the team and drove off.

It was just too good for Orser to keep quiet about—two champion saddle bronc riders, one digging post holes, and the other driving a sheep wagon!

# Runaways

## 10

THERE'S A C.M. RUSSELL picture that has always made a deep impression on me. I'm sure Charley didn't mean it to be funny, though most people seem to think it is, and my bet is that he painted it to show what he thought of automobiles, how much he hated them, and how danger-ous he thought they were. By present standards he didn't know the half of it, but what he painted chills me, and I never see the picture without my stomach tightening in anticipation of what I know damn well is about to happen.

The scene shows a car of early vintage spooking a team that is hooked to a spring wagon driven by a rancher, with his wife and baby as passengers. The team has made a wild lunge and the man is in midair, jarred from the wagon seat. He has lost the lines, and the team is completely loose as they start their run toward the lane fence. The driver's wife, clutching the baby, is toppling out her side. She may clear the wheel, but it's a cinch that she'll hit the fence. In another fraction of a second the man may be stove up, but there's no question what is going to happen to his wife and to that poor little kid! I suppose that the scene affects me so strongly because I have had a damn sight more than a nodding acquaintance with runaways. I savvy not only what's happening at the moment, but what the end result is sure to be—at the very best a rig and harness torn all to hell, and a team that, even if they don't get badly wire cut in the fence, will be boogery and untrustworthy for the rest

127

of their lives. To a man who has been there it's a nasty picture!

When I was a little kid somebody was always getting stove up in a runaway. Men, as a rule, but when a woman got hurt she usually got badly hurt. Their long skirts were bad about getting caught in the wheels, worked like a set of hobbles when it came to jumping clear, and all too often would cause a foot to get caught in the spokes, which is about as unenviable a spot as there is during a runaway.

They weren't usually as fatal as a traffic accident nowadays nor as frequent, but a lot of people got pretty badly crippled and occasionally were killed. I was lucky, for I never got hurt. Just skinned up some.

There were lots of causes for runaways. A close pop of lightning, a rattler, a jack rabbit jumping out underfoot and, particularly, a hail storm. Fortunately a man would have some warning of the latter—from the green color of the clouds or the thrumming roar—and often had time to hunt timber for protection. At worst, in the open, he could unhook, tie the team to a wheel, and he and any passengers could crawl underneath the outfit.

Automobiles, thank God, were pretty scarce, for they sure caused trouble, almost all horses being completely unused to them. As a matter of fact, when my Uncle Jack Scarlett brought the first car into the country in 1905 it was a common occurrence to have somebody call up and ask, "Is Scarlett going to be loose on the roads with that damn thing of his tomorrow?"

If the answer was negative there was invariably a sigh of relief, and "By God, then I think I'll drive to Melville. Just wanted to make sure."

Uncle Jack took one of the first, if not the first, cars ever into Yellowstone Park. However, the authorities made him leave it at Mammoth Hot Springs, just a few miles inside the boundary. It was causing too much hell among the teams, especially the four horse stage hitches.

I remember vividly how, after Dad got a car, when we met a wagon the driver would pull over, get down and hold his horses' heads as we gingerly eased past, and usually he didn't look very happy either. You would have thought we were the Devil himself, too, the way even a gentle old team would carry on. Julius Gunderson, from the Norwegian "Settlement," a man who had a reputation for hot horses, even took to using those old long-shanked U.S. Cavalry curbs on his teams when he planned on being on a county road.

All in all we figured a runaway about like we do a car accident now, only back then you didn't have to worry so much about what the other guy would do; a man usually got in a wreck through his own fault. I don't think I ever had a runaway except where I was to blame; because I got careless, or did some damn fool thing. Like the time I was raking hay on the flat below Melville.

As a rule a kid draws the raking job on a hay crew. It's a lonesome proposition; the mowers are gone and the stacking crew won't arrive for a while. Besides, since the driver on a rake is right in amongst his team, within easy reach of their heels, we always used the oldest and gentlest horses we had. However, our boy had gotten behind and the stacker was crowding him, so I decided to help.

I had another rake, not a real good one fortunately, so I hooked up and started bunching what was windrowed. My team was a pair I'd been using on a mower, going sons of guns, and it took them a little time to get used to the pop and clang when I tripped the rake teeth. They finally settled down, though, and I thought I had it made. Would have, too, if I hadn't gotten careless.

I finished bunching on the first land, but as I drove by the stackyard on my way to the second I noticed a weight—we always had to hang a couple over a finished stack to keep the wind from blowing the top off—lying in the gate, and whoaed up to move it. Like some sort of knothead, instead of tying my team to a post or even driving them up against the fence, I just stepped off, walked over and picked up the weight, and about twenty feet of wire that was attached to it wriggled and rustled through the grass towards me and my team.

I jumped for the lines with a "Whoa!", but I was a day late and a dollar short. Their tips slid through my clutching fingers as the horses snorted and shied from the moving grass, the eveners hit their heels, and they were long gone!

I watched them go, in what looked like a veritable cloud of broken rake teeth, gaining speed with every jump. The gate out of the field up at Melville was open, thank God. The team made it but not the rigging, for I saw a wheel spin into the air and knew they'd picked up a gate post. They swung out of sight up through town, and I cringed at the possibility that there might be teams, saddle horses, maybe a child or two in their way on the street. The dogs and chickens I knew for sure were there didn't bother me.

It was a long trip back; particularly since I had to pass the saloon as I trudged through town. Looked like a Saturday night, the porch and doorway were so crowded, and everybody was packing an idiotic grin and just busting with neighborly remarks.

"Lose somethin', Spike?", "Where you been anyhow?", "Quittin' sort of early, ain't you?" Real friendly concern. But I knew they *had* been concerned until they saw I was all right. I also knew my team hadn't gotten into any wire down by the barn, for if they were in trouble everybody would have been down taking care of them. So I just grinned and went on to the barn.

Dad had a runaway with four horses and a grain drill one spring. He was a fine teamster, but this day he had a stud on the outside next to a big gelding—with a jockey stick between them so the stud couldn't reach him—then another broke horse across the pole with a colt we'd broken that spring outside of him. The stud was blaring and trying to get to his mate, both geldings were flinching sideways and uneasy because of him, while the old gunsel colt was completely bewildered by it all. It looked like a shaky outfit, and Gramp said so.

"We're short of work horses," Dad explained, "and I've got to get these oats in. Hell, I'll get by. The field is soft, there won't be much noise, and they'll cool down."

He'd forgotten he had to cross some hard ground before he got to the field, and the ball commenced with the first rattle of those iron wheels. Pop did fine until they hit a ditch which jarred him off the step, but he kept hold of the lines and was dragged along on his stomach, bellowing, "Whoa!"

They slacked a little, but about then he got over on his back, and they couldn't seem to hear him as well or something, for they picked up speed again. In a short time he got back on his stomach, and this time they slowed and finally stopped.

Dad got to his feet his clothes both front and back torn and dusty. "Damn," he remarked with a grin, "I thought I was going to lose them. It was getting awful hot on my stomach, and when I'd roll over to let it cool a little, I couldn't get much purchase. I'm sure glad there wasn't any prickly pear here, or I'd sure have had to let them go. Well, let's see if they tore up anything, and we'll have another go at it."

They hadn't, he did, and was seeding blithely shortly afterwards!

A neighbor of mine, a Norsk, had a gaudy go-round during haying. He was famed for his teams, anyhow. I helped him thresh one time and he fit me out with a bundle wagon and a pair of horses that had both damn sure been up against the weed some time or other, so I spent most of my time hauling on the lines and cussing fervently, especially when I was trying to unload at the threshing machine. He thought it was a hell of a joke.

Anyhow, he had a couple of mowers cutting down below his place on Hailstone. Somehow one of the mower men got in a bind, his team and machine got away from him and headed for home. The other mower man saw them coming, jumped off his outfit and ran out to try and stop them, but when he saw that cutter bar popping, the sickle whining like a buzz saw, he did what any sensible person would do; he got the hell out of the way. Of course when the runaways went by the second mower its team enthusiastically joined the race, and up the flat the two outfits went, both teams digging for all they were worth, cutter bars bouncing and sickle sections flying like shrapnel. A runaway with a mower is spectacular, but the man that owns the machine is seldom very appreciative. This old Norsk, though, calmly watched his two mowers and teams rapidly going to hell in a hand basket, and as they disappeared around the rise at the upper end of the flat he turned to his crew, which had joined him as spectators. "Heh, heh," he chuckled, "I vonder vich von vill vin!"

Some of those Norwegians sure got off some good remarks, and the thing that really spiced them up was that often the remark was made in all seriousness. Like the neighbor from down the creek who hailed me from the saloon as I rode through Melville one nice spring morning, "Spike, coom and have a drink vid me."

It was pretty early in the day, but curiosity got the best of me for I knew he wasn't much of a hand for booze. So, as we were having the drink I asked just what he was celebrating.

"Ay am not celebrating, Ay am yust getting drunk an' to hal vid t'ings!"

"How did that come about?" I queried.

"Oh, de damn lambing, an' dis here t'ing of putting ayodine on de damn nawels," and he launched into a long heartfelt explanation.

It seems that the vets had come up with a new wrinkle

for lambing—putting iodine on each newborn lamb's navel. It was supposed to keep them from getting some sort of disease or infection which had been killing a lot of them. Each lamber carried a bottle of the stuff, and as soon as each lamb was dropped, the umbilical cord was sacked up in the bottle, the mouth of the latter held tightly against the animal's belly while he was turned upside down so no part of the exposed navel would be missed. It took time, was a nuisance, and the lambers didn't like to be bothered with it. Especially the older ones, who didn't think any new idea could be worth a damn anyhow. So my neighbor had been losing lambs.

"Why don't you get after them about it?" I asked when he finally ran down.

"Ay do, damn dem. Ay fired vun an' vipped anudder, an' still dey von't do it unless Ay am vidin sight an' jelling range."

There was a minute of silence as he reflected on his woes. Then he burst out in exasperation with the clincher, "An' even ven dey do, dey put it on de balls an' not de nawel!"

# Bells, Bears and Lash Rope

## 11

I'VE GOT A THING about bells, and I've gathered quite a string of them. Sleigh bells—hame, backband, bellyband, britching, Santa Claus, single horse, Norwegian, Swiss, Austrian and French. Tongue bells, too, including cow bells which friends have sent me from Europe, Africa and Tibet. I picked up some lovely bells in Spain and have also gotten hold of a couple of cavalry bells, a set of six for the leaders of a jerk line outfit and a set of three for an ox yoke. Barring the jerk line bells and the ox yoke bells, I use most of them on and off, and I sort of think by now my milk cows have begun to wonder just what the hell they'll sound like next month. As a rule we don't have much snow here, and a lot of wind to blow what there is away, so ordinarily I get maybe a week of winter when I can use a bob sled to feed with. I just love the whisper of runners through the snow and the chime of the bells on my team, and I swear their song raises the temperature at least twenty degrees. At that, though, I am not quite as keen since the winter of '69—I *had* to use a bob then for ninety-eight days hand running!

I've a string of horse bells, too—cast brass Swiss bells, each of a different tone—and among the eighty-odd horses we turn out every evening during the summer there'll be about fifteen head wearing them. Horses are class conscious as all hell and cliquey, so the head honcho of each separate bunch of snobs wears a bell, and to hear them all

134

coming down the canyon ahead of my wranglers about daylight is a never ending joy to me. When I move the cattle to the high summer range, and on pack trips, I use the same sort of bell, but bigger and deeper toned, for I think a lower note is easier to hear and locate over the sound of water or wind in the timber. Their sound is pretty comforting, too, during the night singing gently to camp. Everything's all right, I'm not afoot!

A man learns to tell a lot from the sound of his horse bells. A soft, desultory chiming means the stock are grazing quietly or dozing, while a steady rhythmic beat means they are moving, which in the Crazies can only mean down. You can judge whether they are on the trail, which is no problem, since if you are smart you have rolled your bed in the middle of it, and all that is needed is to sit up and yell and pop a slicker at them when they get close enough to where it'll spook them back where they belong. But maybe there's the ring of slide rock, and that'll mean some smart bastard is taking them around the lake and across the slide you figured would stop them. Then's the time to hit the deck in a long lope and right now! Lord God, but I've run miles in my shirt, drawers, boots or untied shoes, and usually in the dark, after horses! Then the ride back to camp bareback, nothing between me and that backbone but BVD's, and if I'd been unlucky it was *quite* a ride. We'd both get sweaty, and that itchy old horse dust would work in.

My Dad had a band of sheep on the head of Sweet Grass when I was a kid, times were tough, and he decided I'd make a camptender. "Good experience," he said, and fit me out with a bell mare who, if she laid over without use for a day, wouldn't be satisfied unless she started the next day by bucking me off, and a Thoroughbred gelding that couldn't be ridden, but than whom there was no whomer as a pack horse. I still have a warm feeling when I think of old Snip, for I packed him in some horrible places. I also drew a small, trim, grey jinny that soured me on mules for the next forty years. Horses and mules are different propositions, to say the least, and unlike the Frenchman who was speaking of the difference between men and women, I damn sure don't shout "Vive la difference!" This jinny—I never did settle on a name for her for fear I'd forget and use it in public when I was out of the mountains—was temperamental, independent as a hog on roller skates and more contrary than a milk cow. I had to keep the stock shod myself, and she could kick the snapper off a bean and never mark the hide. I wasn't as lucky as the bean, and mule tracks still show up on me when I get real cold!

I don't claim to be a sure enough packer, for I have never used a Decker or a manty, but I damn sure learned the rudiments. I started with, and still favor, a sawbuck, sling ropes, and paniers for the loose stuff. Looking back it seems to me that I've packed about everything a man in his right mind, or out of it, can pack into rough country, or out. The diamond and double diamond hitches are pretty and romantic, and when I wanted to impress somebody and had help in getting them pulled down tight, I've used them on a top pack or a bedroll pack. But an old guy taught me the "Basco" years ago, and I quit the rest. It's a one man deal; sort of a glorified squaw hitch, sound, simple and solid.

I learned about hobbles right quick—how a horse that couldn't outrun a fat man loose would give Secretariat a hell of a run with hobbles on, though in those days it would have been Phar Lap; how rawhide hobbles don't go with sharp rocks and wet mountain grass; how the ring of chain hobbles is pretty handy to help locate a missing animal sometimes; and how a smart old pony can handle hobbles, side hobbles or cross hobbles, sometimes all at once, in a way you wouldn't believe. Not until you'd walked and cussed for a few miles, that is! I learned it's always a good idea to carry a couple of gunny sacks in the bottom of the paniers for emergency hobbles, or even blindfolds. About picketing, too, and what a rope can do under the heel of a shoe. Or what can happen to a knot after a night in a wet bottom or in a rain or a heavy dew. Still, picket an old pony by a front foot to a stout, limber, green tree with a good lash rope and you'll just about keep him. I had a bear come through camp when I had four head picketed that way, and though all four ironed themselves out a time or two during the ruckus, when the smoke had cleared I still had my livestock. Or, if worse comes to worst, tie him with a halter, short, to a stout tree. I'd rather count his ribs than his tracks!

I got to know bears, too. Intimately, too intimately. Whenever there'd be a fuss in the band at night the herder, a Norsk, would "Let go a couple of shoots vid de riffle" and send the dog out to investigate. He never downed a bear but then he never downed a sheep, either.

One of Grosfield's herders told me about the time he set his dog on a bear, the bear took the dog, and, to quote, "De dam dog rin to me vid de dam bear yust behind."

"What happened?" I asked, hoping maybe to get a pointer or two for my herder.

His reply I treasure. "Ay pick op de dam dog an' trow him at de damn bear an' rin like hal!"

One morning I went jauntily out to get my horses, whose bells I could hear maybe a quarter of a mile above camp. I came around a big boulder and ran nose to nose with a silvertip, swallowed my chew and froze. He grunted, in surprise I hoped, and reared up, his belly button about level with my eyes, and I came uncorked. Throwing the bridle at him, I hightailed it out of there. The herder was still in camp, and seeing me scrabble for the rifle, he made a run for the nearest tree—a limberpine about as thick as my upper arm—and shinnied up it saying, "Oh Yeesus, dey say a grissel von't climb!" When he was as high as he could go, the tree bent over so he was pretty near upside down, and maybe three feet or so off the ground. He hung there praying fervently, with the dog trying to lick his face, while I watched my back trail, rifle ready. I got to giggling, and when a chipmunk suddenly flirted his tail out of the scrub, the fact that I was so tickled probably saved him from being blown to kingdom come. Finally I went gingerly back up the canyon. The bridle was lying by the rock, and my horses were dozing and calmly switching flies about a hundred yards up the hill, but no bear. Never did see him again, and I was glad of it—I sure never have lost any grizzlies!

Bears are funny, though, and I won't forget old Fletch Weatherman's story about being raided by one when he was prospecting years ago on the head of Big Timber Creek. Said nothing turned up missing except a pair of red gum boots he used in the hole. There wasn't anybody else in the country, but when a skiff of snow came he got to seeing tracks every now and then, so he figured the bear must be wearing the boots. Probably liked the color, or his feet had gotten cold, and Fletch swore that when he happened to run onto the boots a year or so later they were worn plumb out!

One herder I tended for, old Sam Vashus, would have made the average bear look good. He was not only about half weedy, but every time I went out for salt and supplies he'd use the dishes and not wash them—just let the dog clean them up before the next meal! He kept a camp so damn dirty even the flies wouldn't come into it, so I finally got a teepee for myself, set it up out a ways from camp, did my cooking in the open, did the dishing out myself, and let him do what he damned pleased with *his* utensils. *I* kept *mine!*

My post graduate course in packing came when we were hauling for the Belle Mining Company, which was working a lead above Blue Lake. Hard times, and Dad was getting five dollars a day per pack animal and, though I've never understood why, three dollars per packer and his saddle horse. Didn't do much to make a man feel important! It was before the Forest Service had done much work in the Crazies, and trails the old-timers had built were pretty rudimentary. I look at the old traces now—skirting a cliff edge or across a perpendicular, loose slide half way up Granite Peak—and wonder what sort of fools would pack powder there. *We* did. Two hundred pounds of dynamite to the horse, two horses to a man, and we carried the caps, packed in sawdust in round cans a little larger than snoose cans, in our shirt pockets. It was a regular Kamikaze outfit, and I never enjoyed it. Sort of like the old fellow who took his first plane ride, and, when the pilot asked how he'd enjoyed it, replied, "Oh, all right, I guess. But I never did let my full weight down."

Dad was always a great one to have some rank old bronc he figured should be packed. "Does 'em good," he said. Fortunately, he usually put the food on the broncs and led them himself, and as a rule we got by. Not always, though.

He was in the front one time leading a big black juicy bronc loaded with two quarters of beef, and two of us were behind, each with two tailed powder horses and caps in our pockets. We'd made it up the slide to the top of the cliff, along the bench above it that ran around to the camp, and were in the last narrow, steep rock chute when I, who was at the tail end, heard a yell from up front. Here came the bronc, with a quarter of beef popping at the end of about four feet of lash rope. Over the man and his horse ahead of me he came, and over his two powder horses. Somehow I quit my saddle horse and slid halfway under him about at the cinch. Don't know how I did it, but I kept thinking of those caps, those four hundred pounds of dynamite and the blue glare it'd make. My horse squashed down on me, then my two led horses went down, the commotion faded, and I was still in one chunk! We got sorted out and on up to the camp where we got rid of the damn stuff we were carrying and then went to look for the bronc. There was a quarter of beef just below where I'd been, and he'd cut off the trail down one of the draws towards the cliff edge. He must have seen what was coming, tried to stop, fallen, slid and when he was over the edge to about his withers the other quarter of beef jammed between two solid rocks and stopped him. He was quiet when we got there—I'd have been quiet, too, if I'd been looking at the same view he was. After careful work we got some ropes on him, took some dallies around our saddle horns—not too many to throw fast, either—and another with a lash rope around a big rock to hold the purchase as we got it, and finally pulled him back to where he could stand up. Then, as he stood sweating and shaking, we loaded the beef and lashed it down tight.

"Looks like the sonofabitch learned something," said Dad. "Let's go."

A lucky day all around; for the miners and their beef, though it was a little gritty; for us; and damn sure for the bronc. But still I didn't enjoy it!

Years later I had some more salty packing. Not dangerous, but tricky. When the Belle outfit went broke the miners attached the equipment for their wages, and when they in turn finally sold it we got the job of getting it out. There was a full-sized cook stove, a Home Comfort, which we finally slung on one side with an anvil and several bundles of drill steel on the other. The two compressor tanks were no cinch either, but Snip drew them, and when they were slung all you could see of him were his head and his feet tripping daintily along below the tanks. The rails were bad, too, but we slung them in bunches, wrapped in gunny sacks, at an angle and crossed over the horse's neck, which was padded with a sheepskin. The heavy, hundred-foot lengths of compressor hose we whipped by slinging it in coils on either side of one horse, dropping about five feet, and slinging the rest on the following horse. It took three pairs of animals to handle six hose lengths, but the Forest

Service switchbacks were not as abrupt as the old trail had been, and things went fine. The block of the compressor engine was a sticker, for it weighed right at four hundred pounds and was L-shaped. Finally we padded our biggest horse, old Hector, from hell to breakfast, balanced it across him with the longer leg to the outside and lashed out all the sway we could. It worked, though we unloaded the old fellow four times to rest him before we got to the head of the road. It was tough work all the way through and took a matter of ten days, but we got her done. When the going was bad I remembered other loads I'd liked a damn sight less!

Oh, those horse bells, and the memories they sing of! They were chiming from across the lake one night when I was making a last check of a camp full of guests and overheard a girl tell her swain, "I'll give you just a half hour to get out of this sleeping bag!"

Another night we could hear them all the way when a couple of us rode and tied the only horse in camp up over the Sweet Grass-Big Timber divide after some smart boogers that had outfoxed us. Never could see them, but their bells kept us company until we caught up—at the ranch corrals. A matter of about fifteen miles! If it hadn't been for the bells we'd have quit. Literally, we were "tolled"!

I came over that same divide at night from the sheep camp a long time ago, the bells on my empty pack horses chuckling along behind me. I rolled in my slicker and slept till I froze out on the near side of the hump, walked a while to warm up and then rode on home. As we got nearer the ranch I began to hear horse bells as each pod of dude horses spotted us and moved restlessly as they tried to figure us out. When they had done so, the different tinklings subsided one by one, and the creek and the little breeze took over again.

When I had tended my stock I headed for my cabin.

Since we turned off the light plant at eleven there were no lights, but I sat sleepily on the edge of my bed, pulled off my boots and stripped. I did notice that the place didn't smell as much of leather and horses as usual, but I was tired and paid no attention. When I got into bed there was somebody already there, probably my Uncle Bill Perry who was always put in with me when he came down from Helena for a visit. But damn, he was hogging the bed, so I backed off and gave him a hefty boost with my bare seat, and got the hell shocked out of me!

A feminine voice said, "Oh!" and a girl popped up and asked, "Who's there?"

I made a dive for the door, scooping up my stuff as I went, and hit a high lope for the barn, badly unnerved and awful bare, and thanking God she hadn't screamed. I made the hayloft, but couldn't sleep well, seemed like, so before the bell rang I went up to the bath house, showered, shaved and cleaned up. I didn't ask any questions or get too noticeable either, but when I went in to breakfast my mother greeted me with, "My, Spike, I'm glad you got here this morning. We're crowded and I had to put a new guest in your cabin last night," and she introduced me to a good-looking girl at the table.

I shook hands as serious as a tree full of owls, said, "I think we've met," then grinned. She blushed furiously and then smiled back, "Indeed we have."

I'm sure my mother thought we had met at the bath house. Many's the time I have heard her tell how she put a girl in my cabin, with never an inkling of the facts, and I sure never told her! I got to know the girl pretty well before she left. A nice girl, and horse bells somehow always remind me of her.

# The Old Breed

I WENT TO A FUNERAL a while ago. It wasn't what you'd call crowded, the preacher sort of hung fire in his sermon a time or two, and it was a short one. After the doings were over three or four of us bunched and got to talking. Each of us had a story or two to tell about the man we'd come to pay our respects to. Unusual, maybe, for a time like that, but we grinned back and forth as we chatted, occasionally laughed and when we broke up none of us had come to the end of our store of tales. We'll miss him, but when we think of him it'll always be with a chuckle. He was quite a man, but like the old 30-30 saddle gun, his breed is getting pretty scarce now. But damn I'm glad I knew him!

There used to be a lot of old-timers cut out of the same leather who lived "at the head of the cricks" up under the Crazies. Prospectors, trappers, moonshiners, sawyers from the bull team days and old stove up cowboys. They were a special breed, and God sure broke the mold when he made the last of them. They were pretty raspy old customers, by and large, but it was always, "Get down, come in and set up," when you rode in. It was a damn good idea, though, to hello their cabins from out a ways and to make plenty of noise coming in!

We had a few of them as wranglers on the dude outfit years ago, but not too many. They were just too easy going when it came to dirty, and their talk, even when they were doing their best to tone it down, rated a whole lot beyond picturesque. Old Frank wrangled for us for several seasons, and boys, he didn't have to act western—he damn sure was! Tall, thin, one-eyed, a big droopy mustache over a mouth like a wolf trap—but that could surprise you with the smile it hid. No matter what the weather was he wore a flannel shirt, big silk bandana and California pants foxed with buckskin, for he claimed, "If they'll keep the cold out they ought to damn sure keep the heat out, too."

Sometimes he wore a suit vest over his shirt, though I'd bet my bottom dollar he never owned a suit in his life, and there was always a toothbrush in the top vest pocket. I asked him once what about the paste to go with it and was told, "Hell, ashes do fine, kid. Or sand."

His spurs were drop shanked and sharp roweled, and I don't think, by God, that he ever took them off his boots. He wore drop seat long handled drawers and his shirt to bed, always. Damn if I don't think he wore his hat—a tall-crowned, straight-brimmed Stetson, pulled down square just above that one eye—to bed, too. But seeing as how I was never able to catch the old devil asleep I can't swear to it.

He was good with rawhide and horsehair—had learned braiding while serving time in the pen for killing a man, and he was damn casual about it. Right today, if I happen to run into an old boy that's handy with horsehair I can't help but wonder where he learned it, but because those old fellows had a hand in raising me right I damn sure don't get inquisitive.

Frank had a way of saying a lot real quick. Two brothers lived over on Hailstone trying to farm, and they lived rough and dirty. Frank and I took a ride by their camp one time. For the last half mile it'd been like working upwind on a wolf den, and the guests were getting curious. The two came to the cabin door when we whoaed up, they were sure a pair to draw to; their clothes stiff and shiny with dirt and grease, and the wrinkles in their faces and necks marked blackly with grime. We didn't stay long, and as we jogged off Frank observed, "'Magine a man'd have to sand them two to get 'nough traction to get 'em outa there."

He was about right. Lord they were greasy, and I wouldn't have tackled their cabin for love nor money. I had stayed at an outfit of the same ilk a few years earlier when I was bringing home a strayed horse for Dad. It was a sheep camp, and during my stay I picked up some "seam squirrels" and brought them home. I was not popular for a while, and I'll never forget Gramp's remark, "Hell, Spike, it's no disgrace to *get* lousy. But it damn sure is to *stay* lousy."

Well, to get back to Frank. He rode an old A fork double rig, and carried about forty feet of raggy catch rope. He could use every inch of it, too, afoot or ahorseback! We used to cut right at fifty head of two-year-old studs a year, and I remember one time when Frank was sitting on the corral fence watching as we doctored a bunch. Things went fine until we hit one that none of us could forefoot and upset right, try as we would, so finally the old devil dropped off the fence into the round corral and stalked out to the middle shaking out his old rope. "Git out the way an' spook him by," he ordered, rolled out a loop like a wagon tire and stood the stud on his nose.

Of course I had to excuse my misses by remarking that I'd gotten out of practice away at school and had about half forgotten how to forefoot. "Gunsel," says he, "you got to know *how* before you *can* forget." I never forgot that, nor how it shut me up!

He was set in his ideas—figured there hadn't been a cowboy born in the last forty years—and there were a few people he had a pet hate for, and he sure made no bones about it. The last time I saw him was years later when I dropped into the rest home where they'd finally sent him. I brought him a caddy of Bull Durham with a pint hidden under the tobacco, and we talked and chuckled for a long time while the nurses scowled disapprovingly over the language we used. I noticed that he wasn't so damn rabid about those enemies any longer, and figuring maybe he'd mellowed some I remarked on the fact. "Nope," he agreed, "I just don't hate them fellers so bad now."

I asked how that'd come about, and I treasure his answer, "Th' sons of bitches are purt' near all dead!"

Trouble is the more I write about the old rascal the more comes to mind, but I've got one more story I have to tell about him, for sure! One time when Frank was wrangling we had a retired Army man as a guest. Starchy old ramrod, so straight he made you hurt, handled horses real well—like he'd been in the cavalry—and he and the old one-eyed scalawag got as chummy as a couple of high school girls. Frank must have been in either the Rough Riders or the Philippine insurrection, or both; at least he had some hair-raising stories about them. Anyhow, when the soldier left he willed a few things to Frank.

Among them was what I found out later was a leotard. Just why he'd used it—maybe as drawers, pajamas, part of his riding setup—or whatever he did with it I don't know, because most of us boys walked pretty wide around the jut-jawed son of a gun and left him to Dad. But after the soldier'd left and Frank came bragging around, proud as an old gelding with the first spring colt, telling what a fine rigging they'd be, how they'd save socks and not bag at the seat so bad and so on, we hoorawed him as much as we dared. Which sure wasn't a lot.

Well, along that winter I happened to run into him in Big Timber. He'd been holding down a steer camp for an outfit over in the Big Coulee, batching. After we'd talked some I just couldn't help inquiring about the classy drawers he'd gotten from the cavalry.

Just like he'd figured, he said. Socks were plumb elimi-nated and the outfit was sure snug and warm, but there was one drawback. "I'm a hell of a bean eater in cold weather. Trouble is, now I keep blowin' m' boots off!"

Jim Bowman was a great friend of Dad's. He was a Texan who had come up the trail with a herd during the '80s, liked the country and stayed. Soft spoken, polite and dangerous, with a couple of killings to his credit from 'way back, he was a fine old gentleman and a top cowman. I think he also was the greatest all-around roper I've ever seen when it came to range work or in a pen. Ahorseback he tied hard and fast no matter what he roped, and in a round pole corral with broncs he threw the finest forefooting loop I have ever seen. When you were with him you damn sure better be ready to get on that head when he rolled one out, for I never saw him miss a set of front feet. He was cow foreman for the Charley Bair outfit on the upper Musselshell when I was a kid, and since Dad was running cattle for Charley for a while after the winter of '17-'18, I rode with Jim a lot. As a matter of fact it was he who taught me to ride in the middle of a saddle horse; up off the cantle and standing in the stirrups, and I still ride that way. Lord, but he could cover country! Ramrod straight, limber and easy from spurs to Stetson, and at a jog. Always at a jog unless the work at hand happened to call for a change of pace. He was what was meant when they coined the word "cowboy"!

He didn't say a whole lot, but when he did, it was sure worth listening to, for he had a dry humor and a way of getting a lot into a word or two.

We were branding down on Otter Creek that spring, and he heeled seventy-eight calves by both feet, hand running, before he had a miss! I think it was at the same branding that Riley Doore, who had only been married a month or so and was holding down the camp with his new bride, quit the pens and went over to the house about an hour before it was time to eat. Jim noticed he was missing and asked where he had gone. Dad answered that Riley had gone over to get some lunch together.

"Cain't his wife cook?" the tall old Texan asked quizzically.

"Guess not," Dad answered.

"Well, t'was me," said Jim squinting at the cabin from under his hat brim, "I'd get her a outfit an' let her try."

Another damn good man and sure enough old-timey westerner was Jim McGregor. He savvied what a cow said to her calf or a mare to her colt, and he could skin from two horses on up to eight or more 'way easier than he could handle a tractor. Cowman, cowboy, horse hand, skinner and old-time rancher, he was a great guy and a fine friend, and had the most magnificent way of telling the damndest collection of stories of any man I have ever met! I just loved to listen to him, and he didn't lie; for a liar is careless with the truth, and Jim wasn't. He just served it with a lot of dressing!

When he got too stove up to ranch I tried to get him to wrangle for me, but he claimed he was crippled, couldn't earn his keep, couldn't even ride anymore and so on. Finally I realized that, unbelievably, he was shy when it came to strangers, so I quit bothering him. I sort of suspect, though, that I wanted him for my own enjoyment more than for anybody else's. He was a lovely guy!

He used to tell about two old characters—to listen to him you'd have thought he didn't know any plumb normal people, they were all "characters"—who were deer hunting in the foothills of the Belts. It was typical Montana fall weather, and the wind would've blown the hair off a dog. These two old fellows bucked it all day without even so much as getting a chance to cock their rifles, for the game, naturally, was all bedded down out of the wind. By late afternoon the two were getting footsore and pretty disgusted, so they holed up under a bull pine at the head of a long open draw to have a smoke and size up the country. The wind was whooping up the draw, they had trouble getting their cigarettes made and lit, and about the time they did one poked the other in the ribs and said, "Goddam, look yonder!"

A coyote was trotting towards them up the coulee. It was a long shot, and he was headed their way, but these two just couldn't wait; here finally was a chance to limber up at something, anything, and Mr. Coyote was it. So they bellied down, got comfortable and went to work right now.

Well, they were packing 30-30's or some such caliber rifles, and what with the distance and the fact that the wind fixed it so he couldn't possibly scent or hear them, the coyote didn't know there was any excitement going on at all. He just kept poking along towards them, stopping every now and then to investigate something of interest, happy as a hog in a potato patch. By this time, too, these two hunters had gotten blood in their eye and were wasting shells as fast as they could lever them into their chambers. This kept up until one of them went to reload, hunted through himself, came up empty and said to his partner, "I'm outa shells. Gimme a handful."

The other drew a careful bead, touched her off, and the coyote kept coming, close enough now so's they could see his pelt ripple in the wind. "That'n 's my last, too," he said.

Just then the wind, as it very often does, dropped and sucked backwards for a second or two. Long enough, anyhow, for the coyote to get a big whiff of man right spang in front of him, and he high tailed it out of there. The two old fellows watched him go and looked at one another sort of sheepishly. Then one of them straightened up, squared his shoulders and stated, "Well, by God, we stood the sonofabitch off, anyhow!"

Jim used to tell about an old-timer he worked for as a kid. Said the man was pretty old-fashioned and not long on modern conveniences. "Except for alarm clocks an' lanterns; one to get me up an' the other to keep me up. But he was sure a nice, considerate feller to work for. Why, hell, he'd give me eighteen-twenty hours to do a day's work! I'd finally get to the bunkhouse to get to bed, pull off my boots an' drop 'em, an' by the time they quit rockin' 'twas time to get up!"

I was pulling a couple of horses up to the Milk River north of Browning. It was spring and it was rainy. I didn't complain—my granddad always said, "When, and if, it rains in Montana just be damn happy about it"—but I had a lot of tire trouble to boot, so by mid-afternoon I had only gotten as far as Hobson, on the upper Judith. Jim had quit ranching and lived in town, so I headed for the bar to see if I could locate him.

Sure enough, he was there with maybe four or five old fellows of the same vintage and leather, and I spent one of the most enjoyable afternoons I've ever had. Big old room with a pipe running the whole length of it from a box stove in the back. There were bullet holes in the walls and ceiling, and an old dark bar and back bar. I kept quiet and listened while the old guys told terrible lies to and about one another, squabbled, roared with laughter and remembered and remembered. Don't believe anybody had a drink, barring the round I bought when I was introduced. They weren't there to drink. They were there for companionship; to talk, to remember and to relive things of a way of life that was long gone. I sort of imagine it would be pretty hard to match that bar and that bunch of men today, and I'm sure glad I happened to be a part of it!

It got into the evening, and Jim wouldn't hear of me not spending the night with him. When I said I was pulling a couple of horses he said, "Hell, there's an old Missourian got a barn an' some corrals here, an' he'll be glad to put up your ponies."

We went on over, and the Missourian was a quiet, friendly old fellow, tickled to keep my stock. When I unloaded he looked them over, commented courteously on their good points, and I did the same with his horses which were in the corral. Then, after everything had been taken care of and fed, I asked if he would come over to the bar with us and have a short one. He declined with thanks, and I turned to Jim and told him, "You old booger, I've always figured you leaned toward lying, but never could catch you for sure. I've got you now, though."

"What you mean?" he protested.

"Well, you told me this man was a Missourian, and there's no way he can be. In the first place he's wearing shoes, and secondly, he turned down a drink."

Jim just oozed unctuousness. Sounded like a preacher, or a man talking down a well. "He's a Missour'an, pure quill. Sure is, an' far as the drink goes, why he's got hisself a still in the brush back of th' barn, an' what he gets out of it has spoiled him for civilized booze. An', about them shoes, well, I'll tell you.

"It's a long time ago, an' he's just a big ol' barefoot kid mebbe fifteen or so—anyhow he's weaned—an' he's playin' around in the hollow where he's been dropped, back in the Ozarks, when he runs across somethin' he ain't never seen before. Like any kid he gets curious, not knowin' it's a wagon track, an' follers it to see what sort o' critter'd made it. I guess maybe he'd still be follerin' it if the wagon hadn't broke down just up the river here. That's how he come to come to Montana an' the Judith country. 'Course he wanted to go back home, but he was too footsore to make the trip, an' time he'd worked long enough to be able to buy some shoes, an' learned to wear 'em, why, hell, it was a cinch that most of his folks back home had gone to their reward. So he just stayed here." He turned to our companion, "Ain't that so?"

There was the barest suggestion of a twinkle in the old fellow's eyes as he replied softly, "Pretty close, I guess, Jim."

Wonderful people, wonderful people!

# Dad

MY DAD WAS quite a guy! He had quite a temper, too, and every now and then got on the fight about the damndest things. I still grin about some of those times.

I used to have a great big, part Brown Swiss cow. Like every milk cow I have ever known well—and a man naturally does get to know a milk cow right well, you might say intimately—she was cross-grained, independent and overbearing. You could count on her doing exactly what you didn't want, every time, but she was easy milking, didn't kick often and had a sort of interesting personality in spite of everything, so she and I got along pretty well. Dad hated her. I don't know exactly why, but as long as I had her I don't think I ever heard him mention her without adding some genial term like "overgrown sow" or "yellow slut." He sure wasn't fond of her!

Well, anyhow, we had gathered the brushy draws across the head of Dry Creek and came down to my place with a pretty juicy string of cattle. They were mostly bunch-quitters, touchy as teased snakes, and getting them into the pens without spilling them was going to take some doing. So I was tickled to see Swiss Miss amble over from behind the barn to see what the excitement was. I picked her up, stuffed her through the gate all the way into the far corral, and eased back along the cattle, working them towards her.

Suddenly I heard Dad rasp from behind me, "Why in

hell don't you get rid of the damn cow? Just look at the buckskin bitch; she always does something like that."

I looked, and sure enough, square in the middle of the main corral gate stood Swiss Miss, daring any critter to come through and hooking the liver and lights out of any that tried. I couldn't help smiling as I moved her out of the way, but I didn't let Dad see it!

Dad got badly stove up the last few years. Couldn't ride, but that didn't put too much of a damper on him, really, for he used his Jeep for cowboying. I'll tell a man, too, that a trip with him working stock in the hills, especially horses, made for a first class crop of nightmares for the next month, at least. It used to tickle me to see whoever was with him hurry to get the hell out of the Jeep whenever I'd happen to ride up to talk a few minutes. When they'd get ready to leave, too, his passenger invariably acted like a man who was about to crawl into a grizzly den.

One nice spring day we gathered the upper range, about eight or nine sections, to start shaping up the dude string. Buckshot and I handled the rough country, while Dad took the flats.

When we'd made our circle, we passed the Wolf Butte branding corral as we headed for the ranch with the ponies we'd picked up. Although we could see horses strung down the country for two or three miles below us, here was Dad and his Jeep at the pen. We gave our bunch a boost and then loped on over.

Inside was a runty paint mare huddled in the corner, Dad's cane in splinters beside her. His dogs lay in the shade panting, and as we whoaed up he swung around to us, his face red and sweat streaked, and his eyes a chilly white. "You wouldn't happen to be packing a rifle?" he asked hopefully.

"Nope," said I. "What for?"

"So I can kill her!" he chopped out. "I've been to the top of every hill and across every draw from here to the Sweet

Grass three times at least, damn her to hell. My dogs are played out, my cane's broken, and I haven't enough gas to get home. Lope on down, get your Jeep, some gas, and your rifle, and hurry back!"

Pleading that our saddle horses needed to catch their wind, I made a try at cooling him down some, but he just glared balefully at the paint and muttered something either to himself or to her, I couldn't tell which. Finally I said brightly, "I don't know that mare. Looks about half Shetland or Welsh to me. Where'd you get her?"

"Oh," he answered bitterly, "Jack McCormick gave her to me. As a kid's pony. As a friendly gesture."

There was silence for a minute as he thought it over. Then he erupted, "A hell of a way to make friends!"

Behind me Buckshot choked loudly, but I didn't dare look at her. Pop scowled over his shoulder, and then the tight lips quivered into a sheepish grin. "Aw, go on down and bring me back some gas, and call that horse buyer in Big Timber, Hubert whoever he is, and tell him to get up here right, by God, now. She's been loose for the last time, damn her, on *my* outfit."

One day when I happened to come down from our place to the home ranch to see Dad about something, he said, "I've got some cattle to move. Climb in and we'll talk on the way."

I did, and away we went. His old dog, Specks, was in the back of the Jeep wagon with us, and his young one, Nig, loped alongside. When we got to the cattle they were on the yon side of quite a deep draw, so Nig was sent to gather and cross them. Well, on this day the pup wasn't working too well, or at least Dad didn't think so, and the instructions, "Way over," "way back," "Over here," or "Stop, damn you" got louder and more heartfelt.

I'm not a dog man, so I was keeping quiet, wincing occasionally as an order bounced off the windshield instead of out the open window. The old dog with us, of course, was taking a real interest in the proceedings. Ears cocked and mouth open, she started to pant as the excitement grew. Suddenly Dad turned to her, and to my near ear, and exploded, "Cut that out, Specks!"

When my head quit ringing I ventured, "But, Pop, she's not doing anything. Just panting."

His answer broke me up. "I know, I know. But it's from excitement, damn her."

Dad and that Jeep of his! He used to do the damndest things with it, especially after he lost one eye and drove sort of by the lay of the land rather than by what he could actually see. I remember one day when a rather noisy man, a guest at the ranch, went with him when he was helping gather cattle for a branding. We were eating lunch while we waited for the irons to heat when the two of them drove in. As the guest got stiffly out of the vehicle, my mother asked him cheerily, "Have you been taking a lot of pictures this morning?"

"No, Mrs. Van Cleve," he answered in a subdued tone, "But I have been taking a lot of chances."

Pop used his outfit to straighten out recalcitrant cattle, especially bulls, by "bumping" them, as he put it. He finally had a sort of cowcatcher proposition put on it because of the attrition to his fenders. He was along when a young, cocky bull, a typical Angus bunch-quitter, was giving us a lot of trouble. He'd tried to escape us again and again, and was beginning to get snuffy about being turned back when Dad came sailing up.

"Get out of the way," he warned me out his window. "I'll educate the black sonofabitch," and never slackening speed, he "bumped" the bull in the britches. The jar shortened the animal by half, there was a snort you could have heard for a half mile, and he uncoiled in a wild jump for the rest of the cattle. Dad gunned his motor again and Bully shouldered through the bunch to the point. He stayed there, wringing his tail and peeking apprehensively over his shoulder about every step.

"Doesn't take much to teach 'em," Dad observed as he got out to see if he'd broken anything—on the Jeep, not the bull.

If I'd done that it's a cinch I'd have had a cripple. Not Pop, he got away with things. Sometimes, though, it would get too salty for his dogs, and we'd know things were wild when we saw them bail out. He had lost so many mufflers, too, that he finally quit messing with them, but he kept on running his rig wide open, for he'd gotten a little deaf and the noise didn't faze him. It tickled me to watch his stock, especially the horses. He'd come roaring over the hill a mile away, and they'd be in a full run before they got their heads lifted from grazing. Even the horses we were riding kept a wary eye on him. So did I, when he really got wound up.

Somebody talked him into trying a Scout instead of a Jeep, but he didn't like it. He wasn't bothered with it long, though, for he got mixed up setting the emergency brake while he was shutting the gate at the branding pens up on Otter Creek, and the new outfit went down over the hill. It was steep, about a quarter mile down to the bottom, and the last sixty feet or so was straight off a cliff. About halfway down, the dogs popped out through the window like a couple of squeezed watermelon seeds, and the rigging sailed over the edge. Dad was walking home when I came down from salting, so I picked him up, and we drove up to have a look at the wreck.

The Scout had cleared all the trees, must have lit on its nose and resembled a closed accordion. Pop sized it up, poked it with his cane a time or two, looked me right in the eye and remarked conversationally, "Tinny damn things, aren't they?"

# Horse Power

THINGS WERE SIMPLER when I was a kid. Slower perhaps, and easier to live with. We rode or drove horses most of the time, and even after there were quite a few cars in the country, when we'd meet a neighbor on the road we'd whoa up and visit. It might be below zero, but we still took the time to say howdy, maybe have a smoke together, and swap news. Today you meet a friend on the road, and if you even have time for recognition it will be no more than a quick wave, and you're both long gone. Damn if I didn't like the old way better, because I can't see what we are gaining by not sparing some time to talk a little.

Reminds me of the time in the early spring of '20 when Dad was coming out of Big Timber with a load of cottonseed cake and a four horse team. He was running cattle for Charley Bair at the time, for the winter of '18 and '19 had just about cleaned us out. Our country is so damn windy—which makes it a good cow country most of the time—that nobody ever dares to make much of a trip with any kind of a sleigh for fear of losing sledding snow before getting home. This was particularly true towards the Yellowstone, for from January to April the wind usually blows down there twenty-six or seven hours out of every twenty-four, so Dad was using a wagon, with a couple of bells hung on the reach. They kept him company, he claimed.

Mother had gone to town in the car, and they had spent

the night at the Grand Hotel—Gramp said there never was a little western town that didn't have a Grand Hotel and a Palace Saloon—and they had eaten at the Chinaman's. Not exactly a spree, but a pretty gaudy deal for those times, at that. Dad had his load on and pulled out before daylight, and when things opened up, Mother took care of some business around town. In the course of this she found that the lawyer wanted Dad's signature on something or other, so she went after him.

She caught him at Ten Mile and explained the situation. Dad tied his lines carefully on the brake pole, spoke to his horses, and when they were under way he got down and he and Mother went back to town. He signed the papers, they were notarized, and they headed back out.

They found the rigging traveling along fine up the Wheeler Creek Road. The horses had crossed the Wheeler Flats, swung off the main road onto the one up the creek, and had covered a good six or seven miles by the time they caught up in the car. Mother went on by after Dad had pulled to one side, and he came in with his load towards evening.

I asked how he dared to leave his outfit. "Why, they are all good, well broke horses," he said. "They knew where they were headed, and I knew I'd catch them before they had to handle any steep pitches either up or down. There wasn't anything to worry about."

I talked to a man who was on the way to Big Timber with his own outfit that day and had met Dad's. He, too, was unconcerned. "Hell, I knew whose rigging it was; couldn't mistake them horses. So I pulled off, whoaed up, got down an' stopped 'em. Then I gets up, eases them around my layout, wraps the lines like they was, starts 'em off up the road, an' goes back to my wagon. Wasn't no trouble."

Just think of it! Today a man would be pretty leary of leaving his car parked on the shoulder of a main road, or in the borrow pit, for any length of time, to say nothing of sending it on about his business.

I admit that horses couldn't do what machines can, but dammit, they kept a man company; they were alive, something to talk to, and their ears would work as they listened; a man wasn't plumb alone. An engine is about as lonesome a thing to use as I've ever run onto. Also, if a man gets into a jackpot with horses they just might stop if he says, "Whoa." A machine sure won't—just keeps on in massive insensibility.

I used to break a work colt, especially if he had the idea he was some punkins, by using a three horse evener and putting the colt on the pole between two stout, gentle horses. Tied back to their pole strap rings he couldn't do much except just what they allowed, and it didn't take long to iron the wrinkles out of the average youngster.

Modoc and Thunder were two big geldings I had raised and worked for quite a while. A fine, matched team, and a popping good pair to use on a juicy colt, so the three of us broke a lot of broncs over the years. The two had been out since spring and I caught them up a week or so before we figured we'd start feeding the cattle along in early February, thinking I'd have time to give them a little grain and harden them before the work really started. So my wife and I hooked up and drove out to get a load of good horse hay for the barn. Horse hay has to be pretty special— timothy, brome, or wild hay, and put up clean and dry so there's no dust in it, for horses get heavey easily. I was pitching and Barbara was tromping the load when it dawned on me that the damn team kept moving the rack ahead a foot or so every now and then, and I finally told her, "Honey, why don't you get the lines and hold those two old fools, or pretty quick I might just as well be packing this hay home by hand."

She took the lines off the standard and set back on them, but the fidgeting kept on. Even got worse, so I asked irritably, "What in the hell are you doing there, anyway?"

"My very best," she answered. "Thunder keeps trying to rear or lunge and if it weren't for Docko helping me hold him I'm afraid he'd get away. If you think you can do any better, just get up here and try." So I climbed up beside her and took the lines.

I knew right away what was wrong, though it was hard to believe. Thunder was dripping with sweat, shaking like an aspen leaf, and cold jawing against his bit. Modoc was sitting back like a borrowed dog, plainly very uneasy, and horribly embarrassed. "I'll be goddammed, Honey, but Thunder is plumb weedy," I told my wife.

"Oh, no!" she breathed.

"He sure is, poor guy. And poor Modoc, too. He can't figure what's wrong with his partner, and he's scared and ashamed."

Loco is miserable damn stuff! Usually it is the yearlings and twos that it hits, but Thunder was smooth mouthed; at least twelve years old. We have some loco, all right, but nothing like it is below us across the Wheeler and Glasston Flats, but we'd had a wet fall, and under those conditions we can sometimes get a second growth, what we call "green loco," which is fresh and succulent when everything else is dry and cured. It is terribly virulent. Thunder must have gotten into it, though Modoc, who was with him on the same range, either hadn't eaten it, or if he had, wasn't affected. Loco is funny stuff anyhow; unpredictable. Ranchers used to think that there were worms in the plant which crawled up an animal's nostrils into his brain, so turpentine was mixed in stock salt to stand off the worms. We know now that the theory was balderdash, but the queer thing is it seemed to work. They explain loco now as stemming from the chemical makeup of the plant, and I suppose it's a variation in the chemical mixture, due to moisture, temperature, and so on that makes its effects so varied. Whatever, I still feed turpentine and salt to my colts—I'm just a sagebrush vet, but if something seems to work, by God, I use it.

Well, we drove back to the ranch, the trip getting wilder by the minute, unhooked, unharnessed, and fed the two a good bait of grain. When I went to the house for my rifle, Barbara asked tearfully, "You aren't going to shoot lovely old Thunder are you, Spike?"

"Yes, Honey. Damned if I'm going to leave a good friend of ours to wander around stark mad. He was a fine gentleman, and deserves the courtesy and dignity of a decent death."

"I know, I know," was her choked reply.

So I led him over to a nice, warm, pretty spot at the edge of the brush on Dry Creek. I just about lost my nerve. Then I looked at those big eyes, always so sparkling with intelligence, friendliness, and eagerness. They were blank, dull, lifeless. So I shot him and went home.

Naturally with Modoc all by himself now, I broke the colts earlier than I had before. Nevertheless, it took a good horse to act as an anchor for a raspy colt, but Modoc filled the bill. He had the size, the savvy, was unflappable, and no matter what went on he trudged along perfectly happily. A colt damn sure went with him; on his feet or down, astraddle the pole or under it. They learned fast when Docko was giving lessons!

He was a smart old rascal. I had a big good colt hooked up with him one day, and through my own carelessness had a runaway. I was on the ground shutting a gate at the time, and all I could do was stand and watch, and cuss my stupidity. All of a sudden I realized they were swinging around to the near side, Docko's side. Sure enough, they came back in a big circle, the colt doing his damndest to run and the old horse dragging his feet and holding him; for the youngster's halter rope was tied back to his mate. They made another circle inside the first, getting slower all the time, and finally stopped about halfway through a third.

The colt was pretty disgusted—no point in running when you couldn't get anywhere—but Doc was calm and work-man-like. He had just done his job.

The old colt never ran again. He evidently had a bellyful of that sort of wasted effort. I was not only tickled that the youngster hadn't gotten spoiled or hurt, but the times were tough and I hadn't the money to replace any torn up equipment.

Sort of like the first antelope I ever poached, back when that kind of thing carried a five hundred dollar fine. Hell, I didn't have five hundred dollars, or anything like it, and if I'd been caught I'd have had to just lay it out in jail at three dollars a day. It was exciting, though, for I put in more time hunting the warden than the antelope!

I broke quite a few good teams, but the finest I ever raised and broke myself were Bullet and Babe. In every-thing but color—Bullet was a frosty grey and Babe as black and shiny as a crow's wing—they were perfectly matched; honest, eager, friendly, fast and proud; hard on hame straps and tugs, for Lord, they could pull! Whatever they were doing they did with all they had and they enjoyed doing everything. It was fun! I've never had the pleasure of using a team more chock full to brimming over with joie de vivre.

I remember coming up from feeding the cattle one sparkling winter morning. Barbara and I were using a bob-sled with the rack for there was about a foot of new snow on the ground. We had fed and were on the way home empty, the two mares hitting a nice jog, their bells singing in the cold air. About halfway up the flat we ran into a half dozen saddle horses that had gotten the gate out of the upper pasture open and were headed happily down country, tails in the air.

Ordinarily I'd have gone on up and saddled a horse to put the escapees back, but it was such a lovely day that I felt like a little excitement. So I grinned at Barbara and said, "Let's give Bullet 'n' Babe the pleasure of a little run," and pointed the mares at the horses as they started by us.

At first the team was a little hesitant and uncertain, then incredulous joy took over, and after we had bent their compatriots once, they figured things out and built to the job like cutting horses. The upshot was that the loose stock was put back where it belonged, with my wife and me whooping with excitement and holding on for dear life as the bob swooped and swung amid clouds of snow. We never came up the flat with those two again that their ears weren't up in anticipation of another bit of extracurricular enjoyment. Élan, that's the word for what they had.

That Bullet! She raised me some fine colts, and invariably each year as soon as the newcomer had sucked she'd bring it down by the house for us to see. Then, when she'd shown the colt off, been congratulated, and we'd admired and petted her child, she'd take it, disappear into the hills to hide out like a coyote. It would be at least a week until the pair, and Babe, showed up again.

Babe, unfortunately, had cysts, and though she wanted a baby in the worst way could never have a colt of her own, so she did it by proxy. She'd always hold Bullet's hand up until the moment of truth, worrying terribly. Then she'd bustle around as midwife and overseer, always helped clean and dry the baby, and God help any other horse, especially a gelding, that came too close. She wasn't about to have *her* child messed with! The two of them shared the colt, and I really believe that out of sheer maternal happiness Babe may have come to milk, for Bullet's colt sucked them both.

Then there was the time, in November, when I found an orphan colt back in the hills and took him home with me. I'd just weaned Bullet's youngster and she was fairly busting with milk, so I thought she'd be just the ticket to give the poor little fellow a stomach full of the real stuff and at the right temperature, to boot.

So I got the mare working on a feed of grain, sneaked the orphan up alongside and got a tit in his mouth. One taste and he resembled a vacuum cleaner. Since Barbara was at her head, I stepped between the little fellow and her hind leg in case she didn't like what was going on. As the pressure eased on her bag Bullet sighed with relief and through sheer habit reached around absentmindedly to sniff of the youngster.

She had as lovely, intelligent, and expressive eyes as I have ever seen—golden brown, with growths like dark moss deep in them, and set off with fine, silky, grey eyelashes along the lower lid and sweeping, long, dark ones on the upper—and the unbelieving outrage they showed when she realized that, by God, this isn't my colt, was magnificent!

There was a snort and a spray of grain, but Barbara stopped her snakelike open-mouthed grab at the colt and I threw my shoulder into her flank to keep her from kicking, and told her to leave the poor little guy alone. Finally she cooled down; besides it felt good to get rid of all that milk. But every now and then she'd remember and scowl over her shoulder. As a matter of fact, it was Babe that decided the colt was all right, and then Bullet did, too.

I'm strong on using a trip rope when I'm breaking work colts, and I make a point of using it at least a month longer than I really think is necessary, with the result that the teams I broke had a sure enough whoa on them. Bullet's and Babe's was a dandy, and no matter what gait they were in or what they were doing, they set up and slid like a couple of calf horses when I spoke to them. When they were standing, their ears were constantly flickering to catch any command, but when the lines were picked up they never moved—just got a little readier. I had to speak to them to get them to move, but when I did, they sure did, and the eveners would groan.

They weren't a feeding team by any stretch of the imagination—unless they had a driver—for if a man hung the lines on the standard and started to feed they'd hit a run inside a hundred yards. They were up on the bits so much it bothered me until one day when Dad drove for me on the feed ground. I had about half the load off when he remarked, "I damn sure hate to pull a load of hay on the lines, but that seems to be what these two girls want."

"Did I do something wrong when I was breaking them, Pop? Is that why they are so hot?" I asked.

"Not by a damn sight," and he grinned. "Once in a while a man is lucky enough to find, and match, two going boogers like these. Hell, when I was freighting I'd have given anything you asked for them as leaders. The weight of the lead lines would have balanced them, and they'd have made the wheelers and swing teams get out and travel. You just have yourself one of the goingest pairs I've ever thrown a line over. Count your blessings, boy."

Driving them had its drawbacks in real cold weather, for it was hard on a man's hands to hold those two traveling things. If there were a couple of us on the rig we could take turns with the lines and thaw out between turns. Alone it was rough, and I've even wrapped the lines around my wrists to save my hands even though I might be wearing mitts. Cold hands were a small price to pay, though, for they were a pair of very great, eager, lovely ladies, Bullet and Babe. We had a lot of fun doing things together.

# At the Head of the Creek

BARBARA AND I quit college—we were too far apart and I was afraid somebody'd undercut me—and got married in the fall of 1934. It cost me a Harvard degree, but hell, lots of men have those, but I'm the only one who has Barbara. I got 'way the long end of the trade! We spent the next three years in the mountains at the dude ranch by ourselves from September to May. We wintered on thirteen dollars in '34-'35. Was all we had, so we made it do. It bought flour, coffee, sugar, baking powder—and cartridges. It also got us a gallon of moonshine—for medicinal purposes—from a friend. We had anyhow half the jug left in the spring, too. We also had a couple of sacks of last summer's spuds in the root cellar.

We lived well and happy. We might have lived better if I'd known as much about beans as I do now, thanks to the time we spent in Arizona later, but it never occurred to us that we were poor; if somebody had told me so I'd have whipped him, or damn sure tried to. We just knew we had to be careful of what little we had, so we did fine, because in my book "poverty" depends an awful lot on a man's state of mind, not just what he's got. Rifle shells were precious, and it didn't take me long to learn the cardinal rule of a good poacher—don't shoot until you know you can kill what you want to kill, clean. A rifle shot makes an awful lot of noise, too, when it's illegal. We lived on game those first three winters, and Barbara learned to cook meat by cooking venison, which is tricky. The result is that she's the finest meat cook, any meat, I know. She did such a hell of a job with it that we *still* like deer meat; matter of fact I've never seen the time of year when it wasn't good. I got a big old bear the first year, too, and Barbara still claims bear grease is the finest shortening she's ever used. The meat was fine and a welcomed change. It tastes very much like pork, but is dark. Took her some time at first to get over a remark that an old boy who was working for the Forest made when he saw the skinned animal hung up, "Damn if it don't look jest like a man hangin' there, though them legs an' arms is a shade short." Damned if it didn't, too!

I remember an incident along in March when we were out of meat. I lay out on a windy ridge, until I could pick out a dry doe and get a good shot at her with my last rifle shell. I hit her, but the damn wind fouled things—either that or I was so bone deep cold I was shaky—and I didn't hit her where I wanted. I knew that if I followed her right away and warmed her up, she'd quit the country. So I went home, saddled up and rode about six miles to a neighbor who had a phone; ours didn't work in the winter. I called Mother and asked if she'd drive down to Melville and get me a box of 25-35s, and that I'd ride on down to the home ranch and pick them up. She agreed, so I jogged on down another six to eight miles to the lower ranch, picked up my shells, rode back to where the deer was bedded down, slipped up and killed her. When I dressed her I left the heart, liver and other goodies attached, tied her behind the saddle and rode home to the canyon ranch, and we were in business a while longer. To this day I hate to waste shells and I *won't* waste meat!

That first winter about all I got done was getting out wood for our box stove and the cook stove, which were all the heat we had in our two-room cabin, and packing water up from the creek. Big Timber Canyon is narrow, and the buildings are well up the hill from the creek.

I'd skid timber out with Jack and Kelly and cut it up with the only saw on the place, a good Disston two-man crosscut. I figured out how I could hang a weight on the yon end of the saw in place of another man and got by, though it was tough sawing. The first piece of equipment I bought after we were married, and I charged it, was a seven-pound Kelly felling axe, for I had expected to get out some fence posts. However, my two household chores precluded that, but I put the axe to good use anyhow.

The blocks I sawed I split with a maul and wedge. That fit the box stove, but for the cook stove I had to split the blocks again into lighter wood. Then, finally, I'd pack it down to the woodshed I built on the front of the cabin. If I worked pretty steadily at the wood pile I managed to stay a little in the lead.

Of course, since the ranch was a summer outfit and we normally didn't have anyone wintering there, the pipes were either on or near the surface of the ground and had to be drained so they wouldn't freeze. It was quite a climb up from Big Timber Creek with the two buckets I made by cutting the tops out of a couple of those old-timey five gallon gas cans and putting wire bails on them. Ten gallons of water gets to be a load on a snowy sidehill. It was that winter that I told Barbara that woman was man's natural enemy when it came to his ability to split wood and pack water. I found I hadn't seen anything, though, when our daughter Barby arrived the next year!

That second year we were married, '35-'36, was a rank winter. The temperature never got above twenty below zero for almost two months, and one really brisk night it hit sixty-eight below! I saw moon dogs that night and heard trees exploding, even over the creaking and popping of the logs in the cabin as they twisted and shrank from the cold.

That fall I'd had time to plow a furrow from the spring box down to the cabin for the water pipe. I got it in and covered, and for a while we did fine by letting the water run in the sink all night. The brutal weather put a sudden end to that, though, and now I not only had to carry water for us, but for a baby, too, and I soon found that a baby uses more water in a day than a grown man, ten to one. It worked me to a frazzle, for there weren't any disposable diapers in those days. We couldn't have afforded them even if there had been, anyhow. All of us damn sure didn't bathe every night either, for it was a complicated proposition.

First I'd fill a wash boiler on the cook stove. When it was hot enough the two of us would pour it into a wash tub on the floor in front of the heating stove. Then Barbara'd bathe Barby. After that it was her turn at the tub, and then mine. When we were all done she saved the bath water and used it for washing the floor. She's never forgotten either, and right today can go farther on a bucket of water than the average woman can on a barrel full!

A couple of more baby related problems arose, too. One that bothered Barbara some was that every time we lit the candle to give Barby her two o'clock in the morning feeding some kind of a cat would never fail to squall outside. Either a lion or a lynx, for though the tracks were plain I didn't know the difference. I could never get a shot at whatever it was, and Barbara finally got used to it.

It was the oranges that were the real problem. We'd gotten them so Barby would have some fresh fruit or juice, as the baby book said she must. It was a cinch to keep them cool enough so they'd keep—we put the box just inside the cabin door—but when it got so ungodly cold, keeping them from freezing was tough. There was no coal to bank the cook stove, so I tried doing it with green wood and putting the fruit up in the warming oven. It didn't work, for the stove got cold enough before morning that they frost bit. Finally, in desperation, Barbara and I took the oranges to bed with us, and, by God, they didn't freeze, though I must admit they were sort of lumpy bed partners.

The cold sure was a problem, but we kept the baby warm with a hot water bottle and lots of blankets, though many a morning we found a thick layer of frost from our breathing on the spread or quilt by our heads. The damn spuds we had in the root cellar frost bit, too and though I picked them over carefully, we ended up eating frosted potatoes. For anyone who hasn't done the same I can state unequivocably that the slight sweet taste that frosting gives them gets to be horrible! Like mountain goat meat—a man gets a lump in his throat as soon as he smells it cooking; a lump that grows and gets more unswallowable by the minute. However, we did manage to sort of disguise things by laboriously cutting the spuds into shoestrings and deep fat frying them in bear grease. With a liberal dosing of ketchup left over from the dude season, we were able to get them down. It was a lot of work for damn poor results, and if we'd had anything else to eat in the way of vegetables, we sure wouldn't have bothered with them.

I learned that girls were different than boys pretty early, but I had no idea how much different until we spent those three winters in the mountains. Barbara was not a ranch-raised girl, and the adjustments she had to make to the life we led were tremendous. We often laugh now about how she used to figure on a whole day to bake or churn or wash clothes back then. Now she does them all at once, it seems, and has time to work stock with me, to boot. It was the little, funny things I learned about girls that I've never forgotten—feminine mystique, feminine vapors, or whatever, which I had never run up against before. Take the first cake Barbara baked. It either fell, or maybe she took it out of the oven too soon, but we didn't have flour and stuff to waste, so she decided to use it anyhow. So she made a good thick frosting and leveled the top of the cake up with it, figuring, as she admitted years later, that I'd never notice what had happened. I didn't, either! When she cut the cake her skullduggery showed, much to her chagrin, but it made no impression on me—I just thought she'd iced the cake pretty thickly and unevenly. I don't like dry cake. This damn sure wasn't, so I told her, completely truthfully, "Damn but this is fine cake, Honey! Just the way I like it, good and chewy. It'll stick to a man's ribs."

There was no answer, and I suddenly noticed she'd left the room. I had another piece of cake and said something again, and thought I heard a sob. So I hurried into the bedroom and found Barbara lying there weeping.

"What's the trouble, darling? Don't you feel well?" I asked anxiously.

Her reply, between sobs, threw me completely. "You didn't like my cake. Said it was horrible, all chewy and sticky, and I worked so hard to make it for you."

What the hell was a guy to do? I'd told her I liked it, and dammit, I had. I'd been absolutely truthful in complimenting the cake. It sure took some explaining and comforting.

Then there was the time Barbara told me she thought we were eating too much venison and bear meat, because she seemed to get queasy in the stomach when she cooked it. It worried me, so I rode down to a neighboring ranch, borrowed their phone, called up Dad and asked if there was any chance I could get a butcher hog from him. When I explained why, he chuckled. It was a party line and he wasn't the *only* chuckler—the whole damn country knew Barbara was pregnant before either she or I did!

The second year I somehow found time to get out some fence posts. Maybe I had gotten so efficient at getting wood and water that I was saving time. Anyhow, I cut timber into six foot lengths, split it into post size and sharpened one end of each length with an axe. However, at three cents a post, which was all a man could get for them then, I decided the pay sure as hell didn't match the work, so I tried trapping.

There were no beaver as far up the creeks as we lived, for

they need cottonwood or willows for food, and we lived in evergreen country. Besides, they were illegal, though I don't honestly think that would have saved them from my depredations if they had been handy. Weasel were hardly worth skinning, mink moved out of the mountains in the fall, and I had learned a long time ago that I'd starve to death in a hurry if I tried to make a living trapping coyotes. But I knew there were marten in the mountains, for I had seen them once in a while up around the lakes during the summers.

Marten are a North American cousin of the Russian sable, and like most of the weasel family are pretty easy to trap, which gave me a fighting chance. Getting to where they ranged was a horse of a plumb different color. The snow ran from three feet deep in the timber at the ranch to right at twenty feet up at the lakes—at least I blazed a tree at snow level up there in February and the blaze was anyhow twenty feet above ground when I located it the next summer—but I figured out a way to handle things.

I'd ride my saddle horse just as far as he could buck the snow, then picket him and give him the sack of hay I'd carried on my saddle. From there on I used an old pair of snowshoes that had been around the ranch for years, but it was no cinch. I have always been a great believer in my granddad's contention that, "If God had wanted man to walk He'd have given him four feet, but He gave him two—one to put on each side of a horse." On top of that, the webs were those wide, long-tailed Maine propositions that made a man walk all spraddled out, which isn't the ticket for a steep country. The combination stove me up something fierce at first. I stayed with it, though, and finally got so I could make the round trip in a day. Not easily, but I *could* make it—if I rested up for a couple of days afterwards, that is. So I eventually fell into a pattern of making the rounds of my traps every three or four days. Between trips the wood and water kept me out of mischief.

It was about five miles each way, at least three of which I had to make afoot, and during those three miles I gained some two thousand feet in altitude. So I traveled damn light. My traps I had scattered by horse before the snow got bad, so all I carried was a hand axe and a bottle of scent. The upper country widened out a little, but for a mile and a half the gut of the canyon was narrow, high on each side and steep, so snowslides were a threat. As a matter of fact, after a storm or the wind had built snow cornices on the sides of the cliffs and along the tops of the canyon rims, it was damn dangerous. Any vibration could pop them loose, and I'd sure have been a gone gosling if I'd fired a shot down below them. I didn't carry any kind of a gun—there wasn't anything back in that snow country to shoot at anyway. In places I was even leary of snapping a branch, coughing or using the hand axe. It wasn't as bad when the cornices were solid, so I always got away early and made the trip up past them before they had much chance to thaw and loosen.

The trips weren't cold really, for the climb kept me warm, but they were pretty lonesome. I sort of enjoyed them at that. The high country, which I had never seen before in winter, was absolutely lovely. On a clear day the peaks lifted up and up, regal, splendid, and though not a whisper of sound reached the canyon floor, they often flew plumes of snow as the upper winds lashed their heads. Sometimes I would stop and just look at them; pure white except where they were too steep for the snow to cling. Mostly though, they'd be looming dimly in the frost haze or peering through the curtains of a snow squall. I got caught in heavy snowstorms—times when the quiet would be deafening, and the alpine firs so completely stock still under their white burdens that I got the feeling that they never, ever, moved, and that the flakes drifting straight down and I were the only moving things in the world. But then I'd begin to wonder what the hell I'd see if I looked

back along my track. I never did; something might be
there, and I'd rather not know what it was.

Once in a while, toward the middle of the day and after
I'd reached where the upper country widened a little, I'd
hear a snowslide in the canyon below me. There'd be a
crack like a far off rifle shot, followed by a sullen mutter
that stirred the air, and a distant silvery cloud would
blossom above the timber on the flank of a peak and race
down into the canyon. Only once was one ever near me,
thank God, for I damn sure didn't enjoy it. I was just below
lower Twin Lake when the thing let loose high up on my
side of the canyon and maybe two or three hundred yards
ahead with an explosion like a charge of powder. There was
a blast of air and a roar that shook me so that I had to grab
the small tree beside me, and a choking smother of snow
filled air churned over me. When it had settled and the
noise had stopped, I tip toed—or as close to it as a man can
on webs—gingerly forward and inside fifty yards reached
the edge of the slide.

It was nasty! A swath at least a hundred yards wide had
been cut through the timber and was littered with broken
trees and torn up boulders. The tongue crossed the creek
and had driven a couple of hundred feet up the opposite
slope and ended in a welter of trees—thrown at all angles
like jackstraws—boulders and snow, from which came
unpleasant noises as everything settled. As I looked at it I
wondered just what in the hell I was doing back there
anyway, and pretty and pelts suddenly weren't so all fired
important. I headed for home.

It was earlier than usual when I reached the head of the
bad part of the canyon. In my considered opinion too early,
by God, to tackle it, so I built a little fire and hunkered over
it until I figured things had stiffened up. I was pretty
gun-shy about slides right then, and have been a little ever
since. Even so, though mountains can be damn dangerous,
to me, who grew up at their feet, they can also be friendly

and strangely protective; but only if a man respects them. They demand respect. Get careless and they are unforgiving. I have packed out what was left of a careless climber, and I've seen a man who was finally dug out of a slide. There are two things that damn sure have old Spike's respect—mountains and horses.

I learned a little more about girls from one of those trap line safaris. My saddle horse, Irish, liked to buck, and when he did he'd shed me. I found I could cheat him in the deep snow though, so I used him. After about one or two trips he slacked off, and even though I got into the habit of putting more odds and ends on him than Carter has pills, he never bobbled. Though by spring I thought he was broke, when the snow went off I discovered he sure as hell wasn't, so when we moved out of the mountains I traded him to Cremer for Sailor, an honest old cow horse. Irish ended up in Cremer's rodeo string, and I saw him put a couple of good riders down at the Livingston Roundup. Made me feel a lot better.

I took him this day as usual, and a while after I got into my webs it began to snow. It got heavier and thicker as the day went on. I had trouble locating my traps, and finally it got so nasty it was all I could do to find my way back down the canyon. I made it all right, but it took some time, it was full dark when I rode into the ranch.

A bar of light from the Coleman lamp was trying to make some impression on the curtain of heavy flakes outside the cabin window, and I could see my wife, nose against the glass and hands cupped around her eyes, peering out as we came in. Both my horse and I were so covered with snow that I knew she couldn't see us, so to let her know we were back, I rode up outside the window, waved and grinned. She saw us materialize out of the storm, relief replaced the worried look, and she turned away. I rode on down to the barn, tended Irish, milked our cow and bedded everything for the night.

When I got to the cabin, I swept myself off in the woodshed and stepped inside. Barbara wasn't in evidence. Supper was still on the stove, and the table wasn't set, but I called cheerily, "I'm home, Mommy, and 'tain't fitten out."

Not a sound, so I walked into the bedroom, thinking she was tending to the baby, but she already was in bed.

"What the hell, Honey?" I asked.

The response stunned me, for Barbara rared up, her eyes blazing, and in a voice about evenly divided between rage and tears poured out, "I've been worrying about you all day long in this storm. You didn't come back before dark like you promised you'd always do. I thought I could hear snowslides. I went down to the barn to see if that damn bronc you insist on riding had come in by himself. I rang the bell every few minutes, but the heavy snow muffled it. I didn't know what I'd do anyway if I found your horse. We haven't a phone. You let *me* worry all day and *you* knew you were perfectly all right all the time, damn you. I've had supper ready for hours and I don't care whether you eat or not. Just go away!"

My abject apologies for being perfectly healthy and a manful attempt at sweet talk were miserable failures, and I ended by eating my dried-up supper alone. I washed the dishes and, hoping for Brownie points, made plenty of noise as I did so. Then I sneaked into bed to be thrust firmly to the very edge of my own side of the mattress and told bitterly, "Get away. I hate you."

It wasn't a pleasant night, nor was the next day much better, and it was some little time until I was restored to grace. It taught me once and for always, though, that if a girl worries real badly about someone and everything turns out fine, then she'll get on the fight. Be damned if I can understand why, but it's sure a fact, and a smart man learns to live with it—and keep his mouth shut.

It showed up another time, too, when a couple of us left camp on the head of Sweet Grass to do some fishing in

Milly Lake. It was a booger to get into, even after we had left our horses, and when dark sneaked up on us to end our fishing we decided it was too dangerous to try to go out until daylight so we lay out all night. We started early the next morning, got to our horses, dropped down the fork to the main canyon and started up it for camp. They had been worried about us up there, so Barbara and Dad left camp to look for us at about the same time we left the lake and very thoughtfully took us each a couple of hotcake sandwiches; they had run out of bread. Well, they spotted us as they came around a bluff, and as Barbara heard us talking and laughing she realized that we weren't in any trouble, so she got the sandwiches out of her saddle pocket and threw them into the brush down the hill.

Dad asked her what she was doing. She told him, and he ordered, "You get off that horse and go get those sandwiches. Those boys haven't eaten since yesterday morning, and if it rained on us in our tents last night, it damn sure rained on them, too. Hike now." And she did! I never had that much nerve, though I suppose a father-in-law can get away with things a husband can't.

While I'm on the subject of "feminine vapors"—a magnificent Victorian description, that—I must mention something else I learned about girls years later. If Barbara ever really painted for war about something, I damn sure better not mention that something again after she cooled down, especially if she happened to have the tiniest bit of legitimate reason. Even years later, she gets as waspy about it as she originally was. Maybe even worse, so I sure never mention any of those—to use a mild word—controversial issues from the past. And I do my best to head off any conversation that is taking a dangerous slant. I believe in letting sleeping, by God, dogs lie!

Funny, Barbara claims she never would have made a pioneer woman, and I say that she *was* a pioneer woman. A town-raised girl plunked down back in the hills a couple of

weeks after her marriage, living conditions almost completely primitive, and alone for months on end except for
me; and hell, we didn't really know each other when we
first were married. I was gone most of every day, to boot. I
don't know how she stood those first years in the mountains, and she admits now that she doesn't either. Because
they broke the mold when they made Barbara, she not
only stood it, but adapted to it and took care of me and the
children as well; for Tack had arrived by the third year, a
little over thirteen months after Barby.

When winter really socked in, usually right around the
first of the year, the deer, coyotes and almost all the other
animals and birds pulled out for lower country, and we
were alone except for a couple of saddle horses, a cow, an
old three-legged cat that had wandered in and taken up a
claim, some cocky little chickadees—who brightened things
considerably with their cheerful chatter—and an occasional camp robber. We were set down in such a deep canyon,
too, that from November to mid-March the sun never
topped the south ridge until at least eleven in the morning
and went down behind it again between one and two in the
afternoon. Not only that, but clear days were rare, for
there was almost always something going on up at the head
of the canyon. A squall would build up, work down past us
a couple of miles, and then back up, churn around a while
and then here it would come again. Sometimes half a dozen
a day. Or maybe one would just squat down over the place
and storm, while a few miles below things would be bright
and sunny. Possibly we had one day out of ten that it didn't
snow sometime between morning and night, but I doubt it.
Then there was the wind; when it came down from the tops
into the canyon it was like living in the throat of a bass
horn! Maybe I chuckle about some of Barbara's reactions
and tease her about things, but it is damn sure based on
deep, fervent admiration. Courageous and indomitable,
pale words to describe my wife!

Only once did Barbara come apart at the seams. I was off up the canyon and when I got back that evening she was in a state. Between outbursts of tears and fits of uncontrollable laughter on her part I managed to get the story. Then and there I decided we better get down where there were other people.

What had happened was that after I had been gone for several hours and the children were asleep, Barbara was churning when suddenly there came a knocking from the front door of the cabin. Surprised, for we were snowed in and it had been over three months since we had seen anyone, she hurried to the door and eagerly opened it, pleased at the prospect of a visitor. No one was there.

Puzzled, for she was sure she had heard a knock, Barbara went back to her churn. In a few minutes the sound came again, and once more nobody was at the door. The months of solitude began to take over, to affect her thinking. Was somebody trying to play tricks, knocking and then hiding, or was she really hearing anything? Could it be the cabin fever she had heard of, or was she losing her buttons? So she stood beside the door and when the erratic tapping sounded, jerked it open in hopes of catching the culprit. Again a blank, so she ran out the woodshed door and scouted around the cabin. Nothing. Not even tracks, except those I'd made that morning down to the barn and up to the springhouse. Maybe, though, before she had come out of the woodshed, whoever it was had been able to run along my tracks and get out of sight into one of the two buildings. But it was too far to have made it to the barn before she appeared. The springhouse was closer. Perhaps . . . .

Up to the building she went with no thought of overshoes, coat, mitts or anything except to find out who was doing the knocking. Once again, nobody, not a thing, but suddenly the knocking came again from the woodshed on the front of our cabin.

"My God, my babies are down there," came the chilling thought, and down the path she went on high. Just as she reached the shed door out flew a camp robber, and everything fell into place—it had been the bird pecking at the frozen meat we'd left on the shed floor for our old cat, Peg, that she had heard.

Her reaction wasn't plumb under control by the time I got home, and it bothered the hell out of me. This was no place for a girl and two babies. Today, if my children planned on living like we did, where we did, I'd break their damn necks! But we were young and probably the finest, most magnificent thing about youth—at least in our time—is the faith that, hell, everything will turn out all right. It nearly always does, too. But a man learns not to crowd it.

*the head of the creek*

*lived off the land.*

*Mountain man*

*Hot iron!*

Dudes, good horses and big country—Tor, Dad, me (center foreground)

"No Bush" camp, 1938

lucky loop

184

*Feeding—Bullet, Babe, bobsled, Barbara*

*On a Sunday afternoon—work horse pasture*

*Bullet and Babe*

*agers*

*Bringing home
the Christmas tree*

*Bronc pen*

ing one down

Horse breaker Walt Heacock

Filly chasing

*Art Langman's horse sale, Billings*  *We called her ''Lady Luck.''*

*ding the Sweet Grass*

*ing summer range—head of Sweet Grass*

*ling out of "No Bush"*

MADDEN

*Dad always had a race horse handy.*

*Dad and relay mare "Smokey Lady"*

*race—Barby on "Spooks," Dad, Shelly on "Johnny Bones"*

*tch race finish line—Barby and "Chief's Big Pete"*
*, Barby, "Big Pete"*

*Dad and me, 1967*     NORTHWEST MAGAZINE     *My Dad—one hell of a man!*

*A young buck—me, before "Steve"*

*Me, 1970*

Barbara and me—working ranchers

*My wife—*
*"They broke the mold."*

Carol and her mother

*Barby started young.*

*Barby and "Whisht," 1965*

*Gramp and Tack (Paul Van Cleve, Sr. and Paul Van Cleve 4th)*

lly started young, too.

Shelly, sidesaddle on "Lady"

kshot and "Mickey"

Buck and "Ditto," 1959

196

*Three horsehands and one on the way—Shelly, holding son J; Barby; Buckshot*

*The Van Cleves—(standing) Dad, Mother, Spike, Barby, Aunt Mony, (sitting) Shelly, Barbara, Buckshot, Tack.*

# Urban Life

## 6

WE CAME OUT of the hills in '36 for Christmas with my parents at the lower ranch, and we sure were a gypsy looking outfit. Jack and Kelly were pulling a bob sleigh with a set of dump boards for a wagon box. In it were Barbara and myself, with Barby and Tack each tucked in an end of one of those narrow old baby baskets with the handles, a hot water bottle for their feet in the middle. I'd hunted up a good tree, the first of many Christmas trees over the years since, for Mother and Dad. It was in the sleigh, too, along with a big buck deer I'd killed during the season, had kept frozen in the spring house and was taking down as our present to the family. Smokey Joe, Barbara's saddle horse, was tied to one side of the back bunk, and Irish to the other. Cuboss, our cow, trailed along behind. All we were missing was a dog or two.

I had a fine set of marten pelts, for I had been trapping since late fall and was surprised to find when I took them into Big Timber that marten trapping was illegal that season. Oh, I'd jumped the gun all right, but had planned on getting my license during the holidays. Anyhow, after the local hide buyer had been good enough to take the skins off my hands for about a tenth of what they were worth—he had me over a barrel and knew it—I decided maybe ranching, though it wasn't as romantic sounding as trapping or working in the timber, might be a better proposition for a man with a burgeoning family. There have been times since that I wondered just how damn smart I was, but we were pretty tired of the weather at the upper ranch. Besides, we were getting so mountainy that if we stayed back there much longer I was afraid that when the first dudes arrived some spring we might all just high tail it into the timber and hide out like coyote pups. Or like the kids on homesteads back up at the "head of the crick." So I made a deal with Dad on a ranch.

It was the old original "Hub" Hickox holdings surrounding Melville, and in late March of '37 we moved down and started to build a house on the Sweet Grass bottom a little over a quarter mile from the town proper. While we were building the house we lived in an old saloon up town. We were only there about three months, but they were eventful. Good thing, too, for they sort of conditioned us for the normal life we'd lead in Melville for the next thirteen years. I wouldn't trade those years for anything, either.

We slept in the bullet-pocked barroom after we finally got the bar and backbar moved out—like a damn fool I cut them both up for firewood—and cooked and ate in a smaller back room. The same room where Mel Jowell had shot and killed Deputy Joe Brannin in 1911.

Dad had planned some farming for the place, and until it was done Barbara was cooking for about fourteen people, which was quite a change for her. The water situation was a lot like I had been used to, though, for the town had a well, and every morning before I left I'd fill every bucket I could find and I was real grateful for Barbara's early training, for she made it do until noon. When we first moved into the saloon we made the mistake of washing the floors, and it was a month before we got the stale beer smell aired out, so we didn't try it again. We just put newspapers and a sorry old rug down to try to protect the kids from splinters in the floor, and got by.

There was another drawback, too, for I guess the saloon

keepers who had lived there before us hadn't believed in anything as gaudy as an outhouse, so it was a question of just using the all outdoors. I got along fine, but had to rustle up one of those big old-style pot de chambres with a lid for the rest of the family. Each night, after it got good and dark, I'd take "Big Blue," as we called it, down the irrigation ditch a ways and dump it in the water. Worked fine until one night when I was out real late moving a string of cows and little calves. Blue was pretty full, so Barbara put it out so I wouldn't forget to take care of it. Then, when one of the kids wanted a drink, she headed for the water bucket in the kitchen, forgot she'd put the thing right spang in front of the door where I couldn't miss it, ran into it and tipped it over. I got in about then, and damn but I was glad it hadn't been me fumbling through the dark that had caused the wreck! After frantic activity that went on most of the night, we got the rug and papers rolled up and outside, where I burned them the next day, scrubbed the floor, and the hell with the booze smell and splinters. I don't know why we worried about the latter anyway, for when the kids were outside they played among, and with, broken bottles. Tack seemed to favor the pretty blue pieces, but Barby didn't give a whoop about the color, just so long as it was broken glass. Be damned if I don't honestly believe they toothed on the stuff, but they survived. To our amazement.

Two little Frenchmen, carpenters who just happened to come through Melville, and I did the building. The Ward and Parker mill in Sweet Grass Canyon got out the logs for a thirty by fifty foot house, sawed them on three sides, and a man in town who had a little truck and was in the business hauled them for me. The whole works, logs and trucking, cost $350, which came pretty close to cleaning us out.

Eddie and Renee—they were brothers—were good men; quick, cheerful, fine workmen, and everything they did was, as they put it, "Up to snaff." They were also gamblers from away back. They were working by the day, and every evening they'd draw their wages—I'd had to borrow the money from Dad, even though wages weren't very classy in the '30s—and go over to Rader's saloon to play stud with the regular habitues, and by morning, every morning, they were broke.

When our house was done and I paid them off I asked what they were going to do. "Get even, by dam," answered Renee with a grin.

I told them they'd better get their old truck filled before they made their try, and I guess they did, for about dark that evening they went rattling out of town past us, lights pulsating wanly. Renee was driving and Eddie was waving a bottle and assuring me as loud as he could yell, "By dam we sure see you an' fam'ly anudder tam, Spike."

I inquired about the "getting even" at the saloon, and sure enough, they were both broke when they left. But Rader gave me two candy bars they'd left for the kids! Several years later Eddie came by, visited a few days, pointed out all the fine features of our house and left with the same farewell. I hope he does; they were nice guys!

The only real drawback to where we lived until the house was built was that it was right across the street from the post office, and the stage unloaded there. Invariably it would be carrying a man or two coming back to their jobs from a bender in Big Timber or a visit to the "line" in Livingston. Either way, they were usually drunk or hung over. Luckily most of them remembered where the bar was, but if they were strangers or real lit they'd spot the front of our place, and here they'd come. I tried to be handy at stage time, but if I wasn't Barbara'd spot them, shoo the kids inside and shut the door. Mostly though, somebody from around town would come over and point out the real bar, and they'd weave off for it.

Unfortunately we hadn't gotten the new house so we

could move into it by the first Saturday night dance along in June, so I spent the evening warding off strangers who wanted to buy a drink. Most were sober enough so it didn't come to fisticuffs, and as the night wore on and they got drunker they had found where the bar was.

Things eventually calmed down some, the children had gotten used to the noise outside and were asleep, Barbara had gone to bed and I had just taken my shirt off when there was a pounding on the door. I opened it, and here was an old boy that wanted his hair cut. I told him the barber lived around back, but he was insistent that it was me. Said our house had been pointed out to him. Maybe somebody had jobbed him, or me, but I was acquainted with the man, knew that he was a little addled, and that even though he was pretty drunk he was harmless. But damn, he was persistent and kept trying to push by me as we argued. I was just about to where I was going to lower the boom on him, when, as I spun him back to the door, I faced our bed. The covers were all pulled up to the pillow, and there was an eye peeping out from under them, and two interested little faces peering over the edge of the crib behind. Suddenly it was all I could do to keep from howling! About then, the man straightened up and said scornfully, "Ah, go to hell. I wouldn't let you cut my hair if you asked please. I'll go to Big Timber!" and stalked off.

I shut the door and collapsed. It took a little time before Barbara joined me, but she finally laughed, too. I'll never forget that eye!

I have a deep affection for the Melvilleites of those days. They were good neighbors, good people and damn sure not average. No way! One woman I appreciated, but was damn careful of. She was in her sixties, I suppose, not very big, but she threw a long, long shadow and sure had been in the lead when the tempers were passed out. In looks she sort of reminded me of a moulting chicken hawk, and she sure had her husband broke to lead! Once in a while he'd get enough

whiskey courage to talk back, but it usually just earned
him a few bruises, especially if she had been celebrating,
too. I won't forget the time she came up to me at a party at
the Melville hall and asked if I'd dance with her. I said sure,
I'd like to, and away we went.

She'd had a few snorts, and her dancing got chummier
and chummier. Put me in mind of a Swiss movement in a
dollar watch case and thank God it was pretty dark! It got
plumb embarrassing, so I peeled her off and asked just
what was going on. "Oh," she answered frankly, "Al is
tomcatting around with some young girls, and I aim to get
even with the old bastard."

I told her Barbara was at the dance, and she better get
someone else. She said fine, and off she went. Pretty soon I
saw her come by with another old boy. He looked worried
and was beginning to sweat pretty badly, but since it
wasn't me I got a charge out of it.

A few years before we moved to Melville, the same
woman was ironing when a dude boy that was wintering at
a nearby ranch dropped in. He was a weasely sort of pistol
and pretty soon got to teasing her in his usual unpleasant
fashion. That didn't sit too well, and suddenly she picked a
fresh iron off the stove and made a run at him with, "You
little sonofabitch, I'll brand you so's they'll know you in
hell!" Luckily he outran her to his horse, for she meant
every word of it.

If she'd known he would become dean of one of the
country's great cathedrals it wouldn't have fazed her a bit.
Wouldn't today, if she were alive and knew it, either. She
came from Melville!

The local joie de vivre wasn't just confined to town
either. There was an old fellow lived on the head of one of
the creeks up under the Crazies west of Melville. He'd
batched for years and was pretty well fixed, but I guess he
got lonesome and went to writing to one of those lonely
hearts columns in the back of some magazine. Anyhow, he

showed up one day at McQuillan's saloon all slicked up and announced that he was on his way to Big Timber to get married. Everybody was curious of course, and it came out that he and a girl had got to corresponding, had swapped pictures, and he was on his way to meet her train and they'd get hitched. Seems this mail order bride was in her twenties, too, while the groom, though nobody knew for sure, was in his late sixties or better. So the boys got to giving him a bad time about how dangerous it was for a man his age to marry a young woman. Could even be plumb fatal, and so on. Finally the old guy, just as serious as a tree full of owls, shrugged and said philosophically, "Well, hell, if she dies, she dies."

Puts me in mind of another old fellow, a bachelor, over on the Musselshell. He was up in his late seventies when the woman keeping house for him showed up heavy in foal and named him as the daddy. "I been there," he told the judge, and married her. My granddad was a good friend of the old man, and when he heard of the proceedings his remark was, "The old fool. He was just so damn flattered he married her!"

Speaking of brides reminds me of another new one that we had in the country a few years ago. Her husband was a big, pink-whiskered dude boy that had bought a ranch and was doing his damnest to be a cowman. He was plumb serious about the whole deal—charts, graphs, government bulletins, you name it and he had it. Surprisingly, he made a rancher eventually, a good one.

His wife knew as little about livestock as he did, and she worked at learning it just as hard. He'd tackled running some milk cows and got fed up with the demands they put on a man, I guess, for he advertised one for sale, and somebody came to look at her while he was gone one day. So his bride showed the man the cow.

Of course the prospective buyer wanted to know whether Bossy was easy milking, if she kicked, and so on. The girl's answer each time was that she didn't know, but that her husband could tell him. Finally this old boy asked, "What's her production?"

"Beg pardon?" said the bride.

"How much milk does she give?" he explained.

"Oh, I'm afraid I really don't know. But Jerry says she's an awfully honest old cow, so I am sure she will give all she has!"

# Dudes

## 7

I SUPPOSE every dude ranch, at one time or another, has had a guest who just doesn't fit in or enjoy the outfit. Actually they are pretty rare, thank God, and maybe that's why I remember them so well.

This one girl should never have tried a ranch vacation, for she was dissatisfied with everything. The country, the climate, her cabin, the beds, the food, the horses—nothing suited her. I even sicked a wrangler who was quite a hand with the ladies on her. Sometimes that works wonders—though I frown on it as a general rule—but damn if she didn't complain that she didn't like "bucolic types." Anyway, one day, her last at the ranch, we made a trip through the breaks of the South Fork, and as we rode into the meadows to noon she remarked snappishly to everyone in general, "I wish someone would tell me just how I am supposed to get this nag out of a walk."

Well, I'd given her a new horse about every day she'd been there, good horses, and I'd about had it. It took me a little time to try and figure out something tactful, which isn't exactly my long suit, but before I could one of my wranglers spoke up. He was a big green country kid, a real good boy, and he showed it now. Very pleasantly and politely he answered, "You could stop him, Ma'am."

One other woman sticks in my mind—let me hasten to say that I am no chauvinistic male, there have been men, too—but she was salty! In looks and build she put me in

205

mind of a picked hawk, and her temperament was about as warm as a crowbar on a January morning. She was sure a fine horse hand, and she liked the stock I put her on, but even the other guests, after a few overtures, sidled around her. The whole place had gotten a little jumpy by the time her stay was over, and the following day I asked the driver who had taken her to Billings how the trip had gone.

When they had gotten to the top of the Vik hill, from which they could see the whole of the Crazies and all the way up to the head of Big Timber canyon, she had asked him to stop so she could "drink it all in." As he sat there waiting for her, he lit a cigarette. She leaned forward from the back seat, tapped him on the shoulder and said, "Put that out, I don't care for smoking. Gentlemen won't, and servants mustn't."

"What'd you do?" I asked.

"Put it out, by God! But you know, Spike, every time we hit a hill from there to Billings where she could see the Crazies, she'd tap my shoulder and I'd stop while she looked. Then she'd tap my shoulder again, and I'd drive on. Never said another word the whole trip."

The thing has always bothered me. She had loved the country, just as I do, and perhaps if I'd tried harder she'd have limbered up and had more fun. Gotten human maybe. Anyhow, I haven't forgotten, and it's been good for me.

For every cutback we've had, though, there have been a whole lot of fine people and good friends, and many a chuckle. Most of what is done on the ranch is done ahorseback. Our all-day rides, especially in the range country, must average around twenty miles, and sometimes nearly twice that. We use a jog a lot, for it's easy on a horse, covers country, and, when you learn to cope with it, easy on a rider. I remember one day when we had made quite a circle, and so, when we hit a nice stretch of footing, I leaned ahead and put my horse into a lope for a half mile or so. When the smooth ground played out I eased back into a jog. As I did, I heard a guest mutter, "Here we go again. That damn Van Cleve jiggle!"

I just recently got a reservation from a guest and friend of long standing, and he, too, mentioned "The Van Cleve Trot (18 mph?)." I guess a jog is sort of hard to post to, and most people learn right quick to ride western. There's some connection; could be the mileage, or hours, maybe?

Still, I think perhaps we sometimes seem sort of abrupt. Like the time a string of riders were switchbacking up over the Big Timber-Sweet Grass divide—and it's a pretty sizeable hill—when I heard my oldest daughter remark to a guest, "If you don't like heights, just look the other way."

Many's the time I've looked back over my shoulder on that trail and seen everybody, except perhaps some noisy kid, leaning towards the mountain on the up side. I know just how they feel. I had a popping good mare that for some reason always wanted to walk to the left. On a sure enough mountain trail I could look down her near side and see nothing but space. She'd do it where a man could spit a quarter mile and not bend over, too! I sure did some leaning in on her! Then, when we'd swung back, I'd have to fend off the mountain to save my near knee. I finally decided her gaits were too nice to be wasted in high country.

We had a retired admiral and his wife as guests one summer. She was a fine rider and went on every all-day trip from the time they arrived. He was no centaur, but he sure had nerve, and he made every trip right with her. I heard his wife ask a wrangler, when we were bringing out horses one morning, just how long the day's trip would be. The boy told her around twenty-five to thirty miles, which was so. I happened to be tightening a cinch nearby when she enthusiastically reported this to the admiral. His response was a fervent, "Jesus H. Christ!"

We had an English girl with us one summer. A peach of a girl—goodlooking, friendly as a Shepherd pup, interested in everything and eager to do things. She had a sense of humor, and her mammalary facade was magnificent! We were jogging home after a branding when she pulled up alongside. I noticed her sizing me up, and then she said, "I say, Spike, could you teach me to sit a trot as you are doing?"

"Sure, Limey," I answered, and then, because I just flat couldn't help it, "There's one thing you've got to do, though, before we start."

"Whatever is that?" she asked anxiously.

"Well, I think you better get yourself a better bra."

There was silence while she thought it over. Then a broad grin replaced her serious expression. "Haw. Jolly good thought. I shall!"

I remember another English girl who visited the ranch. An awful nice person—enthusiastic, interested in ranching, real good looking and put together right. I liked her, but decided she must have been dropped in a good grass year, for she sure was big. Not fat, just a whale of a chunk of girl.

She was a good rider, and when she arrived I fit her out with a large saddle, and a big, smooth-traveling Thoroughbred mare, and thought she'd do fine. However she kept complaining that she couldn't get comfortable, and after sizing her up surreptitiously a time or two, I figured out the trouble. So one morning I collared her and said, "Empiah," which was short for "British Empire," "I think your saddle is the trouble, and I'd like to change it." She was agreeable, so I made the switch, but as I was fitting the stirrups she asked, "What is the difference between this saddle and the other? They certainly appeah to be the same."

Without thinking I told her that while her old saddle had been a large size this one was an extra large. She bridled immediately, and I had to talk like a Dutch uncle before I finally got her to agree to try the new one just for the day's ride.

I made a point of being at the corral when her ride came

in that evening. I noticed that she was sitting easy and relaxed and talking animatedly to the rider beside her.

When she got down, I stepped up and asked, "How did it go?"

With a smile from ear to ear she answered, "Jolly well! Never an uncomfortable moment. You were right." But then a touch of worry crossed her face. She plucked at my elbow, led me a little to one side and asked in a low tone, "But I say, Spike, is my bottom really *that* large?"

I didn't even try to keep from grinning. "Truth compels me to say, Empiah, that indeed it is. But it sure is becoming, anyhow."

She studied me seriously for a minute, then with a glint deep in her eye, she answered, "Thank you for a veddy comfortable ride, and a veddy nice cumpliment."

We had a real nice little man as a guest several years ago. A bachelor, quiet and sort of shy. He was an appealing little guy, too, and everybody liked him and went out of their way to include him in whatever was going on. I mounted him on old Easy Money, a good, nice traveling horse, and dog gentle. The two got along fine; Easy had the world by the tail with a downhill pull and knew it, while the guest got broken in and braved up and pretty soon was going along on every all-day ride and having just a hell of a time.

Happened one day that we worked cattle on Otter Creek and nooned at Wolf Butte crossing. After we'd eaten and dozed a while, I hunted up the horses, checked the saddles, and everybody got aboard. Everybody, that is, except the little man. He just stood there at his horse's shoulder not saying a word or making a move, forlorn as a kicked pup.

We waited and waited, and finally my mother asked, "Aren't you going to get on and come with us?"

"Yes, Mrs. Van Cleve," he answered apologetically. "Just as soon as Easy Dollar gets off my foot."

Another time we had a woman at the ranch who sure was

a horse hand! She brought her own rigging, and after we'd talked things over, and I'd watched her a time or two, I said sure, use it. Only one thing I sat back like a borrowed dog about—she wanted to use as many reins on one saddle horse as are needed to handle a four horse team. But she could ride, and she had lovely hands. Pretty quick I had her working a couple of good green colts for me, and she sure was making horses out of them! Trouble was that about all she talked about, even thought about, seemed like, was riding and horses. She even reminded me of a clean-built, well-bred Thoroughbred, but all of us in the corrals sure liked her.

Down she came one afternoon, wanted to have a ride, and did I have a wrangler I could send with her? I said you bet but that a hand of her caliber didn't have to take a wrangler along. She said she'd like to have one, so I called one of the boys and told him to bring out his horse.

This was a good boy, but it was the first time he had ever had a job on a dude outfit and he was still pretty much of a big green ranch kid. So, when he came out I told him to go wherever the lady wanted to ride, and do whatever she told him to do. When they were horseback she said something to him and off they went, the lady in the lead with the young fellow behind, looking straight ahead.

A couple of hours later, as we were unsaddling, in they came. She was still posting happily along in front, her horse cool and quiet, the wrangler still behind and still eyes front.

"Ripping ride, Spike," she said. "Thank you," and to the boy, "How did it look, young man?"

The old kid gulped, red climbed up his neck, and his ears started to give off little heat waves. "Looked all right to me, Ma'am," he blurted.

"Thank you," says she, and up the hill to her cabin she went.

You'd 'a thought the boy had been caught stealing

chickens when I turned to him and asked, "What was that all about?"

"Well, dammit, Spike. When we left she told me to ride behind and watch her seat and see if it was satisfactory!"

It's quite a while ago, but I sure remember the morning! Two girls had arrived at the ranch the evening before— good looking girls maybe twenty-one or so, friendly as a couple of hound pups and just busting with eagerness to be western.

We'd just turned a new string into the feed pen and were starting to saddle the horses that had been fed when down these two came. I was changing a latigo when I heard one of the wranglers sort of choke. I looked up and there the two girls were, peering through the corral gate and grinning from ear to ear. I stepped around the old pony in front of me to say good morning, got a clear look at them and saw why the wrangler'd choked. I did, too!

They were sure outfitted! I may be a little vague about their top halves, but it seems to me they had on black hats with tiedowns, bandanas and gaudy shirts. The rest I remember a lot better. Boots, spurs and tight, narrow batwing chaps. But I guess nobody'd told them you wore britches with leggings, for all they had under them were their drawers, pretty pink ones! Talk about the see-through blouses nowadays! The chaps worked sort of like peep sights, too.

Well, I couldn't just come right out and tell them. Maybe I just didn't have the gall to, or maybe I just hated to spoil things. Anyhow they stood around talking and asking questions, happy as a couple of dogs with a hoof paring, while the saddling turned into a shambles. Finally the breakfast bell rang. Away they went, and there was a change of scene. Same color, but broader, and cuter really.

Somebody must have headed them off before they got to the dining room, for there were no repercussions from there that I heard about. I told the boys to keep their damn mouths shut, and that I'd fire the first one that teased the poor devils. The two were pretty quiet for a few days, but then they limbered up and seemed to forget about it. I guess I'm impressionable, for I never did.

I remember one time we were all down at a dance at Melville. As usual every ranch family and hand was there with bells on. There was a popping good looking girl who was a guest at the ranch, and ever since she had arrived she'd had all the young fellows on the outfit, wranglers included, fighting for her attention. She sure lapped it up, and this evening was the belle of the ball. I happened to be sitting next to her between numbers when a big old local boy sidled up and asked her, awkwardly but politely, if he could have the next dance.

Well, this was a good boy and a top hand. Maybe he wouldn't win any prizes for looks, and his Adam's apple was pretty noticeable, but he was clean, his boots carefully scraped, sober and serious. Anyhow, she smiled about as warmly as if she'd had a gas pain, and refused, adding, "I'm afraid I don't know you."

I just itched to kick her, but didn't have to. Before I could make the introductions the old kid said pleasantly, "Shucks, that's all right, Miss. I'm taking just as big a chance as you are." I'd misjudged that girl, too. She got up and danced with him!

A big sheepman, a Norwegian, ran several bands south of our outfit. One nice summer evening toward sundown I happened to pass one of the camps on my way home with a group of guests. The sheep were stringing onto the bed ground by the wagon, and the herder, also a Norsk, was sitting on the wagon tongue playing an accordion.

Scandinavian music sits high on my list of druthers, and he was playing "Balen i Karlstad," a particular favorite of mine, so I whoaed up the outfit for a minute to enjoy the tune. As we sat there a woman from Boston, a lovely person, but like so many Bostonians pretty literal minded, asked what the wagon was for. Without thinking I answered that it was the sheep wagon, neglecting to add that it was where the herder lived.

Silence a moment, except for the lilt of the accordion. Then she said, with a puzzled look on her face, "But, Spike, how do they get all those sheep into that little wagon?"

I'm almost ashamed of myself once in a while about the things I sometimes get away with telling people at the ranch. The outfit is run pretty much ahorseback. We ride every day, as a rule all day, but on Sunday the horses get a well-earned rest, always. Well, I was chatting with a pair of new guests one Saturday evening and mentioned that we wouldn't be riding until Monday. When they asked why not I told them that Sunday was the day we washed the horses. They jumped on the idea like a duck on a June bug and wanted to know the whys and wherefores.

As long as I'd started this I figured I might as well make it good. So I strung out a story of a portable corral set up in the creek, wranglers in bathing suits using brooms to scrub the horses, and how the latter lay basking in the current during the procedure. I mentioned how they washed elephants in India and Africa and said I was sure they'd seen pictures, and they said they had. Then I told them how the horses just loved getting all the trail dust off and practically fought to get their turns; though the last go-round, just before we turned them out for the winter, was usually a chilly proposition. A fringe benefit, too, was the fact that, being all clean, they'd seldom lie down while crossing a creek with a rider. I did a good job, and my listeners' eyes got rounder and rounder.

I forgot about it after they left for their cabin, but it sure was brought to my attention the next morning when I went down to tend the wrangle stock. Here these two were, loaded with cameras, waiting for the washing to begin! Nothing I could do but admit my perfidy, and it was some little time until they fully trusted me again. If ever.

We used to have a block of fifteen or so sections twenty-odd miles below Melville, and we ran our cattle there in the spring and early summer. We'd take a string of guests along and ride down, gather, brand, vaccinate, dehorn and castrate, then get everything mothered up, and cut out a couple or so hundred cows and calves to go to the mountains. We'd string them up to and past Melville, on up the Sweet Grass, into its canyon, and to the head of the South Fork. The whole trip took better than two weeks, and we camped the whole time. At first our commissary was a pickup, and then, when we hit the high country, pack horses. As guests played out we'd bring another group, and the first ones would ride home to the ranch. We called that lower range "No Bush" after a woman guest rode into camp the first evening, looked around and said, "My God, not even a *bush* to get behind!" A fine country, though, plumb on the height of land between the Yellowstone and Missouri drainage.

I remember one morning when we'd eaten and were out of camp before sunrise. We were gathering the top of the divide, a long high bench, and 'way to the north beyond the Musselshell we could see the Judith Gap. To the south the Yellowstone valley lay from horizon to horizon, and at its upper end a thunderstorm was forcing its way out of the mountains perhaps fifty miles away. As the sun peeked over the eastern skyline it tipped the Crazies, thirty-odd miles to the west, with pink and picked out a rainbow gleaming in the dark curtains of the storm to the south. The cattle were getting up out of their beds, a coyote slipped down a coulee, watching us over his shoulder, and some antelope spilled through the cattle ahead of us like blown wisps of cotton. 'Way and away the storm muttered; stock grunted as they stood up and stretched. A horse occasionally blew his nose softly, and among the riders strung out on circle to my right, one let out a squeal and tried a few jumps in sheer exuberance and enjoyment, while the high, wild whistle of a curlew hung like a silver thread in the clear air. The kind of a morning that squares up for many a sorry day!

It was always a good trip, but pretty western. The water was scarce, the rattlesnakes weren't, there were a few horned toads, and it could get *hot*. The country was choppy, rimrocked and interesting, with sweeping vistas off to the Snowies, Belts, Bulls, Big Horns and Beartooth from fifty to two hundred miles away, with the Crazies rising up and up as we trailed towards them. But attrition as to people was pretty high, and one day in particular comes to mind.

We had the cattle strung out and moving by sunup, but it developed into the kind of day that prompted the old cattleman to squint up at the sun and ask, "Where the hell was you last January?" By noon the stock was hot, dry and sulled up. It wasn't a question by then of moving them; we'd be lucky to hold them from breaking back to the last bedground, particularly the calves. We were all busy as bird dogs in a stubble field, and when anybody could be spared they'd lope over to the pickup and snatch a bite to eat and some water. It was about then that Dad spotted this young fellow, up on a rise where there might be a little breeze, lying stretched out in the shade of his horse.

Pop hadn't left the cattle since we'd started them, he'd been riding hard and by now he was as touchy as a teased snake. So he boiled over at a hard run and pulled up beside the boy. "Jim," he rasped, "why in hell aren't you helping hold these cattle?"

The youngster grinned and replied perfectly truthfully, "But, Uncle Paul, I didn't come out here to work."

I thought Dad would explode, but he sat quiet a minute and then rode off. That evening in camp he told me, "That boy was right, dammit. I'm going to remember it, and you do, too."

I have. So now, when guests get tired working stock, we

quit. There'll be another day, and another, and another. What the hell?

When you mix people and livestock, particularly guests who don't know from sic 'em about livestock, there can often be a fine line between tragedy and comedy. The hell of it is, too, that the guests don't savvy the comedy, and I don't blame them. Many a time I have laughed, perhaps in sheer relief, about something which a second or two before had me chilled. Looking ahead to possible trouble gets to be a habit, but things seem to happen in spite of everything, and there are times when a man just doesn't dare laugh even when everything turns out fine.

I've been serious as a tree full of owls while helping to clean up and calm down a rider whose horse had decided to lie down and roll in a nice, cool mudhole. Or the young woman who rode blithely in among the brood mare bunch to take pictures of the colts. I told her to stay away, that the mare she was riding was in heat, but when I next looked up there she was, and the excitement commencing. It could have been bad, only her mare was big and the stud was small, but it sure was funny! She sat there swatting at the stud's nose, which was over her right shoulder, yelling, "Shoo, shoo," and "Spike!" I got things straightened out with no casualties, but keeping a straight, sympathetic face, especially after the smoke had cleared, was rough, rough.

Another time, too, because I didn't use my head, I precipitated one of the damndest examples of sheer chaos I've ever seen. We were jogging along pretty well spread out on nice open country on Middle Fork. My three girls were alongside me, arguing about who had the fastest horse. They were riding their own horses, three good ones, and I was sort of curious as to which one had the most gas, so I finally said, "Hell, my old mare'll jerk the heads plumb off all three of them. I'll match the works of you up to that bull pine yonder."

Everybody jumped on the idea, so, still jogging, we got in line and I said go.

It was a good race. My mare, being used to score boxes, took the lead, but after about fifty yards Barby on Mr. Ed on one flank and Shelly on Fox on the other came up alongside. Just about then, though, here came Buckshot on Ditto, her half Thoroughbred filly. She was on her way by when we came even with the tree and I said, "That's it, hold up."

Buck was starting to object that it was no fair when I glanced behind us and hurriedly said, "Don't pull up too short, or we'll be trampled plumb into the ground. Look!"

Here they came! Every horse in the outfit had enthusiastically joined the race when they saw us start. Naturally their riders had too, albeit unexpectedly! Two of them had fallen off when the race began and were standing, watching forlornly. Pennant, a fine old Thoroughbred horse that we'd used in our relay string in his younger days, and who had become one of our finest children's mounts, was in the lead, digging like a champion. His ears were pinned back, and I could almost hear him say, "Hoo Boy!" It looked like he had a smile from ear to ear, but it probably came from the death grip his rider had on the reins with one hand and a saddlestring with the other, from his seat behind the saddle! Another youngster had been wearing a bandana over his nose on account of hay fever, and here he came wide open with the bandana blown up over his eyes. Plumb blind, but too busy trying to gather his slack, at arm's length above his shoulder, and putting finger nail marks on the horn covering, to pull the thing down. His mare, Victory, had been quite a running horse in her day, too. Two or three others had been wearing tie downs on their hats, had lost them and were purple from the pressure of the thongs across their throats. One real thin girl's hat worked like a parachute, and if it hadn't been for the white knuckled grip she had on the horn, I swear she'd 'a been dragged plumb off her horse. It was chaos pure and simple, and it took the four of us to get the less experienced riders bent in a big circle and finally stopped. Nobody was hurt, for even the casualties at the start had been run out from under of so fast they'd lit easy. We put in some time, though, before we got all the hats, lunches, cigarettes and various sundries gathered, and everybody lined out again. It could have been bad instead of funny, and since then, if I plan on something sudden, I give everybody fair warning. Easier on my nerves.

For some reason that completely eludes me, most westerners seem to have the idea that a dude can't ride. We've run a dude ranch for better than fifty years right along with our cow and horse outfit, and by and large I have developed a hell of a lot of respect for eastern riders. Perhaps I should say horsemen, or better yet, horsemanship. Over the years I have seen a lot of guests at the ranch who will stack up right along with any horse hands in the west. They handle horses differently perhaps, and I am not all that enthusiastic about the riggings they put on an old pony's head—I never thought four reins were necessary to handle one horse—but I'll state right here and now that I enjoy putting a dude who knows horses on the very best of mine, for I know the horse will be ridden right.

Oh, I get some counterfeits, and I can spot them the minute they get aboard, but they are the exceptions that prove the rule. The polo players we've had don't seem all that shiney—sort of like some ropers I've seen—but by God, the dudes who hunt foxes back home, especially the women, sure know how to use a good horse!

Funny, and it's true in my own family, too, but girls seem to make better horsemen than boys. When the latter are good they are real good, but few and far between. Most eastern teenage girls, though, are horsewomen from away back! Maybe they have more rapport with an animal than a boy has, or identify more with their mount, but whatever it is, they can handle a horse. After all, most of them start in "pony" classes at shows when they are about five or six, and back there a "pony" is anything fourteen and a half hands and under, as I understand it. In my day, I've seen some horses that qualified as "ponies" that were damn juicy; little for big but hell for stout. These girls, by the time they are into their late teens, have hands like velvet, no nerves, and can handle a good colt with anyone; better than a lot of men who have their shingles out as horse hands. Trouble is, when they fall in love they aren't worth a damn for a while, and don't really come out of it until they've been married a spell. I've seen it time and again; besides, I raised three daughters of my own.

I remember a girl who had been coming to the ranch since she was a button. She rode a lot back home, and I was always tickled to see her arrive because I knew she would take a good salty colt for me and make something out of him. I guess she was about twenty the last time she came out, and, as had been done for at least six or seven years, I fit her with a fine prospect we'd broken that spring. She'd been there about a week when one evening I asked her casually, "Sis, I'll bet you have a serious beau. Am I right?"

Before she could answer, her kid brother let out a whoop. "She sure does, Spike. Real serious."

"Oh, hush," she said, and turned to me. "Yes, I have, but how did you know?"

"Hell, it was a cinch. You tipped your hand right off the bat, for you haven't been handling that colt like usual. Only one thing could make you that sloppy, a man."

She disagreed violently, but it was a fact—she just hadn't been using the youngster I'd put her on like she always had before.

Every now and then a guest will ask for a horse that will be a "challenge," and my answer is that I can get them bucked off real easy but that I'd rather just have them enjoy a good ride. When I was younger I wasn't as neighborly, particularly if some big pink-whiskered kid wanted to be "challenged." Seems like the boys we had as guests thirty-five or more years ago were all just itching to try a horse that would buck, and we kept some in the string for that very purpose. If a boy wanted a sure enough colt he could have one, but only if he put up the fair price of the youngster before he started with him. If he did a good job we gave him his money back when he left; if not, we kept it and he owned a spoiled horse. Some of those kids did plumb all right, too. Most of them stayed clear of the young stock, but we often had a waiting list for the broncs.

One real long geared boy asked for a "bronco." It was fine with his folks, so I gave him Gunsel, a stocky black who, though he couldn't buck worth a damn, was sure he could and was always willing to give it an honest try.

The old gelding never had it so good. He bedded the big old kid down before he'd much more than gotten un-tracked, once more before we got to the ford and again just across it. I couldn't figure why he didn't do it in the creek, too, but maybe he was a little leary of the footing. It was especially funny to watch because the boy was so doggone lanky and the horse so heavy set that his rider's head and shoulders would be plumb on the ground before either foot came out of a stirrup. After the last wreck I caught Gunsel, and as I led him back I watched the long figure get up off the ground, inch by inch and foot by foot. Reminded me for all the world of a man coiling about forty feet of rope. He backed off as I held out the reins. "You know," he told me gravely, "I don't find a bronco such sport. May I have another animal, please?" I got him one, for he was all right!

We had another boy from New York one year. He was red-headed, never used a hat, but wore a grin continually. He was a good kid, and his ambition was to be a bronc hand. I doubt he ever made it, for he sure didn't at our place, but we gave him a buckskin mare by the name of Fizzy that gave him plenty of practice. The two of them got along fine; she'd buck him off four or five times a day, and he'd climb back on every time still wearing that grin. There were no hard feelings on either side, and I really think he and the mare got sort of fond of one another in spite of their differences. I could always tell when he had come to grief, whether I'd seen it or not, and when he rode in from behind a hill one day, with his grin threatening his ears, I knew what was up. "Spike," he told me, his voice chock full of pride, "I rode her!"

"Good man!" I answered enthusiastically. "I knew."

"How?" he asked. "Did you see me?"

"Hell, no. Didn't need to. There's no dust in your hair or on the back of your shirt!"

It wasn't too much later that things went back to normal, and I bit back a smile as he told me philosophically, "Can't win 'em all, I guess."

We had a stubby, benchlegged kid from New York at the ranch years ago who wanted to be a bronc hand. He got plenty of opportunity, and since he had more sand than a Honolulu beach he tackled everything we saddled for him, and got to be a pretty salty rider. On top of that he was an eccentric cuss and could be depended on, always, to do some knot-headed sort of thing and usually get away with it. He paid an entry in the saddle bronc riding at the Melville Rodeo, a show that sure separated the men from the boys when it came to bronc fighters, and damn if I don't think he'd have been right up there in the money if he hadn't insisted on wearing a solar topee he'd brought out from back home—he was fitting a ride until the nut decided to fan his mount with the thing, as well as spur, and he came down just at the whistle. He got a real hand from the crowd, though most of them hadn't the slightest idea what he was fanning with. He was a good kid, even if he was a little weedy.

A real nice family came to the ranch for years, and I watched their son grow from a chubby little boy into a big, good natured young man, friendly as a pet coon and about as dangerous as a hound pup. He wanted to get in shape for football, so we gave him a job bucking bales with the hay crew on the home ranch a few years back.

It was damp on the third of July, so the crew all went over to the Harlowton Rodeo on the Musselshell. The Fourth was clear and dry so they went back to haying. However, I was in the team tieing, hadn't roped on the first day since there was only one go 'round, so I pulled over on the Fourth, unloaded a little before show time and started to get my rigging ready. Suddenly I heard a voice behind me say hesitantly, "Mr. Van Cleve?"

"That's me," I answered and turned to face a youngster of perhaps nineteen who had easterner sticking out all over him. "What is it?"

"Sir," he said respectfully, "I understand that a Jay Roth is working for you."

"That's so."

"He is a classmate of mine at Deerfield Academy in Massachusetts, and I should like to see him. Is he here in Harlowton?"

Those big innocent eyes and earnest face sort of got to me. Sometimes I'm pretty terrible, though mostly I am careful around our guests; but this wasn't one of ours. It would be a shame not to job a pure-quill greenhorn a little anyhow, so I let myself go. "Yes, he's here."

"I should like to chat with him," he told me hopefully.

"Well," and I started to tie my extra rope to the saddle fork, "I don't know whether they'll let you."

"Let me talk to him? Who is that, Sir?"

I swung around. "The law, son, the law. He's in jail. Got arrested last night."

"In jail!" he stammered. "Whatever for?"

Genius laid its hand on my shoulder; or maybe it was just my odd sense of humor. "For molesting women," giving the words a nasty turn, and shaking my head sadly.

"That's a rank charge in this part of the country, son, and it could go damn hard on him."

It shook the old kid! He batted his eyes like I'd slapped him and backed off a step with a look of horror spreading across his face. "Mo--lest---ing wom - - -. Heavens!"

"Yup. Terrible thing." I swung into the saddle and headed for the arena, saying over my shoulder, "You could give it a try. Maybe they'd let you see him." I knew I had to leave for I was about to grin at the very idea of Jay "molesting women," but boy it had a horrible sound!

I just barely caught his words, "See him. My word, no! But thank you, sir."

I got to thinking, as I waited to rope, what a hell of a thing for a man to do to an honest, green old kid. Probably spoiled the whole rodeo for him, possibly even his whole western trip, but then I remembered his expression and started laughing. My head roper asked, "What's so damn funny?" And at least I was ashamed of myself enough not to tell him.

The incident was never mentioned to Jay, but shortly after he got back to Deerfield I got a note from him. "Damn you," it said, "I'll never live it down—whatever it is!"

# Christmas

CHRISTMAS HAS ALWAYS been special to me. When I was a kid we celebrated it at the Butte Ranch with Gramp and Granny, and when I had a family of my own, we would go down to join Mother and Dad at the home ranch. Now our children and their families join us here, and Barbara and I are the old folks. Christmas has been a lovely, family time all through the years, and still is; the very best time, not just day, of the year. Still, though it might be that I'm getting to the age where the past looks better than it really was, I think the best Christmases of all were when our children were pretty little, and they usually went about like this:

A couple of days early, around the 23rd, the whole family goes tree hunting. If there is snow we take the team and sleigh, if there isn't, we use our old Model A, "Oomphy," and drive as far up toward the head of Otter Creek as we can get. Of course, if somebody had spotted a likely looking tree while riding during the summer, we zero in on it; not too fast, though, for the hunting is the main fun. Outfitted with a hand axe or two, and a felling axe, we trudge through the snowy timber, critically studying each likely prospect from all sides amid much discussion. It always seems that the ones that look the best are way up yonder on the hill, and when we come panting up to them they aren't so darn good at that. Still, during the hunt there will be lots of especially pretty juniper, ground cedar, fir and pine along the way, each with its own scent, color, berries or cones, and some of each is gathered with great discrimination—and not without some slight bickering. Invariably, if I can manage to get the children's attention distracted for a minute, I hurriedly, by clenching my fingers into my palms and pressing my hands into the snow, make tracks, which, I announce in a hushed voice, are surely mountain lion tracks. This results in a great deal of whispering, peeking over shoulders, and best of all, Buckshot holding on to my hand, as well as getting in my way, for the rest of the hunt.

At long last we agree on a tree. I fell it, carry it carefully down to the rigging, and home we go with a load of tree, greens and family. You know, if I were a tree there's nothing I'd like better than to be a Christmas tree for us!

Christmas Eve Day we bring in the tree and put it in the corner of the living room. It stands as tall as the ceiling will allow, with the best side toward the room. The extra branches are used to decorate the house, with the prettiest saved for Nuestra Señora de Guadalupe in her niche over the fireplace. Then that evening, after we've given an extra big feed to the stock—Spike and Big Pete, the stallions; Sam and Tinch, the saddle horses; the weanling colts; Pit Pat, the old brood mare who is kept around the barn for the winter; Bullet and Babe, the team; and Mouse, the milk cow—we have a tureen of oyster stew. Mom and Dad are there, and as soon as the dishes are done, Tack, Shelly and Buck, with Barbara as final arbitrator, trim the tree while I sit and give unasked, and unused, advice. Our tree is loaded, everything it can hold. Some of the trimmings date back to '37 and the first tree Barbara and I ever had for our own family. Finally and reluctantly it's decided that it just won't hold any more, and everyone is called in to admire it. Even Dad and Barby are dragged from the kitchen where they have been making eggnog, Maryland eggnog, from a recipe of Mother's mother. No whiskey in classic eggnog, perish the thought; just a couple of dozen eggs, sugar, cream, a little milk, a couple of quarts of brandy, and one of old, black, strong rum. And a lot of elbow grease with the egg beater! I might add that both Dad and Barby have been sampling their handiwork, and we all demand some. There we are—the tree shining in the corner, the fireplace crackling opposite it, the record player rendering "Silent Night" softly—sampling the nog while Buck sets out a glass for Santy and a dish of sugar lumps for his reindeer. I slip outside with my sleigh bells, which have already been smuggled out of the house, and Santy arrives. First, his bells are in the distance, then they come closer and closer, and at last ring to a standstill in the yard. By that time the little ones are in bed in a swirl of popped buttons, strewn clothes and delicious fright—for if Santy catches a child up and about 'til they are twelve years old, then all he gets is a lump of coal and a switch in his sock. So the kids are in bed with the doors and their eyes shut by the time he comes into the house.

Well, he has a nog, fills any stockings by the fireplace, has another nog, and with a "Merry Christmas," leaves, and the bells on his team fade into the distance. We sit and talk 'til about eleven, and then all go into Big Timber to Midnight Mass.

This, to us, is the high point of Christmas. The candle-lit dimness, the incense, the Bethlehem by the altar rail, the majesty of the age-old ceremony and the joyous notes of "Adeste Fidelis," and above all, the peace and joy that His birth brings us once again. We pray for our family, our friends, for our country and for the world, and we go home to our beds better men and women for it!

It isn't yet light when we are roused by the kids, and as soon as I can start the fire and light the tree we gather in the living room to see what Santy has brought. Barbara tries desperately to keep track of who sent what as Tack and Buck pass out the presents. Soon the room is knee deep in paper. Then, wrenched bodily from a new book, I am sent to chore. Again there is an extra feed for the stock and each is wished a Merry Christmas. After I have milked and separated, I decoy Bullet and Babe into the barn, harness, hook them to the sleigh, and away we go to Mom and Dad's for breakfast, with the bells singing in the cold air.

My sister Dee and her husband Tor and their family are there, and after breakfast we open another batch of presents. By the time this is done I am engrossed in another new book, as is Tor; Barby and Dad are hinting that the sun is over the yardarm, while Barbara, Dee, Mom and the older youngsters are getting things ready for dinner. The little kids are trying out their presents and gorging themselves, and it's a dead cinch at least one of them will be sick before the day is over.

Then dinner! A turk as big as a side of beef, Mom's dressing, giblet gravy, mashed potatoes, cranberry sauce, unimportant things like squash, olives, rolls and last but not least, plum pudding and hard sauce—and I mean the sauce is hard! Everybody concentrates on the latter, and Mom invariably sets several things afire trying to light the pudding.

For a couple of hours at least, everybody is pretty sluggish. The dishes get done and that's about all, but after a while there is somebody who has to try out a new pair of skates on the pond, and the youngsters troop off. I am awake enough to hunt up my book, everybody has another nog, and finally Tor and I go home and chore, taking the kids' presents—those they aren't using, wearing or carrying around—before they get them mixed up.

Then back again to a supper of turkey sandwiches, washed down with—you guess—and probably a game of Liverpool rummy, with Dad trying to change the rules, Barbara muttering about not being able to "buy" when she wants to, and bystanders kibitzing loudly.

The neighbors drop in as the evening goes on. Maybe

fifty or more—counting kids. There are greetings, talk, nog, fruitcake, fancy cookies, pound cake and then more nog. Barby and Shelly are extremely forgetful about just where the mistletoe is hung, as are the other girls. Even the more sedate matrons get caught a time or two.

This is Christmas! A day to enjoy, a day to forget the Russians, taxes, politics and cattle prices. A day now, as it was according to the angels nineteen hundred-odd years ago, of "Peace on earth to men of good will." That's what we are here at Christmas, men and women of good will, with our families and friends.

Then early in the morning it's home again through the quiet night, with no sound except for the chuckling bells and maybe a coyote singing his heart out on the far ridge. In past years Barbara most surely would have to be up a time or two before daylight with a child who was suffering from excitement, exhaustion or a stomach ache.

That's the kind of Christmas we've always had, and I hope, always will have. For those two days and nights we aren't thinking of ourselves alone; we're thinking of all the people in the world who are celebrating with us, even if they can only do it in their hearts. We are thinking about our friends in particular, and most especially of those we love. Yes, Christmas is special!

# Good Horses and Bad

MY WIFE USED TO SAY that I spoiled my horses and claimed that if the cattle left a spear or two of hay I'd growl, "By God, look at what they're wasting! We'll just cut them down a bale or two until they start cleaning up everything."

"But," she would continue, "The weaner colts could be standing knee deep in hay, and when I mentioned it to Spike he'd brazen it out with, 'Well, hell, it's not very good horse hay, and they have to pick it over some.' Just as if they weren't getting oats twice a day."

It isn't quite that bad, but she does have something of a point, though I never really gave it much thought until Barbara and I were caught in a sudden blizzard a few years ago. We were better than six miles from the ranch, which lay directly into the northeast wind. The tiny, icy snow-flakes were so thick it was hard to even see our horses' ears, and we were almost blinded by the whipping white chaos. Suddenly from the murk behind me I thought I heard my wife say something and pulled up so she could ride alongside.

"What?" I asked through stiffened lips.

The horse she was riding is black, but both of them appeared solid white and the ski mask Barbara was wearing was frozen so stiff that her voice was muffled. "I see now why you take such good care of your horses."

"Sure enough. Why?" I mumbled.

"Because sometimes you want them to take good care of you."

"Right," I answered, and grinned inwardly. She had the idea; if we'd had anything but those two big sons of guns that I'd known since the day they were foaled—friends whose instinct, surefootedness, strength and sense of direction we could trust implicitly—the two of us would have been found only after the snow went off in the spring. Even a team couldn't have done it, for the country was too rough for a wagon or even a sleigh and when we got home the thermometer registered twenty-eight below, with the wind still howling.

Funny, for years we ranchers have figured that any damn fool should know it's a lot colder when there's a wind, so all this scary talk we get on weather broadcasts lately about "wind chill factor" is irrelevant. The prognosticators who spout it look so pleased with themselves, though, that it would be sort of a shame to disillusion them.

Though I take care of my horses I nevertheless believe that, next to a cat, a horse is about as self sufficient an animal as there is. All they need is some country, and they'll take care of themselves no matter what the weather. They can get by all winter on snow in place of water, and when things are tough I've run them ahead of my cows so their pawing could open the grass for the cattle. But overstock a range with horses, or overgraze it, and they'll ruin it, for a sheep can't pack water to a horse when it comes to being hard on grass. I've seen horses on short feed paw the grass roots up, slobber out the gravel and eat the roots. They'll eat damn near anything, too, including meat. As a matter of fact, under really rank circumstances they can be cannibalistic.

Like a cat, they are independent as all hell, but they prefer company. A horse alone will hunt up some partners; antelope, deer, cattle or even sheep, just as an antelope alone will take up with a bunch of horses. Some of their equine quirks tickle me; they are the sighingest things I know, but that goes right along with their philosophical attitude towards life. I know of no domestic animal that accepts, makes the best of, and adapts to circumstances to the degree that a horse does. I think that's one reason I think so damn much of them—their no nonsense, "if this is what it's going to be then let's get with it" attitude. That, and my belief that most horses need, appreciate and return affection. God knows I have never had my shingle out as a bronc hand, and I've always been leary of bad ones, but I have rapport with horses. When I get acquainted with them we usually end up getting along pretty well.

I respect them, good or bad. If one of the latter, and there are horses that figure a man is their enemy and never get over believing it, a man better take a good long look at his hole card. For a bad horse is a dangerous proposition, particularly a Thoroughbred because that breed is so smart. When you run into one you are way ahead to either kill him, sell him, or if you hate somebody enough, give him away. Anyhow, get rid of him.

I had one like that, and I should have gotten rid of him a lot sooner than I did. I guess I kept him because I thought he'd get over it, for I couldn't understand why he should be bad. His dam was the mare I rode as a kid, Panama, and his sire a good Thoroughbred stud. But somewhere in building him Nature must have gotten careless, for he was a booger.

I called him Weasel, and the name fit to a T. He was mine, so naturally I had to ride him, and it was only after I figured I had him pretty well broken that I finally appreciated what a dirty, human-hating snake he was. He looked good; bay, clean-built and nice-headed; but I have never since trusted a horse whose ears, when they are pricked, point towards each other. Just like I won't milk a bowlegged cow—she'll kick in spite of hell. The Weasel's ears damn near crossed!

I don't believe I ever got a decent ride out of him. He couldn't buck hard, but he way more than made up for it by the fact that he would buck anywhere, and I mean *anywhere*. The worse the ground the better he seemed to like it, and why he didn't kill me, himself or both of us beats me. Either it was just luck, or he was ungodly handy on his feet. Maybe both.

The last time I rode him was from the dude ranch to the Butte ranch, and he must have blown the plug at least fifteen times during the twenty-mile trip. I guess to say, "I rode him," isn't accurate; I stayed aboard him is about all. Coming up the trail out of Big Timber canyon he broke in two three times, and each time bucked off the mountain through sage, boulders, timber and windfalls plumb to the bottom. Oh, I stayed in the buggy, but not through any great riding ability—I was so damn scared by what he was bucking over, through and down, that I couldn't have been pried loose from him with a crowbar. Then when we got to Otter Creek he pulled the same stunt; bawled and built to it down off the rim where it would have bothered a mountain goat to walk.

By the time the trip was over his mane was pulled out from ears to withers, several saddle strings were missing, the cover of my horn looked like a beaver had worked on it, and my fingernails were worn to the quick. It was as tough a day as I've ever put in on a horse.

A day or so later one of the men working for us quit, remarked on "that good looking shadgutted bay" and wondered if "a man could buy him."

I answered that the horse was ganted because we'd had a hard ride—which from my point of view was damn sure the truth—and the upshot was that the man was leading him when he left the place. I sure wasn't sad to see him go.

I never saw the Weasel again, but I ran into the man a year or so later and inquired about the horse.

"Oh, he's fine," was the response. I could almost hear his

mind working, and then he went on, "I had him down in California with me last winter and turned down five hundred for him."

"Dollars?" I asked incredulously, for this was in the '30s.

"Damn right! That's a hell of a horse."

I already knew that, though it was a question of "hell of a horse" meaning different things to the two of us, and I remarked, "I'd sure like to have been there."

"Why?" he asked with a puzzled expression.

"Because I've never actually seen two fools meet face to face, and it must have been interesting."

That was the last I heard of the Weasel, but my bet is that when he went to his just reward he had an awful lot of brands on him. That is if an owner didn't kill him in blind rage before he'd changed hands many times.

For some reason I have never gotten along with grey saddle horses. I had a white gelding that was one of the best I ever sat on, but never a good grey. One I remember vividly as providing me with what was probably one of my most embarrassing moments, though I've had plenty of them. It happened a long time ago, too.

His name was Steve, a soggy, well-built, iron grey gelding. I'd liked his looks, and he hadn't been hard to break, so I was riding him one day when we were trailing cattle over to Big Timber Creek to summer pasture. There was a good-looking girl, a guest at the ranch, that I'd had my eye on, and, as the Frenchman put it, "The campaign was advancing itself satisfactorily." So much so that she and I were putting in a good deal of time together, and of course I was being the pure quill, sure enough cowboy and making it stick. So she was with me this day when a heifer quit the bunch and dived into the timber.

I took to her on Steve, my girl right with me, and just about the time we headed her we came to a pile of poles that had been cut and decked for hauling. I leaned ahead, spurred back of the front cinch, lifted Steve over them, and the next thing I knew his head had vanished. I noted with fleeting—damn fleeting—surprise that my saddle was plumb gone somewhere, and down I came.

I seemed to slide quite a ways on my back, and when I quit the first thing that registered was my girl sitting on her horse watching with a concerned expression. This turned to amusement, and then she started laughing. Hard.

I went over myself, and what I found sure didn't strike me as funny—I'd lit square on a big pile of fresh cow manure, and had slid through it feet first. From my boot heels up to my shoulders, across them, up my neck and into my hair, I was not smeared, but plastered, with the stuff. Even the back of my Stetson.

There was no earthly way I could clean it off, and when the girl shut her mouth to catch her breath I said stiffly, "Suppose you could knock it off long enough to catch my horse for me?" Rude maybe, but I wasn't in a polite mood, everything considered.

Her eyes were round as a horned owl's as she managed to choke out, "Yes." A gleeful giggle got the best of her, and she rode off doubled over her saddle horn with laughter.

Steve looked completely nonchalant when I got him back, which added to my feelings. I pulled my clammy pants up, my clammy hat down, stepped on him, set my reins where I wanted them, told him, "You grey sonofabitch, think you can buck me off, do you"—as though he just hadn't—and spurred him as high and as hard as I could.

We raised quite a ruckus for a little, for not only did the grey buck loud, but I was calling him everything I could think of at the top of my voice and spurring all the way. I rode him to a complete and absolute standstill, and then we hunted up the heifer and took her back to the bunch.

It was a long trip back to the ranch, for though the guests were nice enough to limit themselves to a few polite queries, I caught glimpses of covert smiles when they thought I wasn't looking. The snide remarks of my fellow wranglers I ignored; a tough thing to do since the girl had quit my company for theirs.

When we unsaddled, Bob Langston, a shirttail cousin of mine who was working for the outfit—and competing for the good-looking girls—allowed as how he'd wrangle horses the next morning on Steve and educate him a little. I took no umbrage, for by that time I was a pretty rich proposition—I'd have made a skunk look at his hole card—and all I gave a damn about was getting a bath and different clothes.

I was cleaning the barn next morning when Bob saddled Steve, grinned condescendingly and led the horse around the end of the building to the gate. I was wondering whether I should have bent the manure fork over Bob's head when he smirked, when I heard Steve tune up behind the barn. I was out and around the end before the fork I'd been leaning on had toppled over, and a heart-warming sight met my eyes.

Bob was sitting in the middle of the road, ditto a cloud of dust, and beyond him the grey was going through one of the most ungodly gymnastic displays I have ever seen a horse put on. As I watched him my sense of utter satisfaction was replaced by awe; I had ridden this horse 'til he quit? Why, from what he was doing I doubted I could tie my pants back of the saddle so they'd stay aboard! Still sort of dazed, I saddled another horse, gathered in Steve and led him back to Bob. "Here you are, and it looks like you better get with that education you were talking about giving him," I told him, suppressing a grin.

The response was gratifying. "You can go plumb to hell, and take him with you," and he borrowed the horse I was on.

After serious thought I decided that rage and humiliation were what made me able to ride Steve to a finish. I must have popped something loose in him when I did, or perhaps he was learning fast and well, because nobody ever got him ridden from then on. I never tackled him again. Hell, I'd ridden him once when he bucked, which was better than anybody else had managed, so why crowd my luck. Besides, I doubted that I could get mad enough to do it again. I never cared a whole hell of a lot for the girl after that, and even now I don't remember her with any overwhelming affection, though I sure remember her—and that laugh.

## 20

# They Were From Melville

WHEN BARBARA and I moved to Melville in '37 the Weatherman Bros. branch of the "YMCA" was on its last legs. Fletch was dead, and Cris had not only mellowed considerably, but seemed to have lost his old joie de vivre as well. Yet, like the Phoenix, a new "Y" arose, figuratively speaking, from the ashes of the old. Melville needed it, too.

I raised a whale of a crop of oats the summer of '37. They snowed down early in September, but I put pickup guards on my binder and cut them all one way. Shocking and threshing those sloppy bundles was a nasty job, but when the smoke had cleared the damn crop went well over a hundred bushels to the acre, and the only place I had for the grain was the old saloon we'd vacated when we moved into our new house. The 5000-odd bushels just about filled the old barroom. Incidentally, I borrowed a fanning mill that winter and fanned all that grain by hand in my spare time for the sweet clover seed in it. Got four cents a pound for the seed. Tough times, tough times!

Anyhow, by the next fall the building was empty, and a deputation called on me and asked if they could winter there. They were a pretty motley crew, but nice guys, so I said sure, but be careful of fire. The fact that the "wintering," and summering as well, stretched over the better part of the next thirteen years didn't seem to bother them a bit, nor me, either. It astounded me that the outfit didn't get burned down, some of the deals that went on there, but I do

237

believe that this, the last of the Melville "Y"s, was also the finest!

"Blue" Peterson ramrodded the outfit, ably assisted by "Broken Nose" Dutch and "Grizzly" Browne. Of course membership varied over the years—old faces disappeared due to death, the law and job availability, and new faces took their places—but there was always a staunch nucleus of some half a dozen that acted as a magnet whenever a live one, with wages in his pocket, hit town. To be truthful, we more mundane Melvilleites took more or less of a civic pride in the establishment, and if a man had a little time to spare, anytime, and things were quiet at the saloon, he'd invariably drop on down to the "Y" to see what was going on; and something was, always. As a social, drinking and fighting club it was tops!

I remember riding back up from working stock below town and being hailed from the doorway with, "Hey, Spike, come on in an' have a drink. Ol' Buffalo jest come in."

I said sure, but that I'd have to hobble my stud first. "Hell, bring th' sonofabitch in. He'll feel right to home 'mongst this outfit!" So I rode on in.

I had the drink, and about then the housekeeper of the moment spotted us, grabbed a broom and charged, "Get that critter to hell outa here 'fore he dirties m' floor!"

We retired hurriedly, but I couldn't help thinking as my stud dodged out the door that a little horse manure wouldn't really have been noticeable.

Another time Barbara and I were moving a string of yearlings through town when they suddenly spooked back at us. We got them held, and then looked to see what had caused the excitement. It was "Blue." He'd lurched out the door of the "Y", and was headed for the store across and slaunchwise up the street from us. He was traveling high, wide and handsome, and his progress could best be described as steady by jerks. Every few steps he'd waver to a halt, lean forward and get his sights lined on the store, and then have another bust at it. We both heaved a sigh of relief when he disappeared through the door.

Barbara wanted to start the stock, but I said no, wait until he goes back. Won't be long, for it's a cinch he's too broke to buy much—the "Y" got damn little credit at the store. In a minute out he came carrying a little paper bag, tripped over the edge of the platform and down he went like he'd been head shot. Try as he would, he couldn't make it to his feet, and Barbara, bless her heart, said, "Poor, poor man. I'm going to ride over and help him get up. You hold the cattle."

I said, "No, by God! Hold fire, he'll make it."

Sure enough, abandoning hopes of walking, "Blue" hunted up his bag, clenched it between his teeth and crawled over and into the "Y!" We had a little trouble pushing the yearlings past where he'd been, but outside of us and them, nobody seemed to have paid any attention.

Another time one of the regulars stole a chicken somewhere. It wasn't from me, for I didn't run any of the damn dirty things. Anyhow, they got it picked and cleaned and were fixing to have chicken dinner when a live one hit town, brought a couple of jugs from the saloon, and everybody tied on a good one!

While they were sleeping it off one of the more conservative townspeople prospected the creek bottom for, and finally shot, a horned owl. He carefully picked it, cut off the head and feet and substituted it for the chicken before anybody came to. Well, when they went to cut it up they decided a little parboiling might improve it. So they stoked up the fire and went to work. Directly someone'd get hungry, have another try at carving it up, get disgusted and put it back, so the boiling went on for pretty nearly three days. Of course everyone but the regular habitues knew about the deal, and people kept dropping in and inquiring, "What you cooking? Sure smells tasty."

Then later, "That bird done yet?" or, "When you fellows

gonna quit boilin' that poor damn hen an' eat her?"

At first the answers were sort of cagey. "Oh, a bird 'Dutch' or somebody come up with, I guess." Then the replies got franker. "Must 'a run th' sonofabitch to death, not got her off'n th' roost," and finally, "Toughest damn critter I ever see. I'll ride round them yaller Orpingtons from now on. Why hell, th' thing's got th' water now so's a man can't even stick a fork in *it*!"

Finally they gave the fight to the "hen," and threw out the carcass amid much profanity and bewilderment. It was a couple of months before they found out they'd been jobbed!

Then there was the time one of the members tangled with a transient and had to resort to Spartan methods to take first money. In short, he cold cocked the stranger with a tire iron! As the body lay on the floor, bleeding magnificently about the head, one of the denizens said reverently, "Christ, you've killed th' bastard," and out the door and down into the timber on a high lope went the murderer.

Well, the corpse revived enough to catch a ride out of town, but toward evening the same conservative I mentioned earlier slipped furtively down onto the bottom, finally located the fugitive, told him the body had been taken to Big Timber and that a posse was being gotten together. But, he added, "We'll keep our eyes peeled. Just keep hid good, an' when it's safe we'll get you away. It'll take time, though."

It was three days before the poor devil discovered the truth, and the nights get cold along the Sweet Grass in late August!

Actually it was a wonder there were so few killings right in Melville proper. Oh, the community had a pretty good record, but there were only two I know of in town; Mel Jowell killed Joe Brannin, a deputy sheriff, out back of the Bennett saloon in 1911, and "Tinch" Hannon was shot out in front of the hotel in 1930. The latter was a family argument among Southdowns, a feud that ran back to Georgia, and about who stole whose moonshine. As a matter of fact, almost all the killings in the Melville Country were over moonshine or water, with women a distant third. Consequently most of them took place out of town; near a headgate or a stillhouse. But in keeping with the Melville feeling for fun and frolic, the saying went, "If you think you got a bucking horse, or a running horse, you can get him rode, or outrun, in Melville. An' if you think you're a bronc stomper, or a fighting man, you can get throwed, or whipped, in Melville." In my day the town wasn't really lethal or vicious. Just high-spirited!

We had some great doings in Melville back in the '30s, doings bred by that high spirit, and since I lived right handy I saw most of them and heard about those I didn't see. Of course everybody knew I was tenderhearted when it came to horses, so when anyone rode into town to spend the afternoon, the night or the week, it was pretty near a cinch that I'd fall heir to his mount down at my barn; they knew I'd take care of it, and I did. Once in a while I'd draw a rollicky booger to babysit, and I got run out of my own barn by an outlaw or two. But hell, I had plenty of hay and grain and I won't let a horse go hungry. Besides, I always got thanked and sometimes given a bottle. Though it was usually shy on booze, the intentions were good.

There was a dance in town every Saturday night from spring until fall, and damn but we were glad our house was set back in the bottom and sort of out of sight. My barn wasn't fifty yards from the dance hall, though, and I learned in a hurry not to let the kids over around it on a Sunday morning until I'd prospected the hayloft first, for God only knew what I'd find. Sometimes, after I'd had a look, I wouldn't even let them go over until Monday.

Those dances were something, and I can't hear "Minnie the Mermaid" right now without being carried back over forty years to the warm embrace of the "Melville Stomp."

Hell, these kids today don't know what dancing can be!

The excitement inside the hall wasn't a patch on what went on outside. When "Tip" O'Neil built the gas pipeline up the Yellowstone valley his crew came out from Big Timber with the avowed intention of cleaning out Melville. They tried, I'll give them that, but the town looked about as usual Sunday morning, and we heard that the crew wasn't in shape to do much but lick their wounds until about Wednesday. According to an elderly banker who was a guest at the dude ranch, he personally witnessed forty-two fights that night, and since damn little is ever gained by arguing with a banker we took him at his word.

It was along about this time that John Garner was Vice President. Montana was building roads hand over fist, and it seemed like every road surveyor in the state was a Texan—with all the endearing qualities they so often have away from home. They came to the dances in bunches, bragged, and I'd hazard a guess that more of them were whipped in Melville than at the Alamo.

The cardinal rule at dances, if you wanted to stay out of trouble, was to keep your hands out of your pockets, your mouth shut, mind your own business and keep your back to a wall. I violated that rule one night. An old boy was sacking out his wife, and I, good old Spike, stepped in and told him to lay off. One thing led to another, and we tangled. I was working him over in pretty fair form when his wife, most ungratefully, went to stroking on me with the heels of her shoes, nice long sharp ones. I was lucky to get the two of them turned loose with no damage except a wad of peeled places down both sides of my head, but all my ears were still attached. Since then, if a man wants to put a swelled lip on his loving spouse, it's plumb all right with me; their own damn business as far as I'm concerned.

It was easy to get into trouble at those dances. A friend of mine, guiltless and clean as a hound's tooth, was twosing with his best girl when a man came out of the hall to relieve himself, and picked the spot right in front of their car to do it. He was going strong when the girl switched on the lights. It startled him and did other things, to boot, for when he got buttoned up and dried off he strode back, jerked open the door, pulled my friend out and proceeded to kick the living hell out of the poor innocent, while the girl wrung her hands and tried to explain. My friend later married her, the damn fool!

Then there was the dance night when a little carnival was in town. It had a wrestler. I had wrestled some in college, and the upshot was that we were matched by popular acclaim. Once wouldn't have been so bad, but as the sporting element got more and more oiled we had rematch after rematch. I have no idea how many times, and by daylight we were both played out. He was in some sort of shape, but I used muscles I hadn't since college, and for the next two days I couldn't even roll over in bed without help, and lots of it. I saw the guy several years later at a big carnival while I was rodeoing in Livingston. He remembered Melville, and suggested that we have another go or two at it and split the purse. The trouble was that I remembered, too, so there damn sure wasn't another match. Wouldn't have been even if I wasn't roping the next day. No, sir!

Billy McMahon was a freighter, a good one, who lived at Melville for years and married Louisa Dahl, one of the first white children born in the "Settlement." One of their sons, Clarence, or "Red," lived there practically all his life. He was a dyed in the wool Melvilleite, and something of a poet. He's long gone now, but I asked his brother if I could include one of his poems. He told me yes, so here it is.

## MELVILLE ON SATURDAY NIGHT

*If you feel in the mood for a frolic*
*Or just simply want to get tight,*
*There is no better place on the face of the earth*
*Than Melville on Saturday night.*

*There are places of far more importance,*
*Small towns and great cities so bright;*
*But they just can't compete with that busy main street*
*Of Melville on Saturday night.*

*If you're craving an evening of action,*
*Or care to see a good fight,*
*Just strap on your gun and come on the run*
*To Melville on Saturday night.*

*You'll meet a lot of good people,*
*But, brother, you better do right;*
*Just step to the bar, order drinks for the house,*
*At Melville on Saturday night.*

*If you come to town just to gamble,*
*And it looks like a game were in sight,*
*Just take out a stack, but they better be blues,*
*At Melville on Saturday night.*

*If for trouble you've always been searching,*
*But failed to find an invite,*
*Don't look any more, you can find it right here*
*In Melville on Saturday night.*

*You can travel the whole world over,*
*You can see all its wonders and might,*
*But you'll not find a place on this side of Hell*
*Like Melville on Saturday night.*

Red had it figured about right, and by God, the Melville
Country is proud of him!

# Filly Chasing

## 21

IN MY CONSIDERED OPINION, one of the greatest pleasures God gave man is running horses—filly chasing. Unlike sex it is of necessity an outdoors proposition, and although it, too, is an all season deal, it can get pretty wild when the ground is iron hard and slick with snow, particularly in rough country, but Lord, it's fun! The excitement of handling a string of half-wild horses in a big open country they know to the last inch is something to experience. Actually, too, it is pretty technical, and you damn sure better know horses, and savvy how they work. To boot, you better be mounted on a big, rapid, hardheaded Thoroughbred, grain-fed preferably, and be plumb ready to point him at anything, anywhere, anytime, and wide open. I've heard horse hands swear by a cold blood, or a mustang, for the job, but personally I prefer a range-raised Thoroughbred—if there's anything that the breed has lots of, it's heart, and in my books the latter is a necessity for the work at hand.

It didn't take a reined animal nor a finished one—a Quarterhorse couldn't cut the mustard for he just wasn't geared for it—to bend a bunch behind some smart old brood mare with sage brush in her mane. It took a horse that loved to run; could gallop all day and bust out for maybe a two- or three-mile, sure enough horse race whenever necessary—which could be right frequent. And he had to have nerve. So did his rider.

245

I'd say the filly chasers were made, not born. They grew up with it, and conditions have changed so that there's not much chance to learn the art any more, but I can sure spot a man who has run them. I wouldn't have to see that he's getting a little long in the tooth, or cripples around pretty much when he's afoot; both of which are brands of the breed. I could tell from his talk, for the old-timey filly chasers I grew up around never spoke of horses as anything but "shitters." Always! Anybody who has ever been on a sure enough horse outfit will know why, too.

Most of us in my generation are getting too stiff or stove up to do it right. Maybe it's a question of nerve now, too, for I raised some girls that are filly running boogers, and I realize how much I've slipped when I find myself shuddering at some of the runs I watch them make, and pulling up my horse in the plumb bad places.

It used to be different! I was after a few head of bunchquitters one January day in the mid-30s, about a foot of snow on the ground, and twenty-odd below zero. I was riding Sailor, and along in the afternoon we got those snorty sons-of-guns pretty well lined out on the Dry Creek flat—some poor deluded drylander had plowed it once and turned up all the rocks, the wind had blown away what was between them, and it was about like running a horse up a dry creek bed. About then this outfit made a last run for the upper country and we built to them. We were in overdrive when we hit something and down we came in a cloud of snow. When I quit somersaulting I got up, pulled down my muskrat skin cap which had been jarred loose, ran to Sailor who was up and waiting with an embarrassed expression, and we outran the bunch till we could bend them.

When things were straightened out I took stock, and outside of my pony having a gimpy foreleg, and my neck feeling like it'd been shortened a foot or so, everything seemed in good shape. I had gotten warmed up in the run, though, and pretty soon sweat began to leak down from under my cap into my eyes. I wiped it away and the back of my mitt turned red, so I looked myself over a little more carefully.

Darned if the front of my sheepskin coat wasn't covered with freezing blood, so I gingerly explored under the cap and found I'd split my head from the hair line above my forehead as far back as I dared feel. Wasn't much I could do about it, and it was a long way from my heart anyhow, so I pulled the cap down as tight as I could to dam things a little, and we finally corralled the ridge runners at the home ranch. Time I tended my horse, worked on his bad leg and got to the house, I was pretty messy and we almost had to cut the cap off me. It was only then that I realized the heavy fur had probably kept the rock I'd hit from killing me. But a miss is as good as a mile, though she smarted some when Dr. Baskett sewed it up in Big Timber the next day, and Sailor was sound again shortly.

Dad was a horse running man; he had the wherewithal to run, and to run it with. We nicknamed him "Many Ponies." One spring—in the early '40s, I believe it was—he, I, and my brother-in-law, Tor Anderson—a horse hand—gathered the "No Bush" range, some 15 sections split into two pastures. All across the two we bounced the lead from one to another of us at a hard run, keeping an eye on the gaps between us and on the outside so nothing could slip back up a coulee or around a hill. Sort of like tennis, with the herd growing with each pocket, draw and flat, for no horse alive can see his own kind running and not join them. When everything was finally in the wide, fenced alley that led around two sides of the last section to the county road, Dad loped across the angle, opened the gate and took the lead up the lane. I don't know how many head we had, but when we got to the lane with the tail end there were horses strung up it as far as we could see, and that was about four miles! It was around eight miles to Melville from the upper end of our range and as we came up the street, somebody called from the saloon door, "How the hell many horses you fellers got anyways? Paul went through better'n a hour ago with the lead, an' they been comin' ever since. Got time for a snort?"

Since our drag was a little leg weary we took the time, but by evening had the works home. The next couple of days we sorted them—dude horses, youngsters, brood stock and work stock, moving each to their respective range, and ended up with around 30 to 40 big, stout, unbroken stuff, ranging from five to seven years old, in the corrals. Pop looked them over, picked out a dozen or so to be broken and decided, "The rest of these snorty boogers would make dude horses, but it would take a lot of time. The Remount has closed up on account of motorizing the cavalry, so let's take these down to Art Langman's big horse sale in Billings. I think it's in about three days."

That night it began to rain, and, because the weather in Montana never does anything halfway, by morning no stock truck could get in, much less out with a load. But Dad was Dad, and when he decided to do something, he did it! So we loaded a portable loading chute and a couple of rolls of snow fence into the ranch truck and sent it ahead down through Melville and out to where the paved road from Big Timber came to an end at a bridge across a draw. We three saddled up and headed the horses after them.

When we arrived, the chute was set up about fifty feet down the highway from the bridge, on the paved side. Snow fence was stretched from the bridge corners to the sides of the mouth of the chute, a stock truck was backed up to it, and others were waiting. Nobody but Dad would have dreamed it would work, but be damned if it didn't!

We cut out about a truckload, lined them at the open end of the bridge at a run, gave them a little time as they hit the wings at the yon end, and they poured up that chute like they'd been born to it! When the lead hit the front of the truck and started the surge back, sort of like water in a bath tub, the gate dropped and there was a truck loaded and ready! The few extra head went back to the main bunch, and we held them as quietly as we could until another truck was ready to load.

There were problems, though. Whenever somebody came by on the highway, if they were in a hurry, we had to dismantle at least half our rigging to let them through. There were some who thought they were in a hurry I'm sure, but after a look at us they decided they really weren't, for by the time we'd made a run or two to bend our stock in the mud, we were a pretty raunchy looking outfit.

Local people, when they came by, would park their outfits and enthusiastically join the proceeding, for just as a horse has to join any other horses he sees running, a rancher just can't resist getting into any stock work that's going on, particularly if people are having trouble. We damn sure were, too, for as each remnant from a load escaped back to the bunch, the whole works got goosier and harder to hold, and the last couple of truckloads were sort of like trying to bunch ants, or hogs. So we were glad to welcome everybody!

One who was especially helpful was Bud Brannin, foreman for the Stevens outfit on American Fork. He'd been to a funeral or something and was all slicked up when he arrived, but he's a hand afoot or ahorseback, so out he got and proved it again and again. Time we were done and he'd charged around in that ankle deep gumbo and steady drizzle, the only thing about him that wasn't mud covered was his grin. That he wore continually, for he was having a hell of a time!

There were fringe benefits, too. Stan Hanson, the Melville saloonkeeper, arrived with a load of stock from the liquor store in Big Timber, immediately tapped it and joined us. So every time we got a truck loaded, we'd have to have a quick one in self congratulation, and maybe another in preparation for the next go-round.

I've never had a wilder afternoon, nor more fun! I've never seen anything quite like it either—guys trying to run with maybe ten pounds of mud on each foot, roaring advice, whooping with laughter or excitement; people, horses, riders going down in a spray of mud, bouncing up and off again as hard as they could go. The mud softened the falls. My horse lit square on me twice when he tried to cut back, but each time he just mashed me into the softness and neither of us got anything but dirtier!

I saw Hanson make a hell of a run to head a pony in the last truck load, part of a gallon jug of wine—it came in gallons in those days—hanging to one finger. The horse turned, but Hanson either tripped or just plumb played out, sprawled full length and slid, the jug arching through the air. I'd been spurring my tired mount from the opposite direction, and as the jug flew by, he dodged, snorted, struck at it and skidded to a stop beside Hanson. The latter looked up, and I swear all I could see of him were his teeth and eyes. "By God, Spike," he grinned, "how'd you like that for footracin'? Pretty limber, hey!" The jug was all right, too. The mud had cushioned it. I've often wondered what would have happened if a highway patrolman had come by. Probably he'd have helped us, though!

Anyway, when the last load was all set to go, we gave the driver a sack of footropes, halters, combs and brushes from our truck to leave at the yards for us, everybody had a last drink in celebration of a job well done, there were thanks and congratulations all around and everybody went on about his business. We jogged on home, unsaddled and cleaned up. I still don't see how we did it! If I hadn't been there I wouldn't believe we *had* done it! Dad was sure something!

After we were presentable and had eaten supper, we loaded our riding gear in the car and ground out to the highway and down to Billings, where we put up at the

Northern Hotel. Lots of horse hands in town, so it was late, or maybe I should say early, before we got to bed.

The next day we spent cleaning up our string, brushing, combing manes, and pulling those long gumbo matted tails, and we put the footropes we'd brought to good use. By that evening those big colts looked good, had learned to stand reasonably well, and all three of us were sporting horse tracks in various places.

The sale started early next day, but since we'd been late in getting entered, our stock wouldn't go for a while. Dad went over to watch the sale, and Tor and I sat on the fence and watched the show that was going on around us. The Billings Livestock Yards were plumb full; all kinds, all sizes, all colors. Good horses, poor, no account. Gentle, wild, locoed, and a few rank, dirty outlaws. What tickled us was that at any time, in any direction, we could see some old boy's head popping up and then down out of sight behind a corral fence as his mount bucked with him. Occasionally a pair of boots would replace the head! *Any* direction and *any* time, and we were congratulating ourselves that *we* didn't have to do *that* when Dad came back and announced, "Those colts'll look better and bring more under a saddle, so we'll ride them through." Real casual.

When the initial shock had worn off, and I could get my voice to working, I expostulated, "Godamighty, Dad, these things aren't even halter broken!"

"I know, I know," he brushed it aside, "we've handled them enough so's they know us, only us, and they remember us from their home range, to boot. Hell, they're big old country kids in a strange place and we're familiar. They won't buck if we're careful. I'll bet on it. But take your spurs off."

Once again we did something I wouldn't have thought possible. Dad decided we could do it, and I be damned if we didn't! The three of us rode every one of those broncs through the ring and not one of them blew the plug! I grant you they weren't in the lead when it came to handling and we sure didn't bust them out, but they looked good under saddle and they sold well, too. Actually the poor devils were scared to death. They weren't alone—so was I, and I know I didn't take a deep breath until I was unsaddling my last one. Dad was as tickled as a pup with a gunny sack and said, "See. What'd I tell you."

I don't think anybody in the crowd caught on except a few horse men, and they didn't tip our hand. Oh, they had some fun with us. Sid Vollin of the "CBCs," one of the biggest, if not *the* biggest, horse outfits in North America, kept making sweeping gestures with his hat as he sat talking to his neighbors in the stands, and grinning each time. Art Orser, a bronc hand from away back and a friend of long standing, was a damn nuisance and kept up a string of loud remarks like, "Let's see him back," or "Pick up his feet," or "How's he stand to git on and off of," or "Hell, let's see him work." All the time with a grin like a skunk eating garlic! Then he came chuckling around after the sale, demanded a drink, and got one! It was horse work all the way, that whole deal, and I learned that you can accomplish the impossible if you believe you can do it, are lucky, and *know* horses.

Somehow the hereafter is the least of my worries. It's a cinch I'll foregather with more than a few of my friends in hell, if I end up there, and some of them will be old filly chasers, with a hitch in their getalong. If not, what could be finer than a bright spring day in the lovely country under the Crazies, at a long lope on a good horse, with the wind in my face, the smell of lupine and sage in the air, and a string of slick, spooky colts to be gathered. Hell, I've already had heaven!

# Child Care

## 22

LOOKING BACK to when my children were youngsters, I wonder how the hell, between Dad and me, they survived. Not so much my son, Tack, for he was always more interested in machinery than in livestock. Oh, he could make a hand ahorseback when he had to, but, since he took to them, I mostly left the tractors and mechanical things to him. I didn't like anything about them, and so we were both happy.

The three girls were a different kettle of fish. They loved stock work, horse work in particular, and Lord knows they got plenty of it. Whenever we get to talking horses nowadays I am sure to be asked, "Remember when you put me on so and so?", or, "Remember when you and Scrumper (my Dad) put me on such and such and she ran off with me?" But always with a smile. The trouble is that I do remember, and remembering, shudder. I guess a man's judgment gets better as he gets older, and I can see now that mine could have stood a lot of improvement when the girls were little. But their judgment, as regards *their* children, sure isn't anything to brag about. I'm afraid it's my fault—but to see my grandchildren ahorseback is like watching an old movie.

We have run lots of horses on lots of country for a long time, and I pressed the girls into service early. Not as kids just to go along, but as hands, to do a job. Barby, our eldest, started when she was about a long five or short six.

253

Poor kid! I was green at the job of being a father and raised her like a boy, making no allowances, I am afraid, for either her age or her sex. The result was that she made a hand too early. I asked too much, and she tried to give it to me and always sort of got the rank end of the deal. Besides she was serious, red-headed, with a temper to match, headstrong and bull-headed enough so we squabbled pretty often. The tough little devil never gave an inch, either.

She couldn't have been much over six when I had to make a trip to Billings, and the roads being what they were in those times, I was gone for a couple of days. A while after I got home, Barby keeled over at supper, so we took her in to the doctor in Big Timber and found that she had some cracked ribs. It was only after threatening the close-mouthed little rascal with a spanking that we found out what had happened; I had been halterbreaking some coming yearling colts, Barby had been helping, and while I was gone she had decided to finish the job for me. One of them had stomped her while she was trying to halter him in the chute, and it was only when she passed out at the table a few days later that anyone knew she'd been hurt or even had gotten into any trouble! I told her that next time she was trying to halter an unbroken horse in a chute to do it from up on the outside, for God's sake, not down in the chute, and it wasn't long until she was riding with me again. As the man says, she bruised easy but she healed quick, though actually she didn't bruise very damn easy.

When she was about twelve I gave her a little bay gelding we called Eddie Bateman. His dam was a fine Hancock mare bred by Mr. Ed Bateman down at Knox City, Texas, and his sire another Bateman horse, Chief's Big Pete, a grandson of Peter McCue. Eddie, though pretty much of a runt, turned out to be the biggest chunk of horse I have ever seen wrapped up in a hide that small—yes, or several sizes larger! Trouble was, like the Hancock blood sometimes does, he wanted to buck, and, once again like a Hancock, when he did come apart he was damn sure hard to ride.

Naturally, when I gave Barby the horse I told her she would have to break him, and she started in the evenings after school. I was calving, so didn't have time to pay much attention to how she was getting along. After a time, though, I did notice that she had gotten him halterbroken, and a while later I saw her with a saddle on him.

I rode in from checking the heifers one evening, and Barby was aboard Eddie in the big round pole corral, walking him around it. I watched a while and then called, "Speed him up."

No answer, so I led my horse over, hobbled him, and climbed into the corral with the youngster and the colt, telling her, "Hell, he'll have to learn to do something besides walk. Get after him."

Once again no answer, so I gathered a handful of little rocks, remarked, "Well, if you won't, by God, I will," and, standing in the middle of the pen, began throwing rocks at the bay's rump.

Barby snarled something at me, and Eddie, after his first startled jump, broke into a trot, and after a few more well-placed pebbles, into a nice free lope.

After a few circles, her mount keeping a wary eye on me, and his rider a glare of raw rage, I said, "Turn him back into the fence and go the other way."

There was something in a bitter tone that sounded suspiciously like "Go to hell," so, just before they got even with me I stepped out and put my arm up as though I was about to launch another stone. Eddie ducked away from me into the poles, came around easily and loped back the other direction. I let them go a round or two, then said, "Now you do it."

There was no sound this time, but just before I stepped in again, Barby turned the colt back. Then after a circle or so, they reversed again, smooth as silk. "See," said I, and started out over the fence.

"Damn you," I heard behind me.

"What was that?" I asked from the top of the corral.

"I said damn you, Dad, and I meant it. Sometimes I hate you!"

Silence except for the thud of the gelding's hooves. Then, ruefully, "I've never gotten him out of a walk before without getting bucked off, and I've tried it lots."

"Well, he's going fine now, and handling some, too. I'll bet he doesn't buck again, either."

"If he does," she returned grimly, "I'll ride him—and Dad, thanks."

"My pleasure, Red," and I grinned. "I enjoyed it."

"I'll just bet you did!"

He did buck again a time or two, but only after he was broke. Once was at a branding when Barby roped a calf on him for the first time, and it was partly my fault. Dad had always claimed anything worth catching was worth keeping, so I grew up roping tied hard and fast. I admit there have been times when I sort of wondered just how damn good his advice was, but I have all my fingers. To be shy one or two seems to be the mark of a dally man. Anyhow, the kids copied me, and I didn't spot the trouble until the wreck had commenced. Otherwise, seeing as she was in a corral and could afford making a present of her rope to a critter in case of trouble, I'd have told her to dally on the first animal she roped. Also I figure there is no use having a back cinch unless you keep it tight, but Barby had always argued the point with me.

Eddie didn't particularly take to that big calf bouncing around on the rope, and when the saddle reared up and the flank rigging grabbed him his disapproval was vigorous. The end result was that Barby took up a homestead, while he ended up wrapped in the rope and down. They both learned, and from then on out the little devil was a popping good rope horse, and right today a man'd have trouble slipping a knife blade between Barby's flank cinch and her horse's belly, anytime.

It turned out that Eddie could run like a dirty devil, and Barby got chesty about it. So I matched her a race one day as we rode back to the dude ranch after working cattle. It was close, and we were about even when she tried for a little more gas and spurred a little far back.

An outraged Eddie immediately turned the horse race into a bronc ride, and Barby took a real poor second money. To add insult to injury he didn't even bother to run off—just stood and waited while she got up, retrieved her hat, limped over and got on. Then off he went, genial as could be. He just, by God, wasn't about to put up with indignities like spurs in his flanks, and he'd let her know it! I suggested that a bat was the usual equipment for a race, not spurs, but at the time, my advice was not received gracefully. However, I noticed Barby had made the trade whenever she raced him from then on.

Actually she got to be a good jockey, and she sure was under pressure the first real race she rode. It was a match race in Big Timber between our Chief's Big Pete stud and a horse a newcomer rancher had brought into the country with him. This man got pretty overbearing about how he could outrun any damn thing in Sweet Grass County for a quarter. I took it for about so long, and then the match was on.

Pete could run, for Mr. Bateman had taken him to Eagle Pass before I got him, and he had done pretty well. I arranged for a local boy who had been up on a few running horses to ride for me, while this other man imported a California jock from Bay Meadows. Then, to sew things up, a couple of his friends conveniently fell in with my boy the night before the race, and by morning he was so hung over he couldn't have laid on a bed without falling off.

There were several other jocks around the track, but I

was leary, particularly under the circumstances, of getting somebody I didn't know. So I collared Dad, explained things and asked him to keep Barbara busy. Then I snuck Barby away from her mother "to help me get Pete ready," and when we were safely down at the paddock, told her she was about to ride the stud for me.

"Gosh, Dad," was her reply. "Thanks. But with that runty saddle aren't you afraid Pete will run out from under me when he starts?"

"Hell, Red, what do you think a mane is for? Get a good hold on it till he breaks, then gather him. He knows what to do."

I prudently stayed out of sight as the two horses paraded to the gate, but I saw Barbara call to Barby and engage in animated conversation, if that is the right word, with Dad. Then she made a run for the exit, but it was too late; the bell clanged and the race was on.

Barby and Pete won by so far the other horse didn't show in the finish picture, and it was a proud little girl on a proud big dun horse that jogged back up the track to me. I was sort of proud, too.

"You're a race horse rider, Red," I told her. "How did it go?"

"It was fun! One second he was standing, the next he was running. I don't think I'd even have needed his mane. He's like a great, big, smooth engine. After a little way I heard noises behind us, so I hit him once with the bat. I thought he had been running, but damn, Dad, then it felt like he'd just been loping. Oh, Peter, I love you!" and she leaned ahead and hugged the bronze neck.

It took some talking to square myself with Barbara. But with Barby so happy, Pete so handsome, Dad busting his buttons with pride and the applause from the crowd, she had trouble staying on the fight—though I was warned there'd better not be a next time.

Shelly, our middle girl, six years younger than Barby,

was a runt, and when she started riding with me wouldn't have weighed forty pounds soaking wet. All big eyes and grin, great rapport with a horse and she never met one she was afraid of. Still hasn't.

I remember an instance gathering horses up along Spring Creek one bright May day. Dad, myself, Barby and Shelly were making the circle. Shelly was about seven and aboard an old grey, half Thoroughbred mare, Snooper. We had split into pairs, and I saw her and Dad chouse a string of horses out of the bottom and make a run to bend them away from the upper country. The ground was ungodly rough, and they hit a cutbank wash I knew was about ten feet wide, and at least as deep, at a hard run.

Dad was in front, and over the rumble of hooves I heard him yell something. Then they were across, the bunch headed, and Barby and I were kept busy holding our side.

When the horses were lined out for the ranch, Dad in the lead, I loped up beside Shell in the drag and was greeted with sparkling eyes too big for her little heart-shaped face, a wide, gap-toothed grin, and "Gee, Dad, that was fun!"

I had been curious, so I asked, "What was Dad yelling for? I couldn't make it out."

"Oh, when we came to that deep place, he yelled, 'Don't follow me. Go around it.' But Snoopy was in the air before Colonel lit, and there we were."

"Yes," I prompted.

"So he said, 'Well, hell, come along then,' cause we had."

Dad was always a great one to keep a running horse or two handy, just in case. He and Barby were so much alike that they bickered pretty badly, so Shelly drew the job of exercising his horses. Barbara took a dim view of my approach to horses and kids, and an even dimmer view of Dad's. So, discretion being the better part of valor, I cautioned Shell not to say much about what she was doing. She learned fast, never got excited, used her head, and she and the horses had the time of their lives. I only let her ride them around cattle, but even so every now and then those big hot horses took that little girl for some rapid trips.

One morning, working cattle on the hill below the ranch, she came by me on a big Thoroughbred like a bat out of hell, and called, "Looks like Johnny's taking me for a little run. I'm fine. We'll be back. Don't worry." Worry I did, though—the stud looked so damn big, and she so little—but pretty quick back around the hill they came, happy as larks.

Dad fit her out with a hot booger of a mare when I was back at the Mayo Clinic getting cobbled together after a wreck I had on the side of a mountain with a horse, a steer and a tied rope. I still chuckle over a letter I got while I was there:

> Dear Dad,
> Latakia ran off all the time. I couldn't hold her. I told Scrumper and he said show her some country. I tried but it was me got showed the country. She ran away today and I was glad when she stopped by the fence. I led her home. Scrumper came by and asked why I was walking. I told him and he said by God he would teach her. He got on her and she ran away with him. Gee he was mad.
> Love,
> Shelly

Dad never mentioned the incident, but I brought it up when I got home later. Then he grinned shamefacedly and said, "You ought to ride a runaway in a kid's saddle sometime," but Shelly never drew the mare again.

I think it was a couple of years earlier that we were making a gather on the head of Wheeler Creek. Up there the creek cuts through a big flat at the bottom of a steep draw that must be a quarter mile wide and about half that in depth. Shelly was mounted on Victory, a fine gentle old Thoroughbred mare that had been retired from our relay string. The stock was fat and snuffy, and we were having quite a run when the old lady suddenly came out of retirement, gathered in the bit, snatched some slack, and away they went. I don't think she realized she had a rider, Shell was so small; just figured she was loose and joined the parade. The horses poured off into the draw wide open, Victory on their tails and closing fast, and when I got to the lip where I could see, she and Shelly were right in amongst the leaders halfway up the yon side. They must have hit the creek laid straight and jumped it right in the middle of a hundred or more horses. Damn but I was glad to see that little figure still in the buggy!

The run eased off before they got to the far corner of the pasture. Victory had shot her wad, and we found Shelly busily trying to move the horses back the way they had come. As we rode up she chirped, "Golly, Vic can run, Dad. And jump, too. I had a great time!"

"Honey," I told her, "You'll do," and I meant it.

Shell and Barby had many a match race around the place, and I got used to a horse coming home empty occasionally; followed in due time by a shamed girl afoot and a gleeful one ahorseback. They even matched one at the county 4H fair that added considerably to the pro-ceedings.

There was a kids' race advertised, so we sacked up a green broke filly Dad was high on, and as company in the trailer, Dad's Thoroughbred stud, Red Eagle, affection-ately known to the family as Johnny Bones. When we got to the grounds there was only one other entrant in the kids' race besides Barby on the filly, but the board said they'd have the race for the two of them anyhow. About then the other pair pulled out, and they were fixing to cancel the event, much to Barby's disappointment, when Dad asked, "Does it matter who the other rider is, or what they ride?"

The response was that it didn't matter as long as it was a kid, could ride, and it was all right with the parents.

"Hold fire then," Dad told the board, "I've got another entrant. We came to run horses," and to me, "Hurry up and get her, Spike." The damn coward!

Well, I went over to the stands where Barbara was with the children and invited them to come have an ice cream cone. Carol was a baby then, so her mother demurred, as I had hoped she would, but Tack and Shell came along with me. When they had the cones I sent one for his mother back with Tack, and asked Shelly, "How'd you like to ride Johnny against Barby and Spooks?"

She grinned from ear to ear, "You bet!" On our way to the paddock she confided, "I knew what you and Scrumper wanted, Dad."

"Sure enough?"

"Yes, 'cause you'd never take me away from watching a race for," with complete scorn, "an ice cream cone." Then, thoughtfully, "Gee, I'd think Mom could figure that out." She was only eight!

We had quite a time with that race, and it's still talked about around the country. If it were now I suppose we'd be had up for child abuse or something. Anyway, Spooks was green and excited, and Barby bucked off in the paddock. After she was back aboard and had straightened out the filly, we set Shell up on Johnny and a judge asked, "Can that child ride that big horse?"

"You damn right," answered Dad; Shell was *his* jock.

"But can she stop him?"

"Hell, no," said Pop, "but he'll run down after a while." So, pretty dubiously, the race was allowed.

We slipped the two up back of the stands to the start at the head of the quarter mile straightaway, and Barbara didn't know Shelly was in the deal until they hit the finish line. Barby and the filly won, but John was just getting into gear, and on around the half mile track he and his jockey went.

As they came around the first time, both just having a ball, some well-intentioned busybody started out to try and stop them. Dad grabbed him, told him to stay the hell out of things, and the big stud and his small rider went on for another circuit. When the two of them had had a nice mile and a quarter run Johnny pulled up beside us; we'd been calling to him all down the stretch. Everybody was pleased but Barbara!

When our youngest girl, Buckshot, six years Shelly's junior, was too little to ride with us, she would repair to the corral and join Big Pete. When she was three years old I had let her sit on him as I cooled him after a race, and they became sidekicks. They were the damndest pair! The first I knew of their relationship was when I went down to the barn to feed one evening and heard Buck talking like a magpie somewhere inside. I called her, and out of the stud stall into the corral she came at a hard run, squealing loudly. At her heels, his ears pinned back and his head snaked out towards her, came the big dun, the picture of a stallion on the fight!

Spooked to the core, I opened my mouth to bellow, but before I could make a sound, the child stopped, turned and held up her hand. Pete set the brakes, reared high over the little figure, and as his fore feet dropped gently to the ground, reached out and carefully took the stock pellet she held in her hand. "Peter and I are playing, Dad. What do you want?", she grinned at me.

"Nothing, I guess, Bucky," and I wiped my forehead. It damn sure needed it, too!

I found the two of them sleeping together in the sun several times, Pete flat on his side and Buck either pillowed against his neck and shoulder, or cuddled against his chest behind his forearms. I came in with a string of horses one day when they were like that, and that damn stud just lifted his head and cocked his ears, but never moved a hair until the noise woke the little girl and she got up to see what was going on. Then he bounced to his feet and blared around the corral like a booger. Never a move, though, until his partner was safely out of the way!

Another time I watched the two of them from the kitchen window. The big dun was stretched out flat, and Buck climbed onto his ribs, started talking to him and thumping her heels. First an eye opened, then he lifted his head, and with a philosophical sigh finally tucked his legs under himself and rolled up on his stomach. Buck straddled him, if you could call it straddling when her legs stuck straight out, kept talking and thumping, and pretty quick he got carefully to his feet. She fumbled in her pocket, leaned 'way ahead and held out her hand. Pete craned around and took a pellet from the little fingers. When he'd eaten it, the thumping started again and soon he was loping easily around the corral, stopping occasionally to reach back for a tidbit from his happy rider. When I mentioned it to Buck she told me seriously, "Peter thinks he's a people, I think, Dad." Possibly it was the other way around!

When Buck was finally big enough to go along with us I put her on old Mickey, who, while a first class cow horse and a very great lady, was not exactly a fireball—after all, in her time she'd started the other two girls—and we all got tired of wails of, "Wait for me," from behind us. Besides it was hard on Mick, so we fit Buck out with Candy.

The latter was a surly acting, cross-grained, independent runt of a mare. She was overwhelmingly opinionated, but she was tough and couldn't have been hurt with anything less than a pick handle. She and Buck went round and round at first and finally ended in a Mexican standoff, but they were good for one another. To watch the two of them, Buck bareback, wrangle my saddle horses out from among the cottonwoods and willows in the horse trap was a sight to behold! How that little mare usually stood up, the turns she made, and how that little girl stayed aboard her, beat me! It made a hellish rider out of the child, though, and gave her nerves that have scared me ever since, for they had a few spectacular wrecks. The only trouble was that

Candy was so short-legged that when we got to working horses in the open she kept getting outrun. By that time, too, Barby was away at college and Shelly was off at high school except on weekends, so I needed Buck badly; Dad was too stove up to run horses except in his Jeep, which naturally limited his scope—though damn little—and there was just too much country and too many horses for Barbara and me to get the job done alone. So Buck, when she was ten, drew a newly broken, four-year-old filly.

We couldn't have made a better match. Funny, too, for the filly actually belonged to Buck. Her dam was Barbara's fine mare, Sleepy, and when I bred the mare to Big Pete her mother promised Buck that the colt would be hers. So, when I came in from tending the stock one wet, misty May morning and announced that Sleep was fixing to foal right quick, Bucky begged off from school and midwifed the great event. Reminded me of an old gelding the way she fussed and worried, and when a fine chestnut filly had finally struggled to her wobbly legs and was noisily getting her first meal, I asked the small girl, "What you going to name her, Honey?"

She looked up from where she was petting the slick little shoulder and answered, "I've been thinking while Sleep was having her, and I believe Misty Morning would be nice, don't you?"

"Yes, but it's sort of long, and we already have a Misty. What do you say, Barbara?"

"Well, Carol,"—that was Buck's given name, but only her mother used it—"she looks exactly like Sleepy. Why not call her Ditto?" and that was her name from then on out. Of course she was registered differently, but for the twenty-odd years of her life the filly, and mare, was Ditto, or Dit, and she was instrumental in developing Buck into a filly chasing thing.

Lord, but they were a pair. The words, "joie de vivre," were invented, I swear, to describe the two of them! They complemented one another, and taught each other. To Buck's delight Dit had a way, when she was loping along and nothing exciting was going on, of jumping straight in the air with a squeal of sheer delight. Not a mean hair in her, just exuberance.

I remember one day in late May, not long after we'd matched the two, when Buck and I were taking the coming yearling colts from the ranch, where they'd been fed since being weaned in October, to their summer range some four miles up under the mountains. Yearlings are home-loving little devils, and as soon as we got them across the creek the strangeness and size of the country got the best of them— there *had* to be boogers everywhere, and they weren't about to leave their known and safe surroundings. So we had undiluted hell. At least I did; Buck and Dit were enjoying every minute of it!

I had just built a new ditch below the house, and it was probably six feet deep and perhaps ten feet wide where it crossed a hump just off from the creek. The colts made a run back for the corrals. A yearling is hard for a horse that is packing a man to outrun, but I got it done and turned them at the creek. Down along it they went, tails in the air. Forgetting the new ditch I bellowed, "Bend 'em, Buck," and she built to them as hard as her horse could run.

I suddenly remembered that damn canal as she and the colts poured toward it, and my neck turned chilly. All ten yearlings, watching over their shoulders, fell into it in a magnificent cloud of spray. Dit jumped them and the ditch effortlessly, and as she did Buckshot looked down at the chaos below and giggled!

The wreck sort of sobered the little bastards, and we got a good go until just as we put them into the pasture. Then one gelding missed the gate, tried to jump the fence, hit it with both front legs and turned a complete somersault. It knocked him a little silly, so I jerked down my rope, boiled in, caught him as he got unsteadily to his feet, and we looked him over for any damage.

There wasn't a mark on him for a wonder, so we turned him loose. As he lined out for his partners Buck told me with a grin, "I don't believe I'd sell that colt as a steeplechaser, Dad. Might hurt the reputation of your stock."

Buck was always full of wise remarks, but she was such a cheerful child that they were never unpleasant. When she was in high school she borrowed a ride with a classmate on his motor scooter, and her leg was badly broken when a woman driver hit them. When the hospital called we beat it to town and hurried into her room where she lay smeared with blood and dirt, for she hadn't been worked on as yet. Her face didn't seem to have suffered any damage, and I made the usual inane remark about, "It could have been worse."

An impish grin crossed her dirty face, "Yup, I know, Dad. It could have been you."

I got even a few years later. I had a hell of a wreck with a big stout gelding back in the hills. When the smoke cleared I stood up, my ribs gritted wickedly, and I dropped back to the ground with a grunt. Buck had been with me and hurried up to lean over me, a tear slowly rolling down each cheek. "Are you all right, Dad? Does it hurt?" she asked anxiously.

I managed a weak grin at the solemn face above me, "Only just when I laugh, Bucky," and added, "We're even now, by God!"

"Dammit, be serious, Dad. You've always said it was more gentlemanly to be crippled by a horse than by a machine, though, so you ought to be happy," and the corners of her mouth lifted in a tremulous smile.

Barby, Shelly, and Buckshot, hands from away back, all three. They know what a cow or a horse is going to do before the animal does, for they savvy how a cow or horse thinks. Moreover, when I send any of them to check on something they damn sure cover what a stockman should notice: if, and where a fence needs work; whether there's enough salt; the state of the feed and water; if there's a cow that hasn't been sucked, and why; does a calf look poorly, and for what reason; what, if anything, needs doctoring; perhaps a youngster's curiosity has ended in a snake bite or a nose full of porcupine quills. Why, hell, if too many magpies should fly out of a brush patch those girls will go in and find out why; and they know what *are* too many magpies!

They know cattle and handle them right, but first, last and always they are horse hands—always *where* they are supposed to be and *when* they are supposed to be there, in a corral or in the open. They were raised on good horses, appreciate them, and God knows they can use them. When they have something to bend it's a question of "damn the ground and the devil take the hindmost"! I raised them and taught them, but I haven't the sand to stay with them now. Even Dad, a horse-running man, remarked to me shortly before he died, "Those girls of yours are sure hands. But sort of wild." That, from him, than whom there was no wilder!

# Muy Hombres

## 23

GRAMP ALWAYS SAID he'd never hire a man that wore gloves and smoked; claimed they would always be taking time out to take off their gloves to roll a cigarette and light it, and then waste more time putting the gloves back on again. A pipe smoker is worse; a damn pipe is always going out. Gramp's theory was good, but I had a hay crew of Mexican boys that would have made him look at his hole card. They were working boogers, and I never saw any of them without a cigarette in evidence. Of course they didn't wear gloves. I don't believe they even knew what they were.

During the second world war ranch hands were hard to come by, so, with the hay ready to put up on my place, Tor's and Dad's and nobody to do it, in desperation I made a trip to Billings to see if I could come up with somebody. The upshot was that I came home with eight Mexicans. They'd been thinning sugar beets, and were all done. At the time I didn't know that the deal was illegal, and that they'd been waiting to be shipped back home when I ran into them. Turned out it didn't really matter, for I took them so far back to the head of the creek that the government lost track of them.

They were from a little town, Angamacutiro, in the state of Michoacan. Sure enough country boys who had never been away from home before, let alone from Mexico, and not a one could say as much as, "sic 'em," in English. We

269

had lived on the border for three winters just before the war, had bought and shipped home a string of Mex cattle, "corrientes," in '39, and I had gotten acquainted with, and liked, the country people. I also spoke pretty good cowpen Spanish, albeit a little dirty; which sure as hell never fazed a Mexican; so we got along fine.

They were sure good men, and they afforded me many a chuckle, to boot. They all claimed they had milked, so I put a couple to tending our two milk cows morning and night. I dropped in to see how they were doing the first time, and here was one on each side of the same cow milking to beat the band. She wasn't happy about this newfangled double barrelled proposition, and was testing their air first one and then the other. They just hunched in under where she couldn't get a square lick at either of them, and when they spotted me one of them said matter of factly, "Ayee, mucha bronca," and they both grinned broadly. I'm here to state that my cows sure had learned to stand hitched by the time haying was over.

My work horses learned to savvy Spanish I am sure, though at first they had some trying times. I had to learn never to send more than one man with a team unless I specified who was to do the driving. Otherwise each man would be handling a line, sometimes a couple of men. I found, too, that if I told one guy to drive he'd lord it over the other. Besides, the one who wasn't driving would figure I didn't think he *could* drive, and his pride would be hurt. Mexicans are hell on pride, and courtesy, which suits me, so we got things straightened out to everybody's satisfaction. Particularly the work teams'.

These eight never paid a bit of attention to the weather. Rain or shine, when it got light enough to see they'd be on the porch, sitting wrapped in their serapes and carrying their "loonchays," ready for work. Outside of building a little fire to eat by at noon, even though the day might be a scorcher, they never looked up until the sun went down.

Then it was time to call it a day, and when we got in from the field a couple would chore while the others cooked supper. They were boarding themselves, for they got more wages that way. By request, after the first go round at the Melville store, I did most of their buying for them, mainly onions, pinto beans, flour, salt and macaroni. They were working steadily and got by on so damn little that I slipped them some meat when it was handy; a dry doe that had been bothering the oat crop; and I took to carrying a .22 rifle on the bullrake for jackrabbits.

Their first trip to the store tickled the hell out of me. I dropped by Hanson's for a short one while they shopped. When I went over to the store a while later the clerk, with a harried look to him, was enunciating each, by God, syllable of each, by God, word of English, and at the top of his lungs, to my guys.

As he spotted me he shouted happily, "God damn, Spike," caught himself, and went on in a normal tone, "What do these dumb bastards want? I can't make them understand me."

I turned to Alfonso, a quiet, grey headed Mexican who was standing with his hat in his hand and a bewildered expression on his face, as were the others, and asked, "Can I help you?"

"Thank you, Patron," he answered gravely. "This man seems stupid, for he believes us all to be deaf. Or so it would appear. Inquire, please, if it is possible to buy this food here. We have money."

I got things straightened out, and by fall the clerk had learned to recognize a few Spanish terms. Once in a while they would come up with something new, though, and he'd high center until they got me to explain.

These boys, perfectly naturally, considered a bull team real up to date equipment. So it took me a while, working by guess and by God, to find out who was capable of handling a tractor, and there were several false starts before I got them lined out. One of my attempts toward creation of an instant tractor man involved Manuel. He was a small, voluble individual whose looks put me in mind of a mountain rat, and who, according to him, knew all about tractors. So I put him on a Ford-Ferguson and side delivery rake, and we went over the hill to a pocket of mown hay that was ready to windrow. The two of us made a couple of rounds together, with me explaining operating procedures and he seemed to have the hang of it. Except for a propensity to drive like the mill tails of hell, that is, but I eventually got him to understand that the idea was to get the hay "en lineas" and not scattered every which way. Finally, with more than a few misgivings, I went back to my bullrake and the stack, sort of happy I didn't have to watch what Manuel was doing.

We were using an overshot stacker, and Luis, a big, good natured boy, was on the stack. He must have stacked something or other some time or other because he was doing a good job. Esteban was handling the stacker team, and he was making a hand. Having a hell of a time, too, for every time I'd buck in a load he'd pass my bullrake with a gunny sack, saying, "Ha, Toro," deep in his chest, and striking a statuesque pose at the end of the pass.

An hour or so later Manuel appeared, afoot. I was out after hay when he reached the stack, but could see him in animated conversation with the other two. Then, although I was on the way in with a load, here came Luis at a high lope. As he pulled up beside me I asked what had happened. With furrowed brow and worried eyes, and in a tone worthy of the proximity of Doomsday, he announced; and I translate literally; "Patron, the tractor of Manuel does not wish to walk itself!"

We went over the hill to the tractor and it was out of gas. My fault, for in the bustle of getting the Mexicans lined out I had forgotten to fill it. But the trouble was that Manuel had run the battery completely down trying to get it going again, for he'd remembered how I'd started it. So I decided to try somebody else on the tractor and picked Cornelio, which was a fine choice. He was a young, intelligent man, and took to it like a duck to water. In fact I learned that, if he was shown one time, he could handle any job. A good man by any standards, and shortly he became a mower man, and was pleased as Punch to be able to spend the evenings sharpening his sickles rather than helping with the cooking. Gave him "casta," too, which is dear to the Mexican heart.

I mentioned Luis. He was the damndest, best natured guy! The others wore guaraches mostly, though a couple had work shoes. He, however, was the proud possessor of a pair of dress Oxfords much the worse for wear, and, since none of them wore socks, a man could always see his big old brown toes through the network of cracks.

One field we put up was about half Canadian thistle. Cows really go for it when it has been stacked half green, but it's vicious, prickly stuff to handle. Even feeding it in the winter a man almost needs a suit of armor. Anyhow Luis was knee deep in the thistle, tramping around building the stack when I came in with a load and shoved it up on the stacker teeth. He was peering down at me as I backed my team and bullrake away from the overshot, and I asked, "How goes it?"

"Very well, Patron," was his reply. Then he grinned from ear to ear and added, "Muchas espinas," and, thinking about those cracked shoes and bare ankles, I shuddered. Damn if I don't think he could have played football barefooted; with a porcupine for the ball!

Since we had had to hire all eight Mexicans, or none, there were more than we needed for the hay crew, and I put them to building a roping arena I'd been thinking about. There were two Joses, one a big quiet man who went by "Largo," the other a chesty little likeable guy who, when he spoke, was serious as a preacher and sounded like he was talking down a pickle barrel. He was known as "Chicelo." I started them digging post holes, Largo handling the bar for a while and then Chicelo scooping out the dirt with a sardine can. This intrigued me, for I had always used a bar and a shovel, but these two were throwing dirt like a couple of badgers and be damned if it didn't look like a good method. As a matter of fact, later, when nobody could see me, I tried a bar and a can, and it sure works. Except in rocks, of course, but I use it a lot. Anyhow, the bar Largo had was about seven feet long and an inch and a half thick. He was using it like he was taking a short cut to China, so as I left I warned him, "Don't break it."

They both looked puzzled, and Largo asked, "Pardon, Patron. What did you say?"

I repeated my words, and added, "I mean the bar."

He sized me up seriously, then looked at the bar in his hands, and with a slightly startled expression assured me, "I shall be very careful," and Chicelo burst into giggles.

Largo never forgot. Each evening, until they were done with the arena, he would produce the crowbar for my inspection and tell me, "See, it is not yet broken, Patron."

I always raised a patch of potatoes out by the yard around the house, and Lord God but I hate to hoe spuds. These guys were the answer to my prayer; I rustled up a couple of hoes, and Alfonso and Concepcion did a better job by far than if I'd used a cultivator. Concepcion, incidentally, was about as country boy as they come, and he might have been mute from the amount he talked around anybody but the other Mexicans, and always had such an embarrassed expression that I wondered if possibly he'd wet his pants. Expression or not, though, he was a bear for work, and when haying really got to rolling he helped Luis on the stack. Poor guy, he lost his hat one day, and said nothing until I asked him that evening where it was. Looking for all the world as though he'd just come from his best friend's funeral he told me, almost inaudibly, "In the stack, Patron," and when I inquired why the hell he hadn't told us so we could have taken time out to look for it he whispered, "I did not wish to disturb the work."

Bothered us so much that Tor and I took him up to the store and staked him to a new hat. Every time either of us looked at him from then on he'd take it off, brush it carefully, and redent it. I liked the shy little guy.

For a while after the tractor episode, I put Manuel to working around the yard and flowers. He did a peach of a job, but got into Barbara's bad graces by giving the children a cigarette; with predictable results. After that he reminded me of a whipped pup—he was so eager to please—and when I tried him out on the rake again he did fine, though he used grease like it was going out of style. Since I had told him to keep his equipment greased I consoled myself with the thought that a lot was sure better than not enough.

About the time we finished haying Dad asked if I'd bring the boys up to the dude ranch in Big Timber Canyon to put a cement floor in the saddle shed. Surprisingly I ran into problems getting them to go to the mountains. After some discussion I realized that they were afraid, honestly afraid, of "la sierra." Alfonso put it bluntly, "Patron, we do not wish to go where there are osos (bears), lobos (wolves), leones (cougars), possibly even tigres (jaguars). All these exist in Mexico, and molest the people of the monte."

I told them that, though no tigres came this far north, we did have the other three, but that in my lifetime none had ever attacked a human. They sat mulling this over, until Cornelio volunteered to come with me. Then Chicelo stood up, threw out his chest, and announced sturdily, "I, also!" Supressing a grin, I told him he was a veritable "cuñado" of Pancho Villa. Everybody chuckled, came with me to "la sierra," did a fine job on the floor, and no "animales" made an appearance. Very much to their relief, but they kept a weather eye out until we were done.

A few days later I told them they had finished all the work and that I would take them to Billings the next day. They held a short, quiet pow-wow, and Alfonso turned to me, "Patron, if it is possible, we would like to remain here tomorrow, and return to Billings the following day."

I said that was fine with me, but curiosity got the best of me and I asked why the extra day. He answered simply, "We wish to cleanse and put the house in order."

Well, the house looked like a beehive the next day. I was gathering cattle, got in late, and when I drove the truck up to the porch the following morning, their gear was ready to go. As I got out of the cab all eight filed out the door and lined up. Alfonso bowed and said, "Enter, Patron."

I stepped through the door, they all strung in behind me, and I got the surprise of a lifetime spent around bunk-houses, most of which ordinarily look, and smell, like a boar's nest. Surprised, hell, I was thunderstruck! These guys hadn't been fooling when they said "lavar" and "regular." The floor had been scrubbed till the grain of the wood showed clear and pretty, the windows and woodwork washed until they shown, and even the ceilings and walls had been swept down! Sure, I've seen a few bachelor ranchers that were fussy as a schoolma'am when it came to their houses, and once in a while a man who kept a plumb clean camp, but for a crew of men to clean a bunkhouse voluntarily, and especially when they were leaving, was damn sure a new one on me. Hard up for words, I turned to my guys.

There they stood, a trace of worry and a tiny bit of expectancy in their faces, their hats in their hands. Then Largo stepped forward and hesitantly asked, "Does it please you, Patron?"

Funny, but I couldn't find much to say except, "Ay, Chihuahua! It does indeed please me, amigos mios." Each man relaxed, and a broad smile spread over every face. Damndest string of men!

We got to Billings, the boys taking turns, two at a time, riding in the front of the truck with me, and hunted up the government office that handled Mexican national workers. The head man was a little huffy at first, but was so damn tickled to find the eight and get his count straight, that he simmered down, warning me, however, that I could get into trouble for just up and taking them away without telling him. I paid the boys in full, which wasn't a whole lot, because every two weeks since they'd started work on the ranch I'd been sending their wages, except what they'd kept for food, by bank draft to their families, wives, or novias down in Michoacan. The man was suspicious when I told him, and brought in an interpreter to question the boys. I had trouble keeping my face straight at their answers after they got the idea behind the questioning. Mexicans are fine swearing men.

We finally got things squared away and I told the boys goodbye. Each gave me the abrazo, and the government man remarked, "You know, that's the first time I have ever seen a Mexican national do *that* to their employer."

His tone rasped me a little, so I told him, "Hell, we aren't employer and employees. We're friends."

A thought struck me, and I asked the boys, using Spanish for the first time since we had gotten to the office, if they'd have a beer with me before I headed home. They accepted, and the man's face tickled me as we trooped out talking animatedly.

We went to a Mexican bar south of the tracks, and I ordered a round. Somebody, knowing Mexican music is one of my favorites, loaded the juke box with money. It's a cinch he turned it to absolute top volume, too. Alfonso bought a round when we'd finished mine, and I discovered that each one planned to do the same. I certainly wasn't going to hurt anyone's feelings by refusing to drink with him, and the upshot was that we each downed nine bottles of beer. Mostly in silence, for the juke box precluded any possible chance of conversation. Billings, south of the tracks, had a pretty gaudy reputation, but only one small incident occurred. A strange Mexican, drunk, hit me up for a drink, and, when I said no, got nasty. Before he knew what had happened he was surrounded by eight men and escorted out the door. To my complete amazement Concepcion, of all people, produced a knife from somewhere, and damn sure looked like he knew how to use it.

Time we'd finished our ninth beer I knew I'd better call it a day or risk trouble with the Highway Patrol, so we went through the goodbyes and abrazos once more. They escorted me to the truck, and stood silently, hats on their chests, as I drove off.

I never saw any of them again. They wanted to come back the next year, but I think they must cut Mexican nationals at the border about like they were handling cattle, and to hell with where they happen to want to go, for I got a letter from Cornelio the next summer telling me that they had all been sent to North Dakota.

They were a good bunch of men. Not only as to work, but as people. I liked them and I'll remember them. Someday, when Barbara and I can get away, we are going to drive to Mexico and poke around for a month or so. We'll make a special trip to Angamacutiro, even if we have to do it by muleback, in hopes of seeing some of them again. We'd enjoy that, and I think they might, too.

# Two Layer

THE AMAZING THING about the years I have spent dude ranching is what fine people and friends the guests have been, almost without exception. Oh, there have been a few times when I got on the fight, but I have always tried to remember that these are guests and should be treated as such. There was once, though!

We had the string just about saddled when the corral gate banged back against the fence, and here came this man. Didn't bother to close the gate, but just strode into the saddle shed and demanded, "Who's the ramrod of this twobit outfit?"

To begin with, I don't like my gates left open with a corral full of horses, nor do I want anybody but the crew in the saddle shed. But I ignored the open mouths of my boys and admitted that I guessed it was me, and he barked, "My wife and I got in last night. We've been at a *real* ranch in Arizona, and I want the wildest booger you've got," Well, hell, in my prime I wouldn't have gone onto an outfit plumb cold and begged for trouble like that, so I rared back and sized the man up. And swallowed hard.

Talk about western, why it was plumb scary! If I'd seen him in the open at a distance I'd sure have taken him for a giant toadstool, for his hat not only stood tall but had at least a sixteen inch brim, to boot. His shirt made a man squint like a heavy May snow on a sunny day, and around his neck was a big old bandana that was locked loudly in grim conflict with the shirt. I couldn't see too much britches thanks to a pair of bright orange batwing chaps and the fact that he was sporting a paunch like a leanto roof. Below the leggings were a pair of boots of the caliber that, after a rain or two, resemble a couple of old buffalo horn shells, and on them were a pair of nickel plated Chihuahua spurs, big ones.

Took me a minute to get adjusted, but I got my footwork to going and told him I just took care of the average guests, that Dad would be down in a little and see to him. Sure, I was a damn coward, but I didn't dare trust myself. About then Dad showed up, the old boy headed him off at the gate, and the whole ranch listened—or at least was within earshot—as he explained what a hell of a hand he was. Directly Dad came into the shed, where the whole crew had discreetly gathered, and in a shaking voice asked, "What have we got that'll do this sonofabitch?"

"Two Layer?" I ventured.

"By God, yes!" said Dad.

Now Two Layer was a popping good looking, beautifully put together paint that we'd raised out of an old Indian mare and a remount stud. Fine gaited and nice handling, too. Trouble was, he was insane. Not weedy, just plain insane! There wasn't one of us in the crew that he hadn't bedded down at least once, and it was never a question as to *if* he'd buck, just *when* he'd buck. His name came from the fact that when he laid you away he did such a hell of a job that it was equal to bucking off most broncs twice! A few mornings before, when I'd felt full of vinegar and took him to wrangle on, I'd let him stop for a drink at the creek as I came in behind the dude string. I was watching him pretty close even though he'd been like silk, but maybe I had begun to figure "well, what d'you know" a little. Anyhow, when he finished he never even lifted his nose from the water, just let out a bellow, blew the plug and stuck my head into something like two feet of water in the middle of Big Timber Creek. Softer landing than usual, but a damn sight wetter. I really don't know why we kept him around except that every so often Dad would ride him, and I mean to a fare-you-well, just to show us boys that there was still a lot of music in an old fiddle, I guess. None of us could've tied our pants on back of the saddle tightly enough so they'd have stayed till the smoke had cleared. We knew it, too, but we had to have a try at it every so often, anyhow.

Well, the whole crew nearly came to blows about who'd catch the horse, so I put all but one to leading out saddled stock for the guests, and while Two Layer was being caught—it was easy, as always—I got out the biggest saddle we had. Dad, feeling his responsibilities, had gone out to have a try at getting along with the man, so I carried the saddle out and joined them. Between the two of us we talked him into letting us put the saddle on a different horse while we fit the stirrups. I got a closeup of those spurs while we were doing it, and every time I looked at them I either grinned or shuddered. I might add, too, that by the time the man settled down into it the saddle became a muley, and if he'd been roping hard and fast it'd have looked like he was doing it with his umbilical cord!

When we got around to saddling the paint, he stood like a rock—he never believed in doing anything unless it counted—and the man said, "This sorry thing the toughest you've got?"

"Sure is," I assured him, "but I think he'll do you."

Dad chimed in with, "I believe I'd go easy with those spurs until he gets the kinks out." They'd been bothering *him* some, too.

Our guests are a pretty savvy bunch, and most of them that were there had eased their horses around the bend of the corral where they'd be out of the way but could see real well. The boys sort of worked the rest of them over there, too, while I got aboard Peepo and built a loop down out of sight, and Dad eased over on the other side with Colonel. Reminded me of the hush that comes before a bad storm, with the thunder growling 'way off back in the peaks.

One of the boys walked over to hold the paint and the man snapped, "Get out of my way, dammit," pulled down his hat and tried to pull up his pants. He succeeded only in momentarily showing a belt buckle big enough so it's a cinch he'd never get gut shot. Then he climbed on—and I mean climbed—clucked, and Two Layer walked off like a doll!

In stunned silence we started off. Nothing happened at the ford where I'd been homesteaded, nor up the hill to the gate at the laundry. There are a couple of big fir trees there, one of which has something of a lean to it, and as we waited for the lead wrangler to open the gate Two Layer suddenly burst away from the group and I thought, "Here goes!" Not really, but he did the damndest thing. He charged over to the tree, and far as I could see, tried to climb it! His front end went up the trunk, and the bark flew as he tried to go higher. Then he fell back, turning as he did, and stood. There'd been a strangled "Whoa" from the man, and at the top of the climb he'd tried to bail out, so he ended up on the old pony's ribs. But Two Layer just stood while we got him back up in the saddle and gave him his hat.

When he got settled and dusted off, glowered around and growled, "What the hell."

A lady from Delaware, a guest of long standing and a fine hand, said casually, "Oh, he always does that when he goes by that tree." A couple of people coughed, and we strung off down the canyon.

We were working cattle over on Dry Creek just below the Forest line that day, shaping up cow and calf pairs to go to the summer range on the head of Sweet Grass. It was a fair trip over, so we moved right along. Be damned, though, if Two Layer so much as looked crossways. Traveled like a champion, even with the man fighting a bitter battle with his cantleboard as we jogged. Pretty soon, the guy braved up to beat hell, got up in the lead so he could ramrod the outfit, and you could hear him plumb at the tail end running down the country and his horse compared to where he'd been and what he'd ridden in Arizona. So, time we got to the cattle Dad was dangerously quiet.

The stock were ready for the mountains and were gathered at the fence line waiting for us. They handled well, and outside of our man being in the way most of the time, things went fine. I noticed him a time or two hit Two Layer in the ribs with those Chihuahuas to jump him out to turn something, then hold him up where he couldn't do it, so I'm afraid I didn't make too much of a hand; it's sort of hard to cut cows and calves and watch for a bronc ride all at the same time. And I wasn't about to miss it, for it was a cinch what was going to happen, and right quick, though I couldn't figure why it was taking so long.

We had things about shaped up when Barbara arrived with the hot lunch. Leaving a few riders holding the cattle and the cut, the rest of us went up to eat. The man was along, in the lead, and lunch wasn't plumb pleasant. First he endeared himself by blustering into the kitchen area to supervise—Barbara really took to that—and as we ate he alternated between complaining loudly about the food and booming about how he'd work the stock if he were running the show. So everybody was tickled when he finally belched comfortably and announced, "I better get over to the herd and see how they are getting along with the critters," clanked over to his horse and busted him out of a standstill at a run—at least a run was what he'd figured on.

I forgot to mention that Two Layer bucked loud, so by the second, and last, jump everybody's attention had been caught, and we all saw the wreck. I'm sure the old pony had been thinking things over during lunch, and at long last had decided to hell with it. Anyhow he threw our man so high the sun winked on that belt buckle before it disappeared back into the dust cloud. I jumped on Peepo, gathered Two Layer in and led him back to the man. I handed him the reins without saying a word, or grinning, and rode back to the kitchen. Everyone there was poker faced, quiet and watching.

Well, the man dusted himself, poked the dents out of his hat, sneaked a look at our group by the fire, said to the paint, "Just took me by surprise, that's all," and climbed gingerly on. Keeping those hooks well away from the ribs and sort of pushing on the reins, he eased in the direction of the cattle. Just as he was about there, here it went again. He must have been sitting tighter—I'd'a damn sure been— or maybe because Two Layer was at a walk he couldn't get as much leverage as the first lick. The man lasted three jumps this time.

His wife was sitting at the fire still eating. She'd been pretty quiet all morning. I had put her on a good horse, and she rode well. Seemed like a real nice woman. One of the guests remarked, "Your husband just got thrown," and she never said a thing, just went on eating. After the second go-round the guest volunteered the same information, adding "again."

The wife looked up, and with all the interest she'd have shown if somebody'd handed her a wet gunny sack, said, "Oh, really," and went back to her plate!

I've been accused by my wranglers, especially in the spring when they are topping off right at a hundred snuffy boogers that have been in the hills all winter, of being behind the door when the milk of human kindness was passed out, but before the day was over I began to feel pretty nearly sorry for the man! It didn't take long to finish working the stock, but he came down twice more while we were doing it. Of course he had quit cowboying after the second wreck, but I guess Two Layer got bored just watching. Besides, it was like taking candy from a kid, and he knew he had a dead cinch. But he wasn't operating like his usual insane self, and it struck me that he was doing things in a—for him—sort of halfway friendly way. Matter of fact, after the fourth go-round he didn't even run off. Just stood there and sort of dared the man to get back on.

Part of the outfit was spending the night at the Bar B cow camp back across the creek towards the ranch, so they could get an early start with the cattle the next day—it was a good four-day trip to get them up Sweet Grass, situated and salted—so we headed on back. The man bucked off at the horse trap gate at the camp, and then, as those of us who were going back were saying goodbye at the corrals, he came down again. I suggested that maybe he better let me pack his spurs, and he didn't fuss a damn bit about handing them over, but all the same, when we hit the gate at the yon side of the trap, Two Layer came uncorked and laid him away. It was kind of pitiful, but he'd made his brag and he had to ride the horse, or walk. Root hog, or die! As I said, the paint wasn't performing normally but be damned if there didn't seem to be a pattern to his actions, so, time the man got his hat straightened out and ahorseback once more, I decided to play a hunch. My bet was that Two Layer just wanted to get home, be done with things even as easy as they were and was against just standing around. There were a couple of more gates before we hit Big Timber canyon, and at both of them I loped ahead, opened them, and as the people went through told them to keep on going, I'd catch up. It worked, too, for as long as he could keep moving the old pony seemed plumb genial!

I did hump up some when we hit the ranger trail off the ridge down into the canyon, for it's a little rollicky and not exactly what a man'd hunt up to fit a bronc ride. I damn sure know, too, for I've had it happen there a time or two; though, like a prickly pear flat, it makes an old boy ride way above his usual average! I hoped Two Layer wasn't about to throw a fit on a place like that when he could get his exercise, easy, on good ground. Just to make sure, I hurried a little before we hit our pasture gate about halfway down, had it open, and was ahorseback again before anybody got there. I don't think the man enjoyed the trail, for he sat stiff as a chunk of wood with every muscle tight and his paunch sucked in to where it was easy to see the white knuckled grip he had on the horn. It wasn't a hot day either, but he was sweating pretty badly, and in places the dust on his shirt had turned to mud. Be damned, though, when we hit a nice bottom up the creek a ways, if he hadn't braved up enough to puff out his chest and rein up to wait for the rest. I suppose it was plumb instinctive, after we'd gotten by the juicey spots and were almost home. And, of course, Two Layer bedded him down. I watched the man's eyes when I handed him his reins after the fracas, and he came within an ace of telling me to go to hell. Believe he would have if he'd known what I knew— that there was still one to go!

It was about a mile to the ranch corrals, and nothing untoward happened before we got there. The man was sitting pretty tight since the last deal, but as we came in sight of the saddle shed he straightened up, relief, gratitude and self importance, in that order, ran across his face like wind puffs across a still pond. As we pulled up at the corral he stood up to get off and started to say something. He never finished doing either, for Two Layer stood him right square on his head in front of the gate! The old pony had flat made up his mind some time ago that he wasn't about to stand unless he was empty, and he'd sure made it stick!

There were an unusual number of guests in from other rides still down at the corral, all my boys and even some of the cabin girls, so the final exhibition was sure a case of in front of God and everybody. I didn't dare look around at anyone so I looked at the man, and I have always been proud of the fact that I could keep my face straight! He was still pretty gaudy, but it was lessened considerably by smears of cow manure, grass stains, dust, mud and sweat from one end to the other. Even those boots were scuffed. But the payoff was the hat! The last dismounting had jammed it down on the bridge of his nose, the brim had his ears bent pretty nearly double, and the crown was mashed and telescoped to the exact shape of his head. He was a sight to behold. Then some smart guest inquired brightly, of no one in particular, "How was the day?"

His wife answered enthusiastically, "Magnificent!"

The man never said a word, just started off for the cabins. Didn't even mess with his hat, just tipped his chin up so's he could see and paid me no mind when I told him I'd bring his spurs up to the store. He didn't come down to supper, and they left the next morning before breakfast. I never heard of him since but once; a guest told me a few years later that he'd seen the man at a ranch in Arizona the past winter, and that he'd had a new wife. I've still got his spurs somewhere.

Two Layer survived the trip in great shape, barring ending up a little short on mane, and I had to replace a couple of saddlestrings the man tore out sometime during the day. Actually I am not what you could call plumb proud of the occurrence, but it's the only time either Dad or I let temptation get the best of us in a case like that in better than fifty years of dude ranching. No, it wasn't right, just needful, and damn sure funny!

# One of Those Days

IT WAS ONE of those days. Even before daylight, when I went out to chore and gather the horses, things went bad. The smart sons of guns figured there was work in the offing, and it was nearly sunrise before I was able to pen them in the corral off the corner of the pasture. I was afoot, having been so sure the evening before that I could catch them easily that I hadn't kept in a wrangle horse, so by the time I shut the corral gate behind them I was shaking with rage, had run myself to a frazzle, and my voice was reduced to a croak. The latter was probably good because the words I'd used so freely had been pretty choice, and it was only a couple of hundred yards from the pasture to Melville.

I don't know anything more exasperating than three or four good saddle horses that have decided they'd rather be kittenish and play than stand to be caught. Particularly when they know they are going to be caught eventually. For about the time a man heads for the house for a Winchester they will suddenly be brimming with friendliness and busting their buttons to get into the corral so they can be fed. Most horses don't carry grudges and seem to figure men don't either, and as I crossed the corral they hurried over to say howdy and then crowded around the feed trough whickering expectantly. So, though they didn't deserve it, I got a bucket of grain for them from the oat box—which they'd known all along I would do.

I was still a little owly when I sat down under Tickle, our

milk cow, and along about the time her front tits were half milked—it's a matter of preference, but I favor milking the back ones first—she swatted me across the side of the head with her tail. My grouch got the best of me. I growled and thudded her in the ribs with my elbow; and got kicked flat on my back into the manure trough.

I sweet talked her into letting me finish milking, but I was pretty messy when I arrived at the house, and Barbara wasn't real happy about my state, my lateness and the shortage of milk. I wasn't enthusiastic about the cold breakfast, either, but I learned a long time ago that a man is smart to always get along with the cook, particularly when she's his wife, so I changed my clothes, ate and kept quiet. But it was a damn poor beginning to a day.

We had finished the dishes when Dad and my brother-in-law, Tor Anderson, drove in. They had ridden down the day before, left their saddle horses overnight, and the four of us were riding down to the lower range to gather and vaccinate the last of our horses.

There had been an outbreak of equine encephalomylitis, sleeping sickness, with quite a loss over the country and since we ran a lot of horses, we had been vaccinating for nearly a week at the home ranch, Tor's and our Melville place. Now the last we had to do were a string of unbroken young stuff running in the hills some fifteen miles below Melville.

When we saddled up—Barbara on Smokey Joe, her wedding present from me, and Dad and Tor on the two they'd brought down—I decided to ride our Quarter Horse stud, Picacho. He was a sure enough grandson of Ben Hur, and Ben Hur stock has buck in them. He wasn't mean; he was just having his idea of fun, though not always his rider's. He tried it once with Dad when he was roping and got whipped over and under with the loop so thoroughly that he decided that here was somebody that didn't enjoy fun. From then on he never turned a hair with Dad.

Tor had ridden him quite a bit, and invariably had to put up something of a bronc ride. One time 'Cach had him bucked off, but then the son of a gun came to the edge of a deep irrigation ditch and evidently figured this was a poor place to play, for he stopped bucking and walked sedately across. When he got to the other side, be damned if the dirty devil didn't start again, but Tor was back in the buggy and got him ridden.

I have never had my shingle out as a bronc rider, but this morning I felt full of vinegar. If the others had ridden 'Cach, I guessed I could, too. Hell, he was a broke horse, and a good hard ride would be just the ticket for him.

When I cinched things down and pulled up the flank rig, the stud humped up to where I could have thrown a cat under the back of the saddle and gave me a jaundiced look over his shoulder. I untracked him and led him 'round a time or two to see if I couldn't get the kinks worked out. I'd have led him longer, but Dad said impatiently, "Hell's fire, get a move on," so I hoisted up my pants, pulled down my hat, swung into the saddle, and 'Cach stepped out like a gentleman!

Everything wasn't peaches and cream yet, not by a long shot. He wasn't a big horse, but he was sure a lot of horse, and I could feel him under me like a cocked gun, all wound up into a tight, brittle ball of muscle, traveling tippy-toed, with one ear and eye turned back waiting for me to make a mistake. I did my damndest not to, taking a deep seat in the saddle, a short rein, and with my right hand on the fork. Handy to the horn; for as far as I'm concerned a saddle horn wasn't put there just for roping. We jogged easily for about a hundred yards, and then Dad moved out at a long trot. So did we. Everything stayed hunky dory, so, since we were headed up a pretty good hill to the bench, I broke him into a lope, and then, my powder getting dryer by the minute, into a run. A hundred yards at this gait and I could feel him relax. I did, too, and tried not to look as relieved as

I felt when I slowed down and the others caught up.

Dad remarked, "Well, you got by."

Tor added, "For a while," but Barbara looked pleased. It wasn't such a bad day after all.

We moved out across the flats below Melville at an easy lope, jogging where the ground was bad for we had some miles to go and country to cover before we started our work. As we rode we discussed the best way to make our gather, for the horses were in the upper of the two pastures which constituted our lower range. There were seven sections in this pasture, about five thousand acres, but no pens stout enough that we could work unbroken horses in them. So, since our neighbor, Leo Cremer, had his head-quarters, with big corrals and a chute he used for handling his rodeo stock, several miles north of the east end of our pasture, we decided to bunch our horses in the northeast corner. Then we'd string them across to the corrals and vaccinate there.

By the time we had made our plans we had reached the Cayuse bottoms. This was boggy ground, so we took the county lane across it. The road here was built up higher than the surrounding ground, with rough gravel and rocks in its center, baked gumbo—which was badly pitted and chopped by cattle tracks, dating back to the spring thaw—at the edges and a deep borrow pit on either side from which the county crew had gotten the material to raise the road. These borrow pits had at least two feet of water and three feet of mud in them, for the road crossed a good half mile of soggy bottom land. Naturally, with its rocks and gumbo, the footing wasn't easy on a horse, so we pulled up to a slow jog, Dad and Tor in the lead and Barbara and I behind. We were all talking casually, relaxed and enjoying the bright morning, when suddenly things came apart.

Picacho's little pin ears disappeared, the reins jerked through my fingers, and with a squeal he blew the plug. I have no idea to this day what set him off, but something sure did, and he caught me all gapped open, with the result that he got a half jump ahead of me from the word go. I lost my hat immediately, and he was bucking so fast it hit me in the face a time or two before it dropped to my chest for a couple of jumps, then to my stomach and then somewhere. When a man's hat bucks off he's usually next, but I was so busy trying to keep track of my saddle and horse—they seemed to be doing things separately and in several different directions—that my hat was at the bottom of my list of worries. How that little devil could buck! Not strong nor rough, really, but so ungodly fast and squirmy that I never did get back that half jump I'd lost right off the bat. Matter of fact, I dimly realized that he was getting even further ahead of me and that I was on the verge of taking up a homestead, when, as suddenly as he had opened the ball, his head came up and he stopped.

The first thing I did was to get the slack out of my reins and swap them to my right hand. Then instead of holding them in my palm again, I brought the right rein into my hand between my third and fourth fingers, the left up between my second and third, then both reins up between my thumb and forefinger, with the ends down over the back of the hand. Then, when I closed my fist, I'd have enough purchase on them so they couldn't get away from me again, and I would have something to ride against. Some support. I was using a hackamore bit—I have always had to try any new horse equipment—a rigging supposed to give especially fine control over an animal. At least that's what the advertising flyer had said.

Then I looked for my three partners and was surprised to see that they were all behind me, for I hadn't the slightest recollection of passing anybody. Then the thought of how damn foolish I must have looked—beating my horse from end to end with the seat of my pants, and Barbara watching it all—made me forget to count my blessings.

"You little bastard," I told 'Cach, and spurred him, hard.

I had expected him to be sort of sobered by our go-round, but not by a damn sight. With a squeal of outrage he kicked my foot out of the off stirrup and blew up, high, wide and wild. Not for fun, either. He was mad!

There hadn't been any surprise to the deal this time, but with the empty stirrup threatening to beat me to death, and trying to keep the near one when I was all out of balance, in no time I found myself a half jump behind again. This speedily developed into a full jump. I threw pride to the wind—by that time I had thrown everything else that was loose there, too—and reached for the saddle horn, but the damn thing was moving so fast I had trouble locating it. Anyway, when I did find it I couldn't keep hold of it and just succeeded in mashing my knuckles viciously. I got some mane for a while, but it pulled out about the time I lost my near stirrup, and even though I still had a good grip on the reins, it dawned on me—and not as any great surprise—that I was flat bucked off.

Ordinarily getting bedded down by a horse doesn't hurt anything but a man's pride, but here, with those damn rocks and baked gumbo points and ridges, I was sure to get pretty well peeled, if not stove up, when I came in for a landing. That left the borrow pits, and to get mud off is easier than to get hide back on. Better odds any way I looked at it, though there was the chance that if I lit on my head I might smother before the others could dig me out.

The hell of it was that though there was a choice, in the shape I was in, it wasn't mine. It was 'Cacho's, pure and simple. This was all she wrote, and it wasn't a borrow pit I was headed for, so I tried to light easy.

I didn't light at all. Just as I went off the stud bucked under me, picked me up, and I was back in the saddle again being rattled from hell to breakfast. We went through the whole rigamarole—me getting looser and looser and more battered by the minute. Then I was bucked off, and got picked up a second time.

By now, 'Cach should have been getting tired from all the exercise. I sure was, and I was anxious to give him the fight, if he'd only let me. Suddenly, glory be, his acrobatics smoothed out, he hogged a couple of desultory jumps and stopped. I slid hurriedly off, worn plumb out. As I was catching my wind the others rode up. Dad, with a quizzical look remarked, "That was some ride."

Tor handed me my hat and said unctuously, "You forgot something." I made a mental note of it—there'd come a time.

Barbara was all concern. "Are you all right, honey?," and being a little vague on that point myself, I did some exploring.

My shirttails were out, fore and aft, and my shirt was split across the shoulders. I hadn't been wearing leggings, and both pant legs were wrinkled up around my knees, and both my legs were skinned from my boot tops up. From the feel of it, all the way up, across and down. I picked a few remnants of mane hair out of the blood on my left hand and discovered that all the joints and the knuckles were cut—that damn saddle horn. My right hand was bleeding, too, and on closer examination I found it was coming from under the nail of the third finger. My reins, one on each side of the finger, had put such pressure on it when I was trying to hold up my horse's head that the nail split loose. When the pressure stopped, it had begun to bleed. Hackamore bits—I've never used one since, and a man couldn't run fast enough to catch me to give me one!

My scars seemed to be a long way from my heart. So, marveling at the fact that we were well east of the Cayuse bottoms—for I had thought, though I was by no means sure, that I had only been picked up twice—I reset my saddle and stepped aboard.

"We're late," Dad said, and we hit a long lope for the pasture, I being careful to keep my spurs away from the stud's ribs.

When we reached the upper end of the pasture we split up. Dad rode south to within sight of the south line fence. Tor was next to and within sight of him. I headed east within sight of Tor, and Barbara was to my left where she could see the north line. Dad started first, then each of us in turn, so that the horses we were after would move with a northerly slant ahead of us. These were young horses from three to five years old—in those days we never broke colts until they were full fives at least—and though they were spooky they weren't as smart and hard to gather as old horses. Youngsters like to run, and if a man gets them pointed in the right direction there is little problem. Old horses, especially mares, are pretty cute, and as soon as they figure what is happening will try to sneak up or down draws or behind hills to get away. They know every inch of their range, to boot. Unless a rider does, too—especially their favorite escape routes—and stays pretty high where he can see what's going on, he's in trouble. When the gather is over he'll have damn few horses and lots of dust 'way yonder behind him.

We had no trouble. Occasionally I would see a rider on one side or the other when I hit a ridge, and now and then some youngsters who would boil out of sight ahead of me. When I topped the next ridge they would be waiting, heads and tails in the air, to see what had become of me. Then away they'd go again, bucking and playing. Just having a hell of a time.

Picacho, of course, took an overwhelming interest in the proceedings. Deciding he had covered enough miles so that his humor wouldn't be so damn brittle, I let him make a run or two at them, much to their delight.

A Quarter Horse is not geared, nor intended, for filly chasing, so it didn't take long for him to shoot his wad. From then on out he was a good, reasonable saddle horse, not even shying when a jack rabbit got up underneath him. It was a nice change!

When I could see the corner of the pasture I held up until Tor, and then Dad, showed up with their gathers. We drifted them to the angle of the fence where they joined Barbara's bunch. Dad rode through them quietly, opened the gate, stood it up against the outside of the fence where nothing could get tangled in it and started for the corrals at an easy lope. The horses poured through, Barbara and Tor following. I shut the gate and headed after them.

The colts handled first rate. As soon as they were through the gate they were in unfamiliar country, and therefore, to their way of thinking, dangerous. Consequently, seeing a rider ahead, the lead moved up and fell in behind his horse. Barbara moved up on one side, well away and halfway to the drag, and Tor did the same on the other, lining them rather than driving them. I eased along behind. Feeling secure with us to look out for, and tend to, any boogers that might infest this new country, the colts lined out smoothly. A time or two, crossing a draw or coulee, Dad had to speed up to keep ahead, but most of the time all he had to do to keep them behind him was to raise his hand and speak to them. An antelope popping up from under a sage bush where he had been bedded down caused a momentary panic, which subsided as we three closed up a little. The trick of working horses on open range is to handle them quietly, not crowd them and give them time to use their brains and herd instinct. We four savvied horses and half an hour later had everything safely in the corrals.

We loosened the cinches and turned the saddle horses into a small pen. 'Cach I put by himself so he couldn't pick any fights. Then we cut part of the colts into the corral behind the chute where we planned to vaccinate. Dad and Barbara went to get the vaccine and syringes they had rolled in the slickers on their saddles, while Tor and I went to check the chute, one on each side.

My side of the chute ran through a sizeable pen, and I

noticed an animal, probably a Guernsey from its color, on the yon side, but being in a hurry I didn't pay much attention. As I checked for broken planks, holes and other places where a horse could get hung up or hurt on a stob, I noticed that everything had been worked over. A post or two had been set, and so lately that a crowbar was leaning against one of them. I turned at the end and started back still watching the chute. I had gone about halfway when I suddenly felt something push solidly against my back at belt height. Before I could turn there was a jar like a train had hit me. My head popped back until I expected to see my spurs, and I found myself so high in the air I could look out over the top of the corrals. At that the view was better than the landing. I hit with a grunt in an explosion of dust, staggered to my feet and looked blearily around to see what in God's name was going on.

I caught on quick—there stood a Guernsey bull perhaps two years old, shaking his head and fixing to have another go at me. He didn't get the chance. I got the hell out of there!

Bulls of milking breeds are notoriously dangerous, and as I went over myself I thanked God that the bull wasn't full grown and especially that he had been dehorned. Even so he had jarred every bone and muscle I owned. Suddenly I had had a bellyful of trouble, and I went blind with rage. "I'll kill the spotted sonofabitch," and I remembered the crowbar.

I dropped into the pen, dodged around the bull to the bar and started back to him. I was about four feet from his head and had the spot all picked where I was going to drive the point of the bar when Tor got me by the arm, and Dad called from the chute, "What the hell you think you're doing?"

"I'm going to kill him, God damn him," and I set my feet.

"You can't," objected Tor. "He's Cremer's. These are Cremer's corrals. This is Cremer's place."

I hesitated, and Dad bellowed, "Put that thing down," as he came towards me on a run.

Reluctantly I lowered the bar and turned away. Tor asked incredulously, "Didn't you see him in there?"

"Hell, yes. Wasn't paying any attention and just figured it was a milk cow or something," and I took my hat which, for the second time that day, he handed me. No smart remarks, though, this time.

Everything was ready, so we ran the bull into another pen, filled the chute with horses and went to work.

Vaccinating horses against sleeping sickness is tricky. The injection has to be made between the layers of skin on the neck and the needle used is very fine gauge. So, ideally, the animal must stand quietly—a magnificent combination for vaccinating wild colts, but it had to be done.

Tor and I worked along the left-hand side of the chute, earring each horse's head solidly against the poles until he stopped fighting. Then Dad leaned across from the right-hand side and made the injection. Barbara kept the syringes ready, and as we finished each chutefull we would turn them out and go back to cut in another load.

It went reasonably smoothly, but earring those colts was work, hard work. The older ones, big juicy four- and five-year-olds, were just about all the two of us could hold. In short order both of us, and the horses, were dripping with sweat, which didn't do much toward making for a solid grip. My battered hands were bad at first, but they limbered up, or got numb, and didn't bother much. Even so, those colts were wild, handy with their teeth and front feet, and all I needed was to lose a finger or gather a few horse tracks as frosting for my other bruises.

We were about half done when we ran into a booger. He was one of the fives, a big stout gelding who damn sure wanted no part of it. It must have taken the two of us five minutes before we got him held against the side of the chute where he stood glaring, with his mouth open, squealing with each breath. Tor had him by the ears, while I had both arms around the top pole and his neck just below the throatlatch, with my hands gripped tight. Dad leaned over with the syringe, and as the colt felt the needle he gave a bawl of rage, broke in two and got clean away from us. As he did I felt a sharp stinging low on my arm and heard Dad say, "Damn! I wasted a dose."

"Don't believe so," I said as I rubbed the sweat and dust away, and sure enough, just above my wrist was a tiny red puncture.

Dad peered at it. "Sorry. Anyhow you sure oughtn't to get sleeping sickness."

"Nope," said I. "But I'll damn sure sleep tonight. Probably tomorrow, too, for I don't imagine I'll be able to get out of bed. Unless maybe somebody rolls me out," and we went back to work.

It was getting late in the afternoon when we finally found the colt we had been looking for—the last one—and breathed a collective sigh of relief when we turned him out with the rest. Then, at long last, Dad said, "Let's eat. Spike, you go over and see if you can rustle up some water, and we'll get Barbara's lunches off the horses."

No one had come over to the corrals since we had arrived so I figured there probably was no one on the place, but I walked over to the house anyway, knowing I could get water there. As I reached for the latch on the yard gate I caught something out of the corner of my eye, realized it wasn't a grasshopper I heard and jumped back from a rattlesnake coiled in the patch of shade beside the gate post. Unbelievably he hadn't struck, though I had stepped within a foot of him.

There was a garden rake leaning against the fence. I got it, pushed the snake around with it until he sullenly retreated and finally herded him out onto the range until he found a gopher hole and poured himself into it. Then I headed for the house again.

When I got back with a bucket of water and a dipper we hunted up the shady side of the corral, stretched out and enjoyed a well-earned rest as we ate. Suddenly Tor asked, "What were you doing out in front of the house? Looked like you were chasing something."

"There was a rattler by the gate," I told him, "and I moved it away from the house."

"Why didn't you kill it?"

"Well, I'll tell you. You were all so anxious about that damn Cremer bull that worked me over. Wouldn't let me kill *him*. I'd say this was a Cremer snake that had a fine chance to strike me and didn't. So I wasn't about to kill *it*. What's sauce for the goose, they say, is sauce for the gander." For a wonder nobody argued the point.

When we finished eating and had taken five I took the bucket back to the house, while the others put the bull back where he'd been and shut the corral gates just as they had been when we arrived. Then we cinched up, three riders took a good lead, I opened the gate, and back to the pasture we went. This time the colts knew where they were going, the experience in the corral had shattered their trust in us, and they were in a hurry to get back home. So the trip was rapid.

At first it was a question of outrunning them. Just staying in the lead. But by the time they neared the fence the three riders in front had managed to slow things down enough so the colts could be held while the gate was opened and put through it at a reasonable speed. When I came in sight they were headed across the hills as hard as they could run. Home again, and safe!

The trip back was uneventful. All of us, including the horses, had put in a long day. While the light lasted we pushed along at an easy lope, but when darkness came we pulled up and our horses fell into a steady jog. No one had much to say, and there was little sound except the jingle of spurs, creak of saddle leather and whisper of hooves through the grass. A full moon pushed over the hills behind us, dimming the stars as it climbed over our shoulders. From the Cayuse Hills to our right a family of coyotes carried on an intermittent serenade, the pups' voices breaking when they tried to reach the low notes. We crossed the scene of my morning's workout to the Melville flats, golden under the moon. Beyond them the cottonwoods along the Sweet Grass showed as a dark line, and a light or two marked Melville. We were nearly home, and our horses quickened their gait, ears pricked. Suddenly Dad remarked, "We got a lot done. A good day."

I shifted in my saddle, trying to ease my burgeoning aches, and considered: I'd been everything but bucked off, my eye teeth loosened in the process; hooked by a bull; vaccinated, as my tingling arm bore testimony; and damn near snake bit. A good day?

My eyes followed the lifting flanks of the Crazies in front of us, the peaks silvermounted by the moon. Not a good day, no. But I'd seen worse, though offhand I couldn't say just when. It had been a day with its troubles, but hell, everybody has those. I'd just been a little unlucky a time or two.

"It sure was," I answered, and Barbara riding beside me looked across and smiled.

# Home

Out toward the setting sun there's a land
Where the brawling Yellowstone
Drops snakelike through the foothills
Where Cheyenne and Crow were known;
There's a strong voice calling, calling,
My son, oh come you home.

A far flung, spreading rangeland with
Its grey rims in the sun,
Where the song of the coyote lifts to the stars,
And the slim, fleet pronghorn run;
There is where I wish to be,
For I love them, every one.

Where the winter blizzard whips the snow
On the slow herd drifting past,
And the saddle pony trudges through
The whirling, icy blast;
It's all bred into my heart and soul,
God grant it will always last.

*There the sound of the cowboy's voice*
*As he sings to the bedded steers*
*And the friendly sounds from a roundup camp*
*Come faintly to the ears;*
*They all belong to a son of the range,*
*A heritage great and dear.*

*Where the smoke from red hot iron on hide*
*Mounts in billowing swell,*
*While the struggling cattle bawl in fear*
*And the dusty 'punchers yell;*
*The brand of it all is on my soul,*
*Easy to read and well.*

*When my last circle is ridden and I*
*Have hung up saddle and rope,*
*Put me out on a short grass ridge*
*With a sunny, southern slope,*
*And the stone that rests o'er my sleeping head*
*Will carry this verse, I hope.*

*"The riders are home from the milling herd*
*Which fades in the darkening day;*
*The ponies drink at the cool, clear creek*
*And slowly graze away;*
*While far from the sage blue circling hills*
*Comes a coyote's evening lay;*
*All is rest and peace, at last,*
*For a son is home, to stay."*

—SPIKE VAN CLEVE

BIG SNOWY MTS.

LITTLE BELT MTS.

JUDITH GAP

HARLOWTON

TWO DOT

MUSSELSHELL RIVER

CRAZY MOUNTAINS

COFFIN BUTTE

BIG ELK CREEK

AMERICAN FORK

FISH CREEK

PORCUPINE BUTTE

CAYUSE HILLS

BIG COULEE

BUTTE RANCH

SWEET GRASS CREEK

DRY CREEK

MELVILLE

"NO BUSH"

OTTER CREEK

BLACK BUTTE

HOME RANCH

VAN CLEVE'S DUDE RANCH

WHEELER CREEK

MOUNTAINS

SOUTH FORK

10 MILE CREEK

BIG TIMBER CREEK

SOUR DOUGH

RASPBERRY BUTTE

YELLOWSTONE RIVER

BIG TIMBER

**"THE MELVILLE COUNTRY"**